SCHOLASTIC

Early Learning With Puppets, Props, Poems & Songs

by Lucia Kemp Henry and Suzanne Moore

NEW YORK • TORONTO • LONDON • AUCKLAND • SYDNEY
MEXICO CITY • NEW DELHI • HONG KONG • BUENOS AIRES

Teaching Resources

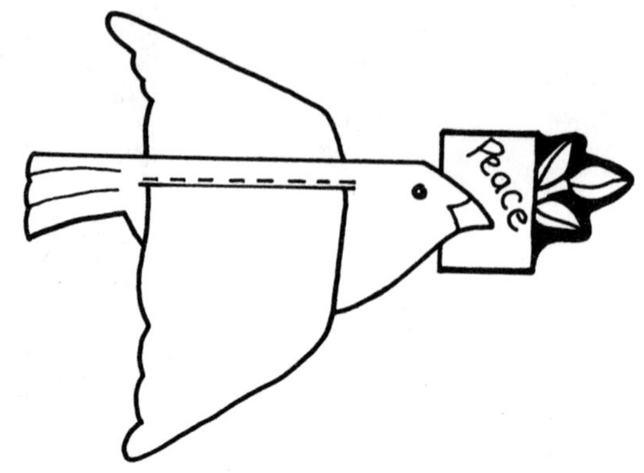

Edited and produced by Immacula A. Rhodes
Cover design by Lillian Kohli
Interior design by Sydney Wright
Interior illustrations by Lucia Kemp Henry

ISBN-13: 978-0-439-65614-6
ISBN-10: 0-439-65614-1

Printed in the U.S.A.

2 3 4 5 6 7 8 9 10 31 15 14 13 12 11 10 09 08

Contents

Seasons & Celebrations

Special Days

Fall

Winter

Spring

Summer

Math

Numbers and Counting

Geometry

Measurement

Contents

Introduction

Welcome to *Early Learning With Puppets, Props, Poems & Songs*! This book provides a variety of easy-to-make projects paired with fun-filled songs and poems that can be used to teach and reinforce important concepts throughout the year.

In *Early Learning With Puppets, Props, Poems & Songs*, you'll find developmentally appropriate projects designed to help children explore special celebrations, seasons, math, early concepts, social studies, and science. The projects and accompanying songs and poems coordinate with standards outlined by Mid-continent Research for Education and Learning (McREL) and also connect to some of the most commonly addressed topics in early childhood classrooms. You can use the projects with children to introduce new concepts and reinforce previously learned information, as well as to build vocabulary, develop language skills, strengthen fine-motor skills, encourage creativity, and much more!

Children can construct the puppets and props in this book from craft items found in your classroom and easy-to-find, everyday materials such as paper bags, paper towel tubes, facial tissue cubes, and detergent bottle lids. For your convenience, each project includes a list of needed materials and simple step-by-step directions. In addition, reproducible patterns are included for many of the projects. As children make the projects, encourage them to add personal, creative touches to make the projects uniquely their own.

But making the projects is only half the fun! After constructing their puppets and props, children can use them with the engaging songs and poems included in the book. With these hands-on projects and fun, meaningful verses, you'll provide children with hours of delightful opportunities to learn important concepts and develop critical skills needed for future learning.

About This Book

What's Inside

Each project in *Early Learning With Puppets, Props, Poems & Songs* focuses on a specific topic or concept. To help you find the perfect activity, each project is conveniently categorized under one of these sections: Seasons & Celebrations, Math, Early Concepts, Social Studies, or Science. In addition, the projects are organized under subcategories for each major area, such as Special Days, Fall, Winter, Spring, and Summer in the Seasons & Celebrations section. Here's what you'll find on the activity pages for each section:

Subject

The targeted subject area is shown at the top each activity page. In addition, a related and more specific topic or concept is identified under the subject.

Meeting the Standards

Each project and the accompanying song or poem is designed to support you in teaching one or more of the benchmarks outlined by McREL* for grades PreK–2. In this section, you'll find the curriculum area and at least one specific benchmark that can be addressed when using the project and activity on that page.

Materials

Check this section of the page to find a list of materials each child will need to complete the project. Often, basic art supplies such as crayons, scissors, glue sticks, construction paper, tempera paint, and paintbrushes are listed here. Some projects include additional craft items such as yarn, pom-poms, and wiggle eyes. Many of the projects require reproducible patterns. The specific pattern or patterns and pages on which these can be found are provided in this list. Other materials shown in this section—such as paper towel tubes and paper plates—are readily available or easy to gather and prepare.

Collecting Materials for the Projects

Materials used in constructing the projects are easy to find and collect. When large quantities are needed, you might want to ask families and school staff members to contribute the items. To help you start getting stocked up, here is a list of the materials most commonly used for the projects in this book:

- paper towel tubes
- paper and foam cups
- small paper bathroom cups
- paper lunch bags
- 6-inch paper plates
- 9-inch paper plates
- facial tissue cubes
- quart-size resealable plastic bags
- snack-size resealable plastic bags
- paper bowls
- plastic spoons
- single-serving cereal boxes
- legal-size envelopes
- plastic laundry detergent bottle caps
- pint-size cardboard ice-cream canisters
- mini-clothespins

Making the Puppet or Prop

These easy step-by-step directions tell you how to make the puppet or prop. You might want to make each project in advance so that you'll be familiar with the steps as well as have a sample to show children. For some projects, you'll find a "Note to the teacher" that identifies steps that an adult may need to complete for the child. As children work on their projects, be sure to encourage them to add their own personal touch to the project or prop being constructed.

STORAGE TIP

Place your sample project in a resealable plastic bag along with a copy of the corresponding song or poem. Then, when you're ready to use the project again, you'll have a sample prepared and ready to go!

* Source: *Content Knowledge: A Compendium of Standards and Benchmarks for PreK–12 Education* (4th edition). (Mid-continent Research for Education and Learning, 2004)

Using the Puppet or Prop

In this section, you'll find suggestions for how to use the puppet or prop with the accompanying song or poem. As children become familiar with the verses and concepts, encourage them to come up with their own creative ways to use their projects as they sing or recite.

Song or Poem

The songs and poems in this section are designed to reinforce specific concepts, skills, or knowledge-building information in a fun and engaging way. The songs are set to the tune of familiar childhood songs and the poems follow simple rhyme patterns. For some of the songs or poems, line-by-line directions are provided for moving the puppet or prop to the words. Before using each song or poem with children, be sure to practice singing or reciting the verses to become familiar with its tune or rhythm.

Building Literacy Skills With the Songs and Poems

Use these ideas to enhance and enrich children's literacy skills:

- Copy the song or poem onto chart paper. Invite children to identify specific letters, beginning sounds, or words on the chart. You might also leave out words as you sing or recite the verses and have children fill in the missing words.
- Write each line of a song or poem on a separate sentence strip. Challenge children to sequence the sentence strips and then sing or recite the lines.
- After singing a song or reciting a poem, invite children to make up additional lines or verses.
- Have children replace key words in the lines of a song or poem to give it new meaning. Or invite them to alter or substitute words in the lines to create new or silly songs or poems.

HOME CONNECTIONS

Here's a simple way to use children's projects to make home-school connections. Simply place their completed project in a resealable plastic bag, add a copy of the corresponding song or poem, and have children take their bag home to share the contents with their family.

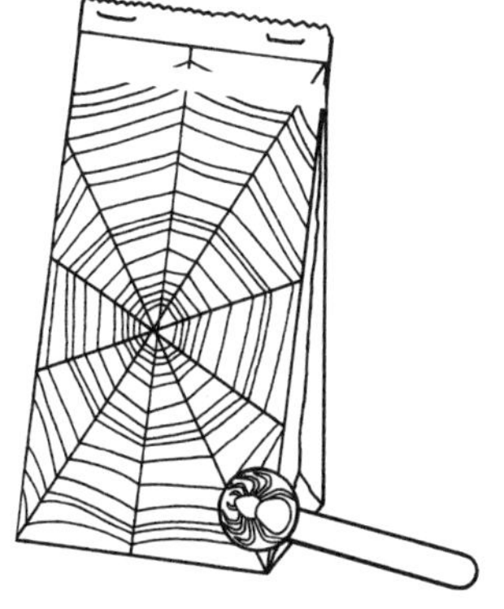

The First Day of School

Children create a backpack to "pack" with supplies for the first day of school.

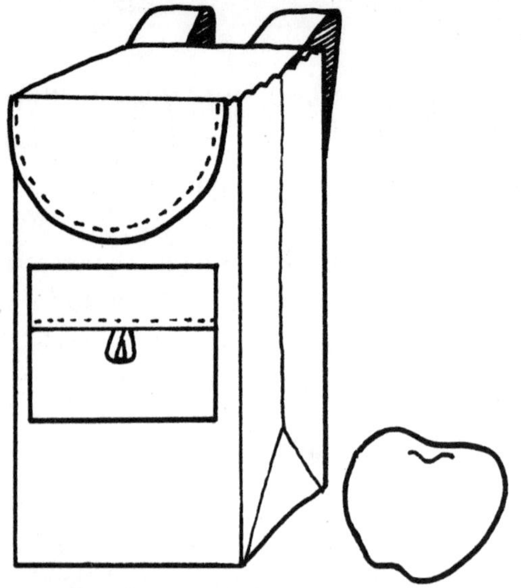

The First Day of School

In go the crayons, the scissors, too.
A pencil, a marker, some paper and glue.
An apple for the teacher—won't that
be cool?
Now I'm ready for the first day of school!

Meeting the Standards: Language Arts

Uses listening and speaking strategies for different purposes:

- Follows one- and two-step directions
- Recites and responds to familiar stories, poems, and rhymes with patterns (e.g., relates information to own life)

Materials (per child)

- backpack and apple patterns (page 115)
- crayons
- scissors
- paper lunch bag
- glue stick
- two 1¾- by 12-inch strips of construction paper

Making the Props

1. Color and cut out the apple. Set the cutout aside for later.
2. Color and cut out the backpack patterns. Glue the pocket to the middle of the front of the paper bag.
3. Fold the flap on the lines. Glue the short folded end to the back of the paper bag at the top opening. Then open the bag so that the flap covers the opening and folds over the top front.
4. For straps, glue the two construction-paper strips to the back of the paper bag.

Using the Props

Use the props and poem to reinforce listening and following directions. To begin, have children gather the school tools mentioned in the poem. Have them place all the supplies, the apple cutout, and their backpacks on their desks. Then, as they recite the poem, ask children to place each item in their backpack as it is named.

It's My Birthday

Children make a birthday cake to use for counting practice.

Meeting the Standards: Math

Understands and applies basic and advanced properties of the concepts of numbers:

- Counts by ones to ten or higher
- Counts objects
- Understands one-to-one correspondence

Materials (per child)

- birthday cake and candle patterns (page 116)
- crayons
- scissors
- glue stick
- jumbo craft stick

Making the Prop

1. Color and cut out the birthday cake and candle patterns. Cut along the dotted lines between the candles.
2. Glue the candles to the cake where indicated. Make sure the bottom of the candles line up with the top of the cake.
3. Glue the cake to the craft stick.

Using the Prop

Use the prop and poem to reinforce counting skills. Before reciting the rhyme, ask children to fold the candles down behind the cake. Then, as they say each number in the first verse, have them raise a candle to make it appear on the cake. As they say each number in the second verse, have children fold a candle down as if it has been blown out.

It's My Birthday

It's my birthday, I can't wait.
Light up the candles on my birthday cake!
One, two, three, four, five, six!

It's my birthday, I can't wait.
Blow out the candles on my birthday cake!
One, two, three, four, five, six!

TEACHING TIP

This activity provides a good opportunity to discuss fire safety with students.

Five Little Loose Teeth

Children practice counting with ordinal numbers with these easy-to-make finger puppets.

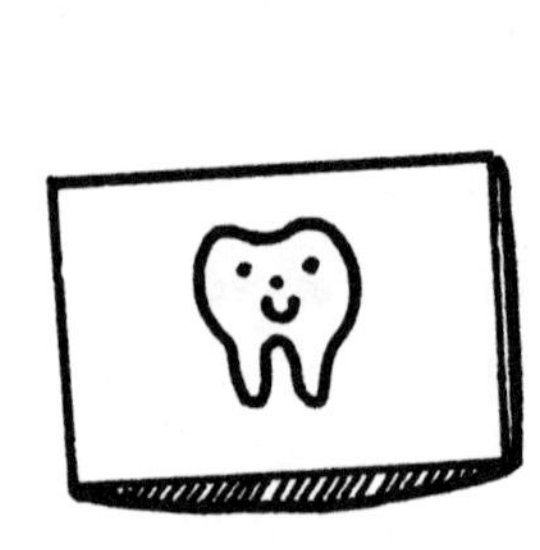

Meeting the Standards: Math

Understands and applies basic and advanced properties of the concepts of numbers:

- Understands the concept of position in a sequence (e.g., first, last)
- Counts whole numbers (i.e., both cardinal and ordinal numbers)

Materials (per child)

- tooth fairy and tooth patterns (page 116)
- crayons
- scissors
- glue stick

Making the Puppets

1. Color and cut out the tooth fairy and tooth patterns.
2. Overlap and glue the ends of the tooth fairy puppet together.
3. Fold each tooth puppet on the line. Glue the sides of each puppet together, leaving the bottom edges open to create a small pocket to slip over a finger or thumb.

Using the Puppets

Use the finger puppets and poem to practice ordinal counting. To begin, have children place all the tooth puppets on one hand and the tooth fairy puppet on the other hand. Then have them move each puppet in order as they recite the rhyme.

Five Little Loose Teeth

Five little loose teeth, ready to fall out.
The first tooth said,
"I'll wiggle and shout."
The second tooth said,
"I don't want to go."
The third tooth said,
"I'll jiggle to and fro."
The fourth tooth said,
"We've got to make room."
The fifth tooth said,
"Big teeth are coming soon."
Then the tooth fairy said,
as she came in the night,
"Come with me little teeth!"
And they flew out of sight.

Celebration Snake

Children create a spiral snake to celebrate the 100th day of school and practice counting by ones, fives, and tens.

Meeting the Standards: Math

Understands and applies basic and advanced properties of the concepts of numbers:

- Counts whole numbers (i.e., both cardinal and ordinal numbers)
- Understands symbolic, concrete, and pictorial representations of numbers (e.g., written numerals, objects in sets, number lines)

Materials (per child)

- snake pattern (page 117)
- crayons
- scissors
- craft stick

Making the Puppet

1. Color all the increments of ten on the snake pattern one color. Choose a different color to color all the increments of five. Choose a third color to color the remaining numbers.
2. Cut out the snake pattern along the dark spiral line.
3. Glue the craft stick to the back of the head, allowing it to extend from the mouth to represent a tongue.
4. Color the tongue red.

Using the Puppet

Use the puppet and poem to practice counting to one hundred. Have children hold the puppet in their nondominant hand as they recite the poem. At the end of the first verse, have them count the numbers on the snake from one to one hundred, pointing to each number as they count. For verses two and three, have children use the snake in the same manner to count by fives and tens.

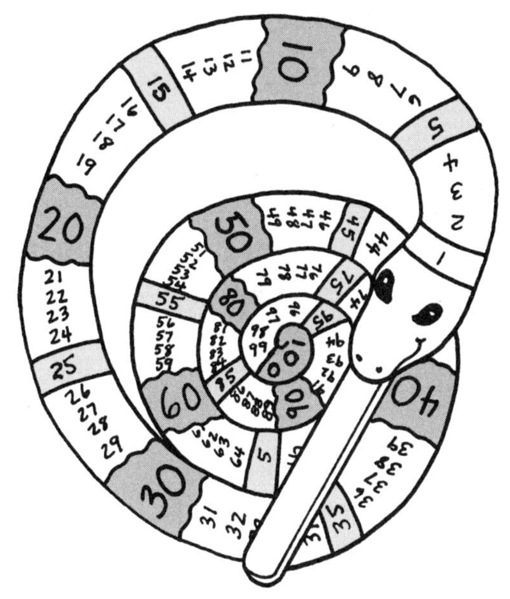

Celebration Snake

How many numbers does it take
To count from one to one hundred on
this snake?
I'll start at the head with the number one,
And count to the tail until I'm done!
One, two, three . . .

How many numbers does it take
To count by fives to one hundred on
this snake?
I'll start with five and you will see,
Counting by fives is easy for me!
Five, ten, fifteen, twenty . . .

How many numbers does it take?
To count by tens to one hundred on
this snake?
Start with ten, it's easy to do.
Before you know it, I'll be through!
Ten, twenty, thirty, forty . . .

I'm a Little Apple

Children create and use an apple stick puppet to share their apple knowledge with others.

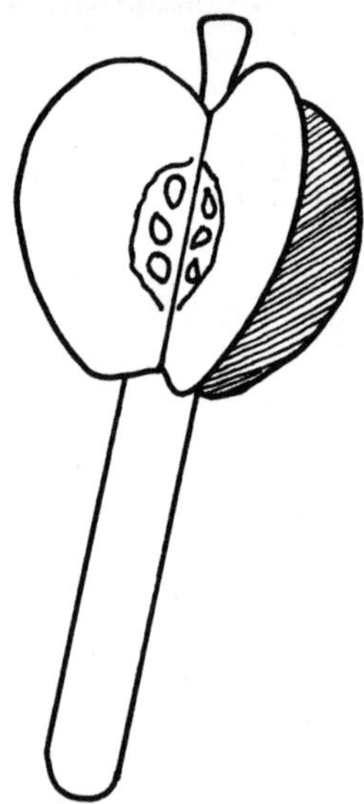

Meeting the Standards: Science

Understands the structure and function of cells and organisms:

- Knows that living things go through a process of change
- Knows the basic needs of plants and animals (e.g., air, water, nutrients, light or food, shelter)

Materials (per child)

- apple and stem patterns (page 118)
- scissors
- crayons
- glue stick
- jumbo craft stick
- 2 wiggle eyes

Making the Puppet

1. Cut out apples A and B, and color the seeds brown. Turn over the cutouts and color the back of each one red. Fold each cutout on the line and then unfold.
2. Place apple A faceup and apple B facedown. Glue B to A only on the right side, creating a flap on the left side of B that can be folded back and forth.

B
Glue B to A
A

3. Color both sides of the stem brown and cut it out. Glue the stem to the back of apple A.
4. For the puppet handle, glue the craft stick to the back of apple A. Then close the flap (apple B) and add wiggle eyes to the front of the puppet.

Using the Puppet

Use the puppet and song to reinforce the parts of an apple and as a discussion starter about plant needs and growth. To begin, have children close the flap of their puppet. Then have them perform the actions in italics as they sing each line of the song.

I'm a Little Apple

(to the tune of "I'm a Little Teapot")

I'm a little apple on the tree.
(Hold apple puppet over head.)
I hang on tight with my stem, you see.
(Point to stem.)
You can reach your hand up and pick me.
(Pretend to pick apple.)
A tasty snack I'm sure to be!
(Rub tummy and smile.)

I'm a tasty apple. I'm just right!
(Nod head and smile.)
Just open your mouth and take a bite.
(Pretend to bite apple.)
There will be a small surprise in sight—
(Open flap on apple.)
Some little seeds all snuggled tight!
(Point to seeds.)

Changing Leaves

Children make a three-sided tree to demonstrate how a tree changes over the seasons.

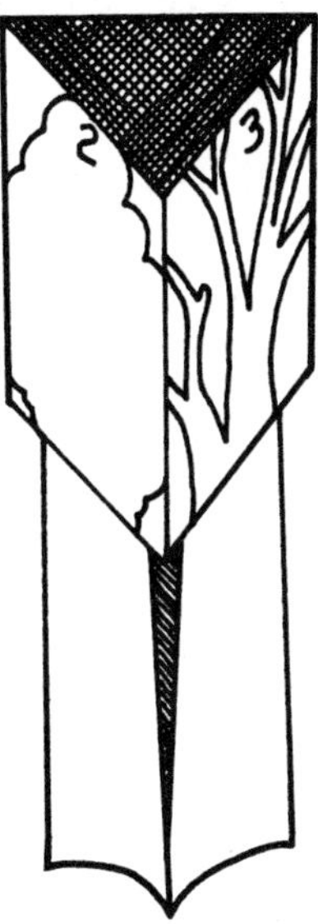

Meeting the Standards: Science

Understands atmospheric processes and the water cycle:

- Knows vocabulary (e.g., rainy, windy, sunny) for different types of weather
- Knows that weather conditions change over time
- Knows how the environment changes over the seasons

Materials (per child)

- treetop pattern (page 118)
- crayons
- scissors
- glue stick
- three 1¾- by 6-inch strips of brown construction paper

Making the Prop

1. Cut out the treetop pattern. Color tree 1 green, tree 2 red, and tree 3 brown.
2. Fold the strip on the lines and glue the ends together to create a three-sided treetop.
3. To make the trunk, glue a strip of brown paper to the bottom of each treetop. Then glue the bottom of the three trunks together.

Using the Prop

Use the prop and poem to reinforce how trees change throughout the seasons. Ask children to hold the prop with the green tree facing them as they recite the first verse of the poem. For the second verse, have them turn the red tree to face them. Finally, have them turn the brown tree to face them as they recite the last verse.

Changing Leaves

In summer, green leaves cover the tree.
On sunny summer days,
Green leaves we see.

In fall, colored leaves cover the tree.
On windy fall days,
Colored leaves we see.

In fall, colored leaves fall off the tree.
So when cold winter comes,
No leaves we see!

It's Fall!

Children create a squirrel puppet and nest to welcome the signs of fall.

Meeting the Standards: Science

Understands the structure and function of cells and organisms:

- Knows the basic needs of plants and animals (e.g., air, water, nutrients, light or food, shelter)
- Knows that plants and animals have features that help them live in different environments

Materials (per child)

- paper bathroom cup
- gray tempera paint
- paintbrush
- squirrel patterns (page 119)
- crayons, including gray
- scissors
- glue stick
- paper lunch bag
- 3 brown pom-poms

Making the Puppet and Props

1. Paint the paper cup gray. Set it aside to dry.
2. Color the squirrel patterns gray, and cut them out. Fold the head along the line and glue it to the bottom of the cup with each side opposite the other side. Fold and glue the tail to the open end of the cup in the same manner. Then glue the legs to the cup.
3. To create a nest, draw colorful leaves on all sides of the paper bag. Open the bag and lay it on its side.

Using the Puppet and Props

Use the puppet, props, and song to reinforce how squirrels prepare for the winter. Have children open their paper bag nest, lay it on its side, and then scatter the pom-pom "nuts" around it. As they sing the first verse, have them use their squirrel puppet to "build" the nest. During the second verse, have them "gather" nuts. Then have them "nestle" their puppet into the nest during the last verse.

It's Fall!

(to the tune of "The Farmer in the Dell")

It's time to build a nest.
It's time to build a nest.
Fall's here, oh little squirrel,
it's time to build a nest.

It's time to gather nuts.
It's time to gather nuts.
Fall's here, oh little squirrel,
it's time to gather nuts.

It's time to nestle in.
It's time to nestle in.
Winter's here, oh little squirrel,
it's time to nestle in.

Columbus Sailed Three Ships

Children create and use character and ship finger puppets to share their knowledge about Columbus Day.

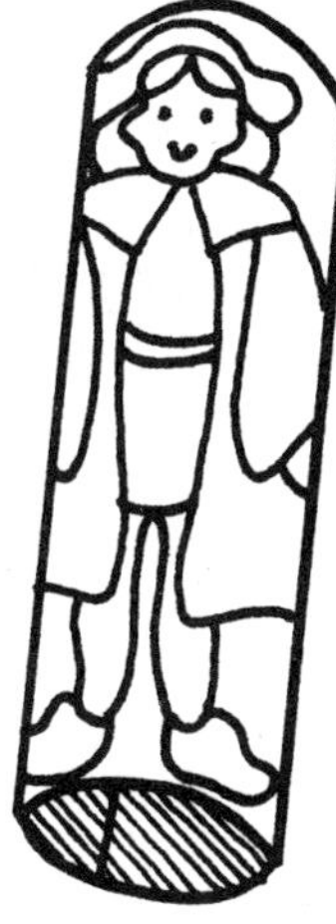

Meeting the Standards: History

Understands selected attributes and historical developments of societies in Africa, the Americas, Asia, and Europe:

- Knows the journeys of Marco Polo and Christopher Columbus and the routes they took

Materials (per child)

- Columbus and ship patterns (page 119)
- crayons
- scissors
- glue stick

Making the Puppets

1. Color and cut out the puppet patterns.
2. Glue the ends of the Columbus puppet together to create a tube.
3. Fold each ship puppet on the line. Glue each of the sides together, leaving the bottom edges open to create a small pocket to slip over a finger or thumb.

Using the Puppets

Use the puppets and song to reinforce facts related to Christopher Columbus's voyage to the Americas. To begin, have children place each ship puppet on a finger on one hand and the Columbus puppet on a finger on the other hand. Then have them move the puppets to the words in the song.

Columbus Sailed Three Ships

(to the tune of "The Hokey Pokey")

Columbus sailed three ships
across the ocean blue.
He was trying to reach Asia,
but he headed west, it's true!
The *Niña* and the *Pinta*
sailed in 1492;
The *Santa María*, too.
(To the Americas!)

Who-o-o's Out on Halloween?

Children make an owl puppet with movable eyes to watch who's out and about on Halloween night.

Meeting the Standards: History

Understands family life now and in the past, and family life in various places long ago:

- Understands personal family or cultural heritage through stories, songs, and celebrations

Materials (per child)

- owl patterns (page 120)
- crayons
- scissors
- glue stick
- jumbo craft stick

Making the Puppet

1. Color and cut out the owl and eye patterns.
2. Cut slits along the dotted lines on the owl's head. (Note to teacher: You may want to do this step for the child.)
3. Glue the craft stick to the bottom of the owl.
4. Thread the eye strip through the slits in the owl.

Using the Puppet

Use the puppet and poem as a springboard to discuss the tradition of wearing costumes on Halloween. To begin, have children position the pair of eyes on the right between the slits in the owl. Then have them recite the first two lines of the poem. On the third line, have them slide the eye strip to the middle pair of eyes. Invite a volunteer to say the last line, filling in the blank with the name of their own or another Halloween character. Then have children slide the eye strip to the pair of eyes on the left.

Who-o-o's Out on Halloween?

Who-o-o, who-o-o's that walking
in the night?
Who-o-o, who-o-o comes near
in the pale moonlight?
Who-o-o! Who-o-o! Who-o-o! Who-o-o!
What a colorful sight!
It's a __________ trick-or-treating
on Halloween night!

The First Thanksgiving Day

Children create and use Pilgrim and Wampanoag puppets to act out a rhyme about the first Thanksgiving.

Meeting the Standards: History

Understands the history of a local community and how communities in North America varied long ago:

- Understands the daily life of a colonial community (e.g., Plymouth, Williamsburg, St. Augustine, San Antonio, Post Vincennes)

Materials (per child)

- Pilgrim and Wampanoag patterns (page 120)
- crayons
- scissors
- four 2¼-inch lengths of paper towel tubes
- stapler
- glue stick

Making the Puppets

1. Color and cut out the Pilgrim and Wampanoag patterns.
2. Flatten one end of each 2¼-inch tube and staple it closed.
3. Glue each cutout to a tube, placing the head at the stapled end of the tube.

Using the Puppets

Use the puppets and poem to reinforce children's knowledge of colonial life and the first Thanksgiving. First, have children place the Pilgrim puppets on one hand and the Wampanoag puppets on the other hand. Then, as they recite the rhyme, have children move the puppets that correspond to each line.

The First Thanksgiving Day

The Wampanoags knew just how to grow
and hunt for food.
They taught their Pilgrim friends how to
do all these things, too.

So when the harvest ended, and the food
was all brought in,
The Pilgrims and Wampanoags came
together once again.

The two groups gathered for three days.
They had no special plans,
But to give thanks for their homes and
food and very special friends.

Back then, the Pilgrims and Wampanoags
played and drank and ate.
And that's why we have Thanksgiving
Day, our thanks to celebrate.

Hide!

Children make a turkey puppet to use with a humorous Thanksgiving Day rhyme.

Meeting the Standards: Language Arts

Uses listening and speaking strategies for different purposes:

- Creates or acts out familiar stories, songs, rhymes, and plays in play activities
- Knows rhyming sounds and simple rhymes (e.g., identifies rhymes and rhyming sounds)

Materials (per child)

- turkey patterns (page 121)
- crayons
- scissors
- foam cup
- clear tape
- ¾- by 12-inch strip of brown construction paper

Making the Puppet

1. Color and cut out the turkey patterns. Then fold the head along the line. Tape each end onto the cup near the bottom rim so that the head stands upright.
2. Fold each tabbed section of the tail along the curved line. Then tape the folded sections to the inside of the cup rim so that the tail on the outside stands up to create a fanned turkey tail.
3. To make legs, accordion-fold the brown paper strip. Tape the middle of the strip to the bottom of the puppet so that the turkey appears to have two legs.

Using the Puppet

Use the puppet and poem to identify and explore words that rhyme. Have children slide one hand into their puppet. Then, as they recite the poem, have them move the puppet to demonstrate the actions of the turkey. Encourage children to use their other hand to form objects in the poem such as the garden, tree, boat, basket, and barn.

Hide!

Hide in the garden.
Hide behind a tree.
Hide in a boat
And sail out to sea.
Hide beneath a basket.
Hide in some hay.
I think I'll leave the barn
And fly, fly away!

Run with a pony.
Roll with a pig.
I'll try to look little.
I'll try to look big!
Pretend I'm a chicken?
Maybe that's the way
To hide myself
On Thanksgiving Day!

My Warm Things

Children create and "dress" a stick puppet for the cold days of winter.

Meeting the Standards: Health

Knows how to maintain and promote personal health:

- Dresses self appropriately (e.g., puts on coat and hat, laces shoes)

Materials (per child)

- 9- by 5½-inch brown construction paper
- white tempera paint
- sponge for sponge-painting
- puppet, scarf, and mitten patterns (pages 121–122)
- crayons
- scissors
- glue stick
- jumbo craft stick

Making the Puppet

1. Sponge-paint white "snow" onto the brown paper. Set the paper aside to dry.
2. Draw a face on the puppet to resemble yourself. Then color and cut out the puppet, scarf, and mitten pieces.
3. Glue the back of each scarf tab to the back of the coat collar, as indicated. Fold the scarf pieces over the front of the coat so the pattern shows.
4. Glue the back of each mitten tab to the back of the corresponding hand, as indicated. Fold the mittens over the hands.
5. Line up the bottom of the puppet with a long edge of the snow-covered brown paper and glue it in place. Then glue the craft stick to the puppet.

Using the Puppet

Use the puppet and song to reinforce wearing appropriate clothing for the winter. Before singing the song, have children fold the scarf behind the puppet and fold the mittens out. Then have them point to the hat during the first verse, flip the two sides of the scarf to the front of the puppet during the second verse, and fold the mittens over the hands during the third verse.

Oh, I Need to Wear My Warm Things

(to the tune of "She'll Be Coming 'Round the Mountain")

Oh, I need to wear a warm hat on cold days.
Oh, I need to wear a warm hat on cold days.
Oh, I need to wear my warm things when
the winter brings its cold days.
Oh, I need to wear a warm hat on cold days.

Oh, I need to wear warm mittens on cold days.
Oh, I need to wear warm mittens on cold days.
Oh, I need to wear my warm things when
the winter brings its cold days.
Oh, I need to wear warm mittens on cold days.

Oh, I need to wear a warm scarf on cold days.
Oh, I need to wear a warm scarf on cold days.
Oh, I need to wear my warm things when
the winter brings its cold days.
Oh, I need to wear a warm scarf on cold days.

I Can Build a Snowman

Children decorate and use a folding snowman puppet to demonstrate how weather conditions affect snow.

Meeting the Standards: Science

Understands atmospheric processes and the water cycle:

- Knows vocabulary for different types of weather
- Knows that short-term weather conditions can change daily
- Knows that water can be a liquid or solid and can be made to change from one form to the other

Materials (per child)

- snowman patterns (page 123)
- crayons
- scissors
- glue stick
- jumbo craft stick

Making the Puppet

1. Draw a face on the front snowman pattern. Color the hat and add other features such as buttons and a scarf. Color the broom.
2. Cut out the snowman and broom patterns.
3. Glue the front and back snowman cutouts together. Sandwich the craft stick between the bottom sections of the cutouts.
4. Glue the broom to the left side of the snowman.
5. Fold the broom back behind the snowman. Then, starting with the hat, fold back each section of the snowman so that only the bottom section is visible.

Using the Puppet

Use the puppet and song to reinforce how changing weather conditions can change the properties of snow. As children sing, invite them to build a snowman by unfolding their puppets one section at a time, from the bottom up, and then unfolding the broom. At the end of the song, have them melt their snowman by folding the puppet in the reverse order.

I Can Build a Snowman

I can build a snowman on a snowy
winter day.
I can build a snowman in my own
special way.

First, I'll make the bottom, then the
middle, and the top.
I'll add a face and buttons, but there's
more before I stop.

My snowman needs a broom, so I'll put
one by his side.
He also needs a fancy hat that he can
wear with pride.

My snowman stands so tall and proud
on a winter day
Until the bright warm sunshine slowly
melts him right away!

Luminaria Lanterns

Children make and use a luminaria puppet to highlight a delightful Las Posadas custom.

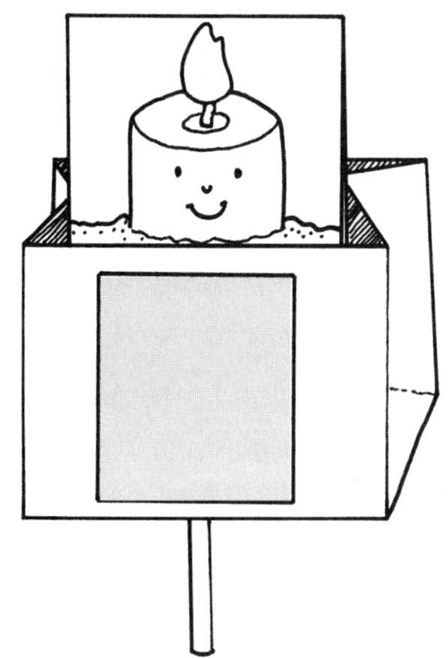

Meeting the Standards: History

Understands family life now and in the past, and family life in various places long ago:

- Understands personal family or cultural heritage through stories, songs, and celebrations
- Knows ways in which people share family beliefs and values

Materials (per child)

- candle pattern (page 124)
- crayons
- scissors
- glue stick
- plastic drinking straw
- white paper lunch bag, trimmed to 4 inches tall
- 3-inch square of yellow tissue paper

Making the Prop

1. Color and cut out the candles pattern. Fold the cutout on the line.
2. Glue the two sides of the pattern together, sandwiching the straw between them to create a two-sided puppet with handle.
3. Cut a dime-sized hole in the bottom of the bag. Glue the yellow square to the front of the bag to represent a glowing light.
4. Open the bag and slide the puppet handle through the hole. Move the handle up and down to raise and lower the candle puppet in the bag.

Using the Prop

Use the puppet and poem to reinforce the Las Posadas tradition of lighting luminarias, also called *farolitos*. As children recite the first verse, have them push the burning candle above the top of the "glowing" side of the bag. For the second verse, have them lower the candle into the bag. During the last verse, have children raise the extinguished candle over the top of the plain side of the bag.

Luminaria Lanterns

It's Las Posadas,
A very special night
With festive candles
Burning bright.

In paper lanterns,
Row after row,
Our pretty farolitos
Shine and glow.

Then lanterns dim
Around the town.
All the glowing candles
Have melted down!

This activity provides a good opportunity to discuss fire safety with students.

It's Hanukkah!

Children make a menorah to use while sharing their knowledge of Hanukkah.

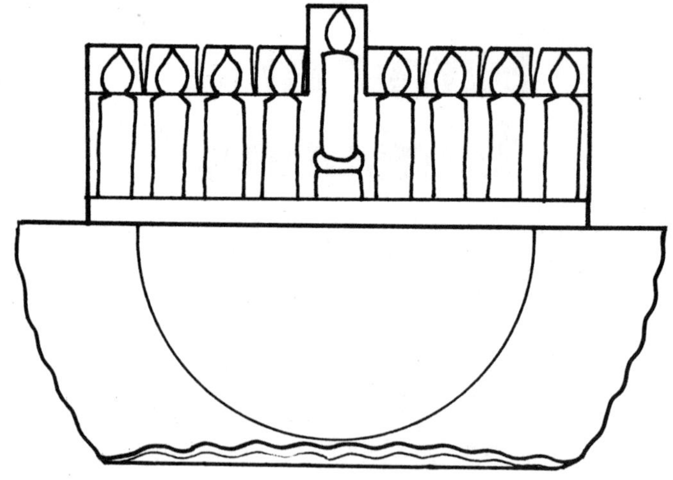

Meeting the Standards: History

Understands family life now and in the past, and family life in various places long ago:

- Understands personal family or cultural heritage through stories, songs, and celebrations
- Knows ways in which people share family beliefs and values (e.g., oral traditions, literature, songs, art, religion, community celebrations, mementos, food, language)

Materials (per child)

- one half of a 9-inch paper plate
- crayons
- glitter glue
- sequins
- glue stick
- menorah candles pattern (page 125)
- scissors

Making the Prop

1. To make the menorah, color the paper plate. Then decorate it with glitter glue and a few sequins.
2. Color and cut out the menorah candles pattern. Carefully cut along each dotted line between the candle flames.
3. Glue the cutout to the straight edge of the paper plate where indicated.
4. Fold the bottom rim of the plate forward about 2 inches to create a base for the menorah.

Using the Prop

Use the prop and poem to reinforce children's understanding of how a menorah is used during a Hanukkah celebration. To begin, explain that the middle candle—the Shamash—is used to light the other eight candles. Then have students stand their menorah on their desk and fold the eight flames down behind the candles. At the end of the poem, have them fold up one flap at a time (from left to right) to "light" each candle as they count.

It's Hanukkah!

It's Hanukkah,
The Festival of Lights!
Light a new candle
On eight Hanukkah nights.

Warm and flickering,
See the Shamash burn.
Use it to light up
Each candle on its turn.

The candles all are glowing.
Let's count and celebrate—
One, two, three, four,
Five, six, seven, eight!

TEACHING TIP

This activity provides a good opportunity to discuss fire safety with students.

Five Little Stockings

Children make a stocking-lined fireplace to practice their counting skills.

Meeting the Standards: Math

Understands and applies basic and advanced properties of the concepts of numbers:

- Understands one-to-one correspondence
- Counts whole numbers (i.e., both cardinal and ordinal numbers)

Materials (per child)

- fireplace and stocking patterns (page 126)
- crayons
- scissors
- glue stick

Making the Prop

1. Color and cut out the fireplace and stocking patterns. Glue the stocking cutout to the back of the fireplace along the top edge, as indicated.
2. Carefully cut along each dotted line between the stockings. Fold each stocking back behind the fireplace.
3. Fold back the bottom section of the fireplace to create a base.

Using the Prop

Use the prop and poem to reinforce one-to-one correspondence and ordinal numbers. To begin, ask students to fold all the stockings back behind the fireplace and then stand their fireplace on its base. As they mention each stocking in the poem, have them flip a stocking forward so that it appears to be hanging on the fireplace.

Five Little Stockings

(to the tune of "Five Little Pumpkins")

Five little stockings, hanging in a row.
The first one says,
  "It's Christmas Eve, you know!"
The second one says,
  "What is that sound I hear?"
The third one says,
  "Dear Santa is near."
The fourth one says,
  "He's good to girls and boys."
The fifth one says,
  "He'll fill us up with toys!"
"Ho, Ho, Ho!" Santa fills every one.
So Christmas Day will be filled with fun!

TEACHING TIP
This activity provides a good opportunity to discuss fire safety with students.

Kwanzaa Candles

Children create a candlestick prop to use in a Kwanzaa rhyme.

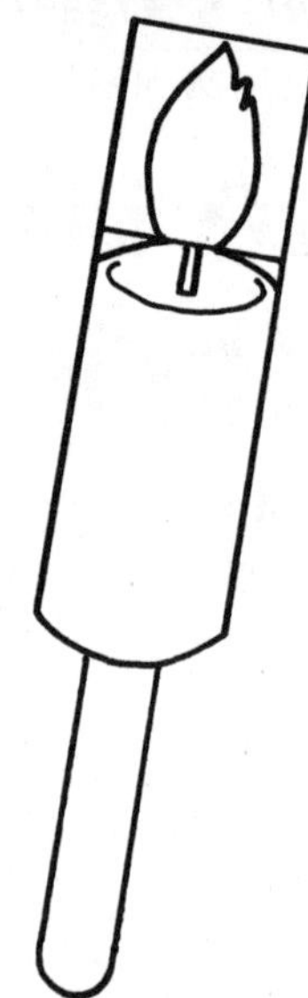

Meeting the Standards: History

Understands family life now and in the past, and family life in various places long ago:

- Understands personal family or cultural heritage through stories, songs, and celebrations
- Knows ways in which people share family beliefs and values (e.g., oral traditions, literature, songs, art, religion, community celebrations, mementos, food, language)

Materials (per child)

- candle pattern (page 125)
- crayons
- scissors
- glue stick
- jumbo craft stick

Making the Prop

(Note to teacher: Divide the class into groups of seven and have three children color their candles red, three color theirs green, and one child color his or her candle black.)

1. Color the candle with the assigned color and color the flame yellow. Then cut out the candle pattern and fold it in half along the center line.
2. Glue the two sides of the cutout together, sandwiching the craft stick between the sides at the bottom to create a handle.

Using the Prop

Use the props and poem to help reinforce understanding of the Kwanzaa celebration. Explain that the kinara is a candleholder and that *mishumaa* is the Swahili word for candles. First, line up a group of seven children from left to right according to their candle color: three red, one black, three green. Have them fold the flame back behind their candle. Then have them recite the rhyme, raising and lowering their prop when their candle color is named. On the last line, have each child—starting with the first red candle on the left—lift the flame on his or her candle as a number is called.

Kwanzaa Candles

We are Kwanzaa candles,
All in a row.
Set in the kinara.
This is how we go:
Three red, one black,
Three green stand tall.
We are mishumaa,
Seven candles in all.

Seven Kwanzaa candles
All in a line.
Time to light the candles.
Time to see us shine!
Seven Kwanzaa candles
Glowing so bright.
1, 2, 3, 4, 5, 6, 7,
Lighting up the night!

This activity provides a good opportunity to discuss fire safety with students.

Happy New Year!

Children create and use a countdown flip sign to welcome in the New Year.

Meeting the Standards: Math

Understands and applies basic and advanced properties of the concepts of numbers:

- Understands that numerals are symbols used to represent quantities or attributes of real-world objects
- Counts whole numbers (i.e., both cardinal and ordinal numbers)

Materials (per child)

- flip sign pattern (page 127)
- crayons
- scissors
- glue stick

Making the Prop

1. Write the number for the new year on the writing line on the pattern. Then color and cut out the pattern.
2. To make the base, fold each side of the cutout back along the fold lines, bringing the two ends toward each other. Unfold and apply glue to the area between the folds (on the back of the cutout). Then refold the cutout, pressing the side sections into the glue until they meet in the middle. (Note to teacher: An adult should complete this step.)

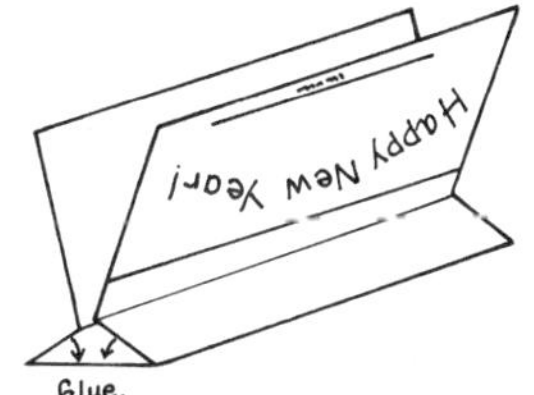

3. Glue the two loose sides together back-to-back. When standing, the cutout will form an upside down T. Allow the glue to dry.
4. Cut along the dotted lines between the numbers to make ten flaps.

Using the Prop

Use the prop and poem to reinforce counting back from ten to one. To begin, have children stand the flip sign on their desk with the numbers facing them. Then have them recite the poem. When they get to the countdown, have children fold down each number as it is named. At the end of the rhyme, their sign will show a surprise new year greeting!

Happy New Year!

Out with the old year, in with the new.
Countdown to midnight, a big to-do!
Toot your horn, and give a cheer.
Ten!
Nine!
Eight!
Seven!
Six!
Five!
Four!
Three!
Two!
One!

Happy New Year!

Golden Dragon

Children make a dragon puppet to greet the Chinese New Year.

Meeting the Standards: History

Understands selected attributes and historical developments of societies in Africa, the Americas, Asia, and Europe:

- Knows the holidays and ceremonies of different societies (e.g., Christmas celebrations in Scandinavia, Germany, or England; Cinco de Mayo; the Chinese New Year)

Materials (per child)

- dragon patterns (page 128)
- yellow, gold, and red crayons
- scissors
- paper lunch bag
- scraps of yellow paper
- six 7-inch lengths of red crepe streamer

Making the Puppet

1. Use yellow, gold, and red crayons to color both dragon patterns the same.
2. Cut out the dragon patterns. Open the bag and glue a cutout to each side of the bag so that the entire mouth extends beyond the bottom of the bag. Glue the loose edges of the cutout together (from the dragon's nose to its chin).
3. Cut scraps of yellow paper into various shapes. Glue the shapes onto both sides of the bag to create dragon scales.
4. For the tail, glue three red streamers onto each side of the bag at the open end.

Using the Puppet

Use the puppet and poem to reinforce children's knowledge about the Chinese New Year celebration. Before reciting the poem, ask children to place the puppet on their hand. Then have them make the dragon twist and dance as they say the poem.

Golden Dragon

Here comes a golden dragon
  moving to the beat.
Twisting left and jumping right
  and dancing down the street.
He's wishing us a year of peace,
  and good fortune, too.
And strength and lots of good luck
  to last the whole year through.
There goes the golden dragon.
  Can you guess what I hear?
Gung Hay Fat Choy! Happy New Year!

Special Presidents

Children decorate and use a flip puppet to share what they know about Presidents Washington and Lincoln.

Meeting the Standards: History

Understands how democratic values came to be, and how they have been exemplified by people, events, and symbols:

- Understands how important figures reacted to their time and why they were significant to the history of our democracy (e.g., George Washington, Thomas Jefferson, Abraham Lincoln)
- Understands the reasons that Americans celebrate national holidays (e.g., Martin Luther King, Jr. Day, the Fourth of July, Memorial Day)

Materials (per child)

- presidents pattern (page 124)
- crayons
- scissors
- glue stick
- jumbo craft stick
- white cotton balls
- brown yarn

Making the Puppet

1. Color and cut out the presidents pattern.
2. Fold the cutout in half along the line. Glue the two sides together, sandwiching the craft stick between them.
3. Glue stretched white cotton balls to George Washington's hair.
4. Cut and unravel short lengths of brown yarn. Glue the pieces to Abe Lincoln's hair and beard.

Using the Puppet

Use the puppet and poem as a springboard to discuss the importance of Presidents Washington and Lincoln, as well as other presidents. While reciting the first verse of the poem, have children turn the Washington side of their puppet to face them. Then have them flip the puppet to the Lincoln side as they recite the last verse.

Special Presidents

We remember special presidents
Each year on Presidents' Day.
So let us cheer George Washington,
Our first president. Hooray!

We remember special presidents
Each year on Presidents' Day.
So let us cheer Abe Lincoln now,
Our sixteenth president. Hooray!

The Dove of Peace

Children create a dove puppet to give flight to the ideas of freedom and peace.

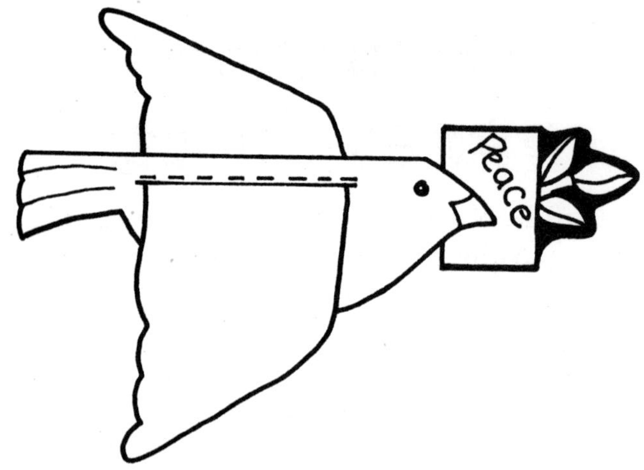

Meeting the Standards: History

Understands how democratic values came to be, and how they have been exemplified by people, events, and symbols:

- Understands how individuals have worked to achieve the liberties and equality promised in the principles of American democracy and to improve the lives of people from many groups (e.g., Rosa Parks, Martin Luther King, Jr., Sojourner Truth)
- Understands the reasons that Americans celebrate certain national holidays (e.g., Martin Luther King, Jr. Day, the Fourth of July, Memorial Day)

Materials (per child)

- peace note, dove, and wing patterns (page 129)
- crayons
- scissors
- glue stick

Making the Puppet

1. Color and cut out the peace note, dove, and wing patterns.
2. Fold the peace note in half on the line. Glue the two sides together.
3. Fold the dove in half on the line. Glue the two sides together, sandwiching the peace note between the two sides of the beak.
4. Cut along the dotted lines to make a slit in the dove. (Note to teacher: An adult should complete this step.)
5. Fold the wings in half along the line. Slide the wings through the slit in the dove.

Using the Puppet

Use the puppet and song to reinforce the message of peace promoted by Dr. Martin Luther King, Jr. As children sing the song, encourage them to move their puppet in creative ways to interpret the words.

The Dove of Peace

(to the tune of "My Country 'Tis of Thee")

The Dove of Peace flies free.
It's telling you and me,
"Let's work for peace."

Peace now for me and you.
Peace for the whole world, too.
Together let our voices ring.
Honor Dr. King!

Groundhog Looks Around

Children make and use a pop-up groundhog puppet to "predict" the weather.

Meeting the Standards: Science

Understands atmospheric processes and the water cycle:

- Knows vocabulary (e.g., rainy, windy, sunny) for different types of weather
- Knows that weather conditions change over time

Materials (per child)

- groundhog pattern (page 130)
- crayons
- scissors
- glue stick
- jumbo craft stick
- paper lunch bag

Making the Puppet

1. Color and cut out the groundhog pattern.
2. Fold the cutout on the line. Glue the sides together, sandwiching the craft stick between them to create a handle.
3. To create a groundhog burrow, cut off 3½ inches from the top of the bag. Then cut a 1½- by 4-inch opening in the bottom of the bag. (Note to teacher: An adult should complete this step.)
4. Open the bag, turn it upside down, and push the puppet up and down through the opening in the "burrow."

Using the Puppet

Use the puppet and poem to reinforce children's understanding of different weather conditions and the seasons. To begin, ask children to lower their puppet into the burrow. Then, as they recite the poem, have them move their puppet up and down through the opening to follow the words in the poem.

Groundhog Looks Around

Slowly, groundhog looks around.
Slowly, groundhog peeks.
He sees his shadow. Run and hide!
Winter—six more weeks!

Slowly, groundhog looks around.
What will the weather bring?
He sees no shadow, he stays out!
We'll have an early spring!

Three Little Valentines

Children make finger puppets to use with a special Valentine's Day rhyme.

Meeting the Standards: Language Arts

Uses listening and speaking strategies for different purposes:

- Uses new vocabulary to describe feelings, thoughts, experiences, and observations
- Creates or acts out familiar stories, songs, rhymes, and plays in play activities

Materials (per child)

- valentine finger puppet patterns (page 130)
- crayons
- scissors
- glue stick

Making the Puppets

1. Color and cut out the valentine patterns.
2. Fold each cutout on the line. Glue each of the sides together, leaving the bottom edges open to create a small pocket to slip over a finger or thumb.

Using the Puppets

Use the finger puppets and poem to reinforce listening skills. Before reciting the poem, have children place each finger puppet on a finger on one hand. During the first verse, have them move each puppet in order as a different valentine "speaks." Invite children to create their own movements to the words in the second verse.

Three Little Valentines

Three little valentines looking so fine.
The first one said, "Will you be mine?"
The second one said, "I love you."
The third one said, "I love you, too!"

I'll sign my name on each of them,
And cross my fingers, too.
I'll send you all these valentines
To say that I love you.

Dance, Leprechaun!

Introduce vocabulary and traditions related to St. Patrick's Day with this adorable leprechaun puppet.

Meeting the Standards: History

Understands selected attributes and historical developments of societies in Africa, the Americas, Asia, and Europe:

- Knows the holidays and ceremonies of different societies (e.g., Christmas celebrations in Scandinavia, Germany, or England; Cinco de Mayo; the Chinese New Year; the Japanese tea ceremony; harvest and spring festivals)

Materials (per child)

- leprechaun and hat patterns (page 131)
- crayons
- scissors
- 4½-inch length of paper towel tube
- stapler
- glue stick
- 2 wiggle eyes
- small green pom-pom

Making the Puppet

1. Color and cut out the leprechaun and hat patterns.
2. Fold the hat on the center line and glue the top and side edges together, leaving the bottom edge open.
3. Flatten one end of the 4½-inch tube and staple it closed.
4. Glue the leprechaun cutout to the tube, with the head at the stapled end. Add wiggle eyes and a pom-pom nose. Then slip the hat over the leprechaun's head.

Using the Puppet

Use the puppet and song to reinforce children's knowledge of St. Patrick's Day. As children sing the song, invite them to skip, twirl, and dance along with their leprechaun puppet partners.

Dance, Leprechaun!

(to the tune of "Skip to My Lou")

Skip, skip, skip, leprechaun.
Skip, skip, skip, leprechaun.
Skip, skip, skip, leprechaun.
St. Patrick's Day in the morning!

Twirl, twirl, twirl, leprechaun.
Twirl, twirl, twirl, leprechaun.
Twirl, twirl, twirl, leprechaun.
St. Patrick's Day in the morning!

Dance, dance, dance, leprechaun.
Dance, dance, dance, leprechaun.
Dance, dance, dance, leprechaun.
St. Patrick's Day in the morning!

From Rain to Rainbow

Children create and use a cloud stick prop to demonstrate their understanding of weather patterns.

Meeting the Standards: Science

Understands atmospheric processes and the water cycle:

- Knows vocabulary (e.g., rainy, windy, sunny) for different types of weather
- Knows that short-term weather conditions (e.g., temperature, rain, snow) can change daily, and weather patterns change over the seasons

Materials (per child)

- cloud, rain, sun, and rainbow patterns (page 132)
- crayons
- scissors
- glue stick
- jumbo craft stick

Making the Prop

1. Color and cut out the cloud, rain, sun, and rainbow patterns.
2. Glue the craft stick to the back of the cloud.
3. Glue the rain cutout to the bottom of the left side of the cloud. Then glue the sun cutout to the top center of the cloud and the rainbow cutout to the right side of the cloud.
4. Fold the rain, sun, and rainbow behind the cloud puppet.

Using the Prop

Use the prop and poem to help children understand the changing conditions of spring weather. To begin, ask them to fold the rain, sun, and rainbow behind the puppet. Then, as they recite the poem, have children use their puppet to perform the action suggested for each line.

From Rain to Rainbow

White clouds grow dark.
(Hold up cloud.)
Down comes the spring rain.
(Flip down rain.)
It's too wet to go out and play.
(Tap cloud to make rain sounds.)

The rain stops falling.
(Fold up rain.)
Up comes the spring sun.
(Flip up sun.)
Look! A rainbow! A beautiful day.
(Flip rainbow out.)

Tulip Garden

Children create a spring tulip garden to practice ordinal number skills.

Meeting the Standards: Math

Understands and applies basic and advanced properties of the concepts of numbers:

- Understands one-to-one correspondence
- Understands the concept of position in a sequence
- Counts whole numbers (i.e., both cardinal and ordinal numbers)

Materials (per child)

- tulip garden pattern (page 133)
- crayons
- scissors

Making the Prop

1. Color and cut out the tulip garden pattern.
2. Cut along the dotted lines between the tulips.
3. Fold the base back along the center line.
4. Stand the tulip garden on the table. Fold each tulip back toward the table.

Using the Prop

Use the prop and poem to reinforce ordinal number skills. To begin, ask children to stand the tulip garden on the table with the tulips folded back. As they recite the poem, have children fold up each tulip as it is named, starting with the first one on the left and moving to the right.

Tulip Garden

Five tulip bulbs planted in a flower bed.
"Wake up now!" the first one said.
The second one said,
 "The sky is very blue."
The third one said,
 "There's sunshine, too!"
The fourth one said,
 "Let's sing, and sing, and sing!"
The fifth one said,
 "I'm happy that it's spring!"

Growing, Slowly Growing

Children make a plant with a rain sleeve to share their knowledge of how plants grow.

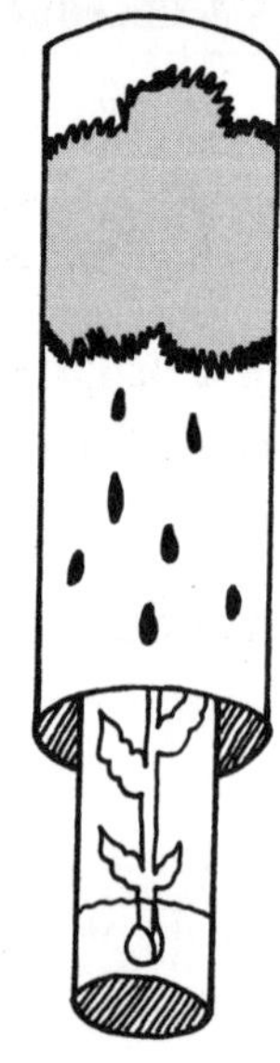

Meeting the Standards: Science

Understands relationships among organisms and their physical environment:

- Knows that plants and animals need certain resources for energy and growth (e.g., food, water, light, air)

Materials (per child)

- plant pattern (page 131)
- crayons
- scissors
- paper towel tube
- glue stick
- 9- by 12-inch light blue construction paper
- gray and blue tempera paint
- paintbrush
- tape

Making the Props

1. Color and cut out the plant pattern. Glue the cutout to the paper towel tube.
2. Place the light blue paper vertically on the table. Paint a gray cloud and blue rain drops on the center of the paper. Allow the paint to dry.
3. Tape together the right and left sides of the blue paper to form a tube—or rain sleeve.
4. Stand the plant on a table. Slide the rain sleeve over the plant. Then slowly lift the rain sleeve to reveal the progress of the plant's growth.

Using the Props

Use the props and poem to explore the relationship between rain and plant growth. To begin, ask children to stand their plant on a table and slide the rain sleeve over it. While reciting the poem, have children slowly lift the sleeve to reveal each stage of the plant's growth as it is described in the poem.

Growing, Slowly Growing

It's spring, and I'm growing.
I start out as a seed.
Growing, slowly growing.
Sun and water are all I need.

It's spring, and I'm growing.
I'm a sprout with leaves so small.
Growing, slowly growing.
My leaves are big and now I'm tall.

It's spring, and I'm growing.
Look, I have some pretty flowers.
Growing, slowly growing.
How I love those April showers!

The Recycle Bin

Children make and use this special wheel to learn about Earth Day and recycling.

Meeting the Standards: Geography

Understands how human actions modify the physical environment:

- Knows how people affect the environment in negative (e.g., litter, pollution) and positive (e.g., recycling, picking up litter) ways

Materials (per child)

- recycle wheel cover and wheel patterns (page 134)
- crayons
- scissors
- paper brad

Making the Prop

1. Color and cut out the recycle wheel cover and wheel patterns.
2. Carefully cut out the box on the wheel cover (Note to teacher: An adult should complete steps 2 and 3.)
3. Place the wheel behind the wheel cover and poke the paper brad through the center of both pieces. Turn the wheel to make sure it moves freely.

Using the Prop

Use the prop and poem to teach children about recyclable items and the benefits of recycling. As children recite each verse of the poem, have them turn their recycle wheel so that the named item appears in the window on the wheel cover.

The Recycle Bin

Put some plastic in the recycle bin,
Find some more and put it in.
When we recycle, we all win!
So put some plastic in the recycle bin.

Put some aluminum in the recycle bin,
Find some more and put it in.
When we recycle, we all win!
So put some aluminum in the
recycle bin.

Put some glass in the recycle bin,
Find some more and put it in.
When we recycle, we all win!
So put some glass in the recycle bin.

Put some paper in the recycle bin,
Find some more and put it in.
When we recycle, we all win!
So put some paper in the recycle bin.

Pretty May Flowers

Children make and use May Day finger puppets to explore colors.

Meeting the Standards: Language Arts

Uses listening and speaking strategies for different purposes:

- Uses descriptive language (e.g., color words; size words, such as *bigger*, *smaller*; shape words)

Materials (per child)

- flower finger puppet patterns (page 133)
- crayons
- scissors
- glue stick

Making the Puppets

1. Color each flower puppet pattern one of these colors: red, yellow, blue, orange, and purple. Cut out the patterns.
2. Fold each flower puppet on the line. Glue the sides of each puppet together to create a small pocket to slip over a finger or thumb.

Using the Puppets

Use the puppets and poem to reinforce colors while celebrating May Day. To begin, ask children to place all the flower puppets on one hand. Then have them move one puppet at a time as it is mentioned in the poem. On the last line, instruct children to bring all their fingers together to make a "bouquet."

Pretty May Flowers

Five pretty flowers growing in the yard.
The red one said,
"Blooming is so hard."
The yellow one said,
"We're really pretty now."
The blue one said,
"Let's all take a bow."
The orange one said,
"It's a beautiful day."
The purple one said,
"It's the first day of May."
Along came some friends to celebrate—
A bouquet for May Day will be just great!

Hang the Piñata High!

Children make these colorful piñatas to celebrate Cinco de Mayo.

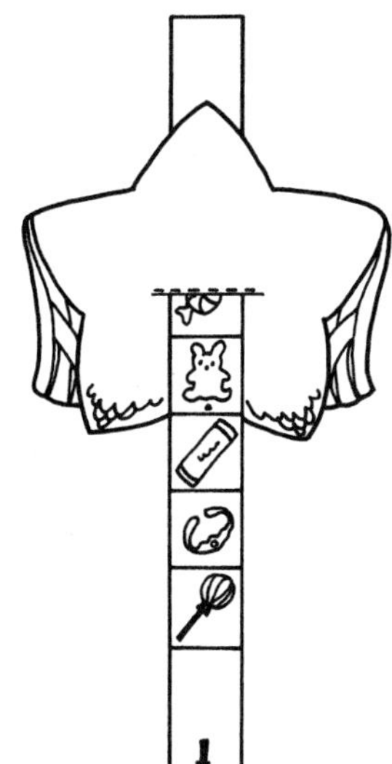

Meeting the Standards: History

Understands selected attributes and historical developments of societies in Africa, the Americas, Asia, and Europe:

- Knows the holidays and ceremonies of different societies (e.g., Christmas celebrations in Scandinavia, Germany, or England; Cinco de Mayo; the Chinese New Year; the Japanese tea ceremony; harvest and spring festivals)

Materials (per child)

- piñata and treat patterns (page 135)
- crayons
- scissors
- glue stick
- 2 jumbo craft sticks

Making the Prop

1. Color and cut out the piñata and treat patterns.
2. Cut a slit along the dotted line on the piñata. (Note to teacher: An adult should complete this step.)
3. Glue a craft stick to the back of the piñata just below the slit.
4. Glue the two treat strips together where indicated to create one long strip. Insert the arrow end of the strip through the slit from the back of the piñata. Slowly pull the strip through the slit to reveal one treat at a time "falling" from the piñata.

Using the Prop

Use the prop and song to help children learn about a Cinco de Mayo custom—breaking a colorful piñata! While singing the first three lines of the song, ask children to bounce their piñata to the rhythm. Have them hold their piñata high during the next three lines. On the next to last line, ask them to gently tap their piñata with the other craft stick. Finally, on the last line, invite children to slowly pull the strip through the slit to reveal all the treats hidden inside the piñata.

Hang the Piñata High!

(to the tune of "For He's a Jolly Good Fellow")

Today is Cinco de Mayo.
Today is Cinco de Mayo.
Today is Cinco de Mayo.
Let's hang the piñata high!

Hang the piñata high!
Hang the piñata high!
Break open the treat-filled piñata,
Treats falling from the sky!

A Flower for Mom

Children create a customized puppet to offer their mom a special Mother's Day gift.

Meeting the Standards: Health

Understands the relationship of family health to individual health:

- Knows the roles of parents and the extended family in supporting a strong family and promoting the health of children

Materials (per child)

- 6-inch paper plate
- crayons
- paper scraps (to share)
- craft items (yarn, ribbon, buttons to share)
- scissors
- glue
- paper lunch bag
- two 1½- by 9-inch strips of construction paper
- four 3-inch tissue paper circles in assorted colors
- mini-clothespin

Making the Puppet and Prop

1. Draw a face on the paper plate to resemble your mother. Use craft items to add details, such as button eyes and yarn hair.
2. Glue the paper-plate head to the bottom of the bag.
3. For arms, accordion-fold the 1½- by 9-inch strips of paper. Glue an arm to each side of the bag. Use craft items to decorate the paper-bag body.
4. Stack the tissue-paper circles and glue them together at the centers. Twist the stack to create a flower. Glue the flower to the mini-clothespin. Clip the flower to the puppet's head or body.

Using the Puppet and Prop

Use the puppet, prop, and poem to help children express appreciation for their mother. To begin, ask them to remove the clip-on flower from the puppet. Then have them use their puppet to act out the poem. On the last two lines, have children clip the flower to the puppet's hair or body.

A Flower for Mom

My mom gives me kisses.
My mom hugs me tight.
Each and every morning,
And each and every night.

I want to tell her, "Thank you."
She does so much each day.
So here's a flower she can wear.
Happy Mother's Day!

Picnic Day!

Children create a picnic basket to "pack" with supplies for a make-believe summer picnic.

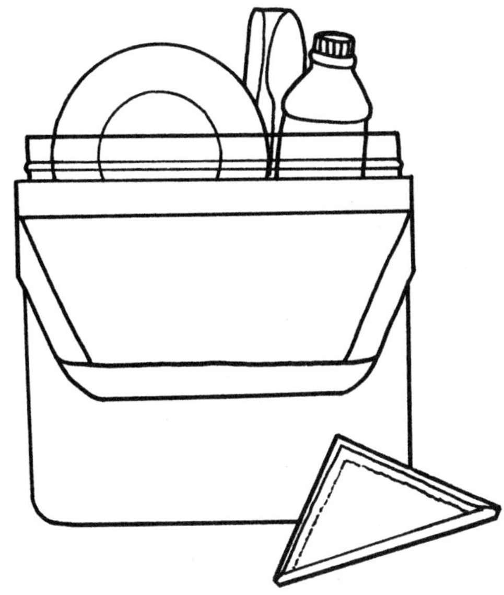

Meeting the Standards: Language Arts

Uses listening and speaking strategies for different purposes:

- Follows one- and two-step directions
- Recites and responds to familiar stories, poems, and rhymes with patterns (e.g., relates information to own life; describes character, setting, plot)

Materials (per child)

- picnic basket and supply patterns (pages 136–137)
- crayons
- scissors
- quart-size resealable plastic bag
- glue

Making the Props

1. Color and cut out the picnic basket and picnic supply patterns.
2. Glue the picnic basket to the plastic bag, placing the top edge of the basket just below the bag's zipper.
3. Open the "picnic basket" and place the picnic supplies inside.

Using the Props

Use the picnic props and poem to reinforce listening and following directions. First, ask children to remove the picnic supplies from their picnic basket and place them faceup on the table. Then, as they recite the poem, have them place each item in the basket as it is named.

Picnic Day!

Forks, spoons,
Napkins, plates,
Pack them just this way.

Sandwiches, apples,
Water, chips.
It's time for a picnic day!

My Favorite Summer Spot!

Children sing about and act out a favorite summertime activity with this personalized puppet.

Meeting the Standards: Language Arts

Uses listening and speaking strategies for different purposes:

- Creates or acts out familiar stories, songs, rhymes, and plays in play activities
- Follows one- and two-step directions

Materials (per child)

- summertime puppet pattern (page 138)
- crayons
- scissors
- jumbo craft stick

Making the Puppet

1. Cut out the puppet pattern. Decorate the figure to resemble yourself wearing a swimsuit.
2. Fold the puppet cutout in half along the line. Glue the front and back sides together, trapping the craft stick between the two layers to create a handle at the bottom of the puppet.

Using the Puppet

Use the puppet and song to reinforce listening and following directions while acting out a fun summer activity. As children sing along, ask them to move their puppets to the words and perform the action named in the song.

My Favorite Summer Spot!

(to the tune of "The Hokey Pokey")

Now that it's summertime,
The days are very hot.
I head out to the pool.
It's my favorite summer spot!
I walk into the water,
Take a breath, and plunge right in.
The pool is my favorite spot!

Now that it's summertime,
The days are very hot.
I head out to the pool.
It's my favorite summer spot!
I walk into the water,
Take a breath, and slide right in.
The pool is my favorite spot!

Packing for Summer Fun

Children make and "pack" a summer bag for some imaginary fun in the sun.

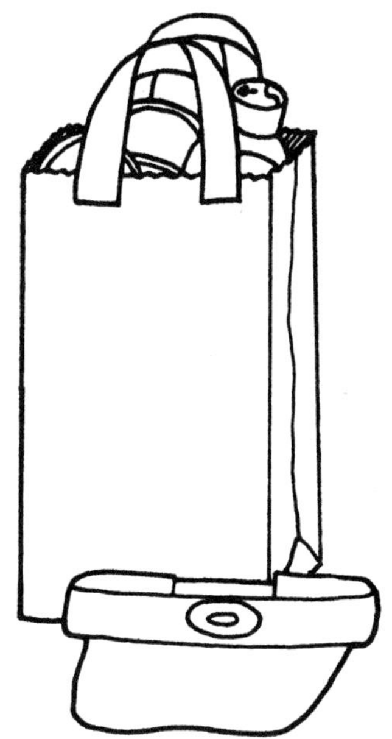

Meeting the Standards: Health

Knows how to maintain and promote personal health:

- Knows personal hygiene habits required to maintain health (e.g., caring for teeth, gums, eyes, ears, nose, skin, hair, nails)

Materials (per child)

- paper lunch bag
- crayons
- two 1- by 8-inch strips of construction paper
- glue stick
- summer item patterns (page 139)
- scissors
- individually wrapped snacks (such as crackers or pretzels)

Making the Props

1. Decorate the paper bag with a sun, summer symbol, or design in bright summery colors. To make handles, glue a 1- by 8-inch paper strip to the top of each side of the bag, as shown.
2. Color and cut out the summer item patterns. Place the cutouts in the bag.
3. Add an individually wrapped snack to the bag. (Note to teacher: Check with families about food allergies and dietary restrictions.)

Using the Props

Use the props and poem to reinforce the importance of eye and skin protection while playing in the sun. To begin, ask children to remove the items from their summer bag and place the cutouts faceup on the table. Then, as they recite the poem, have them place each item in the bag when it is named. Afterward, invite children to enjoy the snack in their bag.

Packing for Summer Fun

Time to pack for some summer fun—
To run and play in the summer sun.

I'll open my bag and put sunglasses in,
My sun visor, and sunblock to rub on
my skin.

In go my sandals, a pack of cards, too.
Finally, a snack, and now I'm through!

I love to pack for some summer fun—
To run and play in the summer sun!

A Hug for Dad

There are plenty of hugs to go around when children make this personalized hugging puppet for Father's Day.

Meeting the Standards: Health

Understands the relationship of family health to individual health:

- Knows the roles of parents and the extended family in supporting a strong family and promoting the health of children

Materials (per child)

- 6-inch paper plate
- half of a 6-inch paper plate
- scissors
- crayons
- 2 wiggle eyes
- yarn (for hair)
- glue
- two 24-inch lengths of crepe paper streamer
- two 2-inch squares of flesh-colored construction paper
- scrap paper

Making the Puppet

1. Cut off about two-thirds of the rim of the whole paper plate, leaving a head shape with "hair."
2. Decorate the head to resemble your father. Add wiggle eyes and yarn hair.
3. Glue the head to the curved rim of the half paper plate, creating a head on a pair of shoulders. Color the shoulders and add other details to resemble a shirt.
4. For arms, glue a crepe-paper streamer to each shoulder. Cut out hands from the flesh-tone paper squares. Glue a hand to the end of each arm.

Using the Puppet

Use the puppet and poem to help children express their feelings for their dad. First, help them bow their puppet's shoulders toward each other until it stands alone on a table. Then have them place the arms out to each side. While reciting the first three lines of the poem, have children make their puppet "hug" them. On the last line, ask children to offer their "dad" a hug in return.

A Hug for Dad

Dad hugs me when I'm sad,
Dad hugs me when I smile.
Dad hugs me when I want to ride
Piggyback for a mile!

So, today is really special.
It's Father's Day, you see.
And I have a special gift for Dad—
A great big hug from me!

I'm a Little Flag

Children can demonstrate their flag knowledge on Flag Day with this patriotic prop.

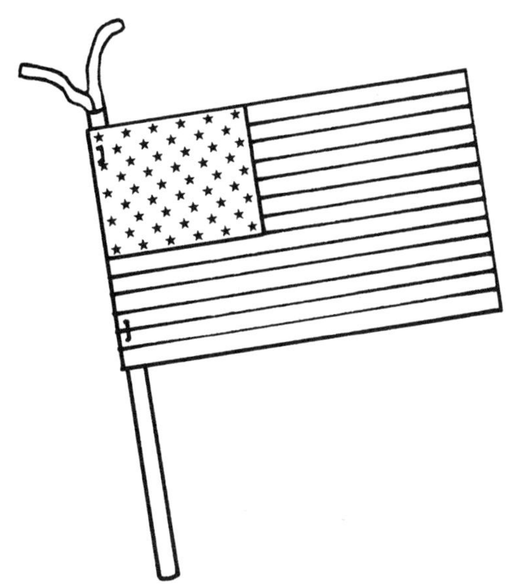

Meeting the Standards: History

Understands how democratic values came to be, and how they have been exemplified by people, events, and symbols:

- Understands the reasons that Americans celebrate certain national holidays (e.g., Martin Luther King, Jr. Day; the Fourth of July; Memorial Day)
- Knows the history of American symbols (e.g., the eagle, the Liberty Bell, George Washington as the "father of our country," the national flag)

Materials (per child)

- flag pattern (page 138)
- red and blue crayons
- scissors
- 6-inch length of gold yarn
- plastic drinking straw
- stapler

Making the Prop

1. Color and cut out the flag pattern.
2. Fold the yarn in half. Poke the folded end into the top end of the straw.
3. Staple the flag to the flagpole straw. (Note to teacher: An adult should complete this step.)

Using the Prop

Use the prop and poem to help children learn about the flag and its importance to our country. While reciting the poem, have children point to each color, the stars, and the stripes as they are named in the song. On the last line, have them raise their flag in the air.

I'm a Little Flag

I'm a little flag.
I'm red, white, and blue.
I stand for America,
And freedom for all of you.

I have 13 stripes
And 50 stars, it's true.
I stand for country pride
On Flag Day and the whole year through!

Independence Day Parade

Children create this patriotic puppet to use in a class Fourth of July parade.

Meeting the Standards: History

Understands how democratic values came to be, and how they have been exemplified by people, events, and symbols:

- Understands the reasons that Americans celebrate certain national holidays (e.g., Martin Luther King, Jr. Day; the Fourth of July; Memorial Day)

Materials (per child)

- drum major and hat patterns (page 140)
- crayons
- scissors
- scrap of white tissue paper
- glue stick
- 4½-inch length of paper towel tube
- stapler
- 2 wiggle eyes

Making the Puppet

1. Use red and blue crayons to color the hat and clothing on the drum major, leaving some areas white. Color the drum major's hair in the color of your choice. Then cut out the patterns.
2. Cut out a small white tissue-paper feather. Fold the hat on the center line and glue the top and side edges together, trapping one end of the feather into a top corner of the hat. Be sure to leave the bottom edge of the hat open.
3. Flatten one end of the 4½-inch tube and staple it closed.
4. Glue the drum major cutout to the tube, with the head at the stapled end. Glue on wiggle eyes. Then slip the hat over the drum major's head.

Using the Puppet

Use the puppet and poem as a springboard to discuss the history and symbols related to Independence Day. Before reciting the poem, ask children to line up with their puppets. Then have them march along and bounce their puppets as they recite the poem.

Independence Day Parade

The parade starts. Hip-hip hooray!
Today is Independence Day!

The American flag leads the way.
Today is Independence Day!

Balloons and floats swing and sway.
Today is Independence Day!

The marching band comes our way.
Today is Independence Day!

Cymbals crash. Horns play.
Today is Independence Day!

The parade goes by as we all say,
"Happy birthday, U.S.A.!"

▪ MATH ▪

Numbers & Counting

Hungry Monkey

Children feed the hungry monkey one food at a time to practice one-to-one correspondence.

Meeting the Standards: Math

Understands and applies basic and advanced properties of the concepts of numbers:

- Understands that numbers represent the quantity of objects
- Understands one-to-one correspondence

Materials (per child)

- monkey and food strip patterns (page 141)
- crayons
- scissors
- glue stick
- 2 wiggle eyes
- jumbo craft stick

Making the Puppet

1. Color and cut out the monkey and food patterns.
2. Cut a slit along the top dotted line of the monkey's mouth. (Note to teacher: An adult should complete this step.)
3. Glue wiggle eyes on the monkey. Then glue the craft stick to the back of the monkey just below the slit.
4. Glue the two food strips together where indicated to create one long strip. Insert the arrow through the slit from the front of the monkey. Slowly pull the strip through the slit so that the monkey appears to be eating one food at a time.

Using the Puppet

Use the puppet and poem to reinforce one-to-one correspondence. As children recite the poem, have them pull the strip to make each food disappear into the monkey's mouth as it is named in the poem.

Hungry Monkey

One little monkey, sitting in a tree,
All by himself and hungry as can be.
He ate one banana, one ham and cheese
on rye,
Then the hungry little monkey ate
one pizza pie!

He ate one apple and one coconut, too.
But the monkey was still hungry, and
that wouldn't do!
So he ate one lemon and one slice
of cake.
Then the full little monkey had one bad
tummy ache!

■ MATH ■

Numbers & Counting

My Treasure Chest

Children count their treasures and store them in a special treasure chest.

Meeting the Standards: Math

Understands and applies basic and advanced properties of the concepts of numbers:

- Counts by ones to ten or higher
- Understands one-to-one correspondence
- Understands symbolic, concrete, and pictorial representations of numbers (e.g., written numbers, objects in sets, number lines)

Materials (per child)

- facial tissue cube
- brown tempera paint
- paintbrush
- treasure chest lid pattern and treasure cards (page 142)
- crayons
- scissors
- glue stick

Making the Props

1. Paint the facial tissue cube brown. Set it aside to dry.
2. Color and cut out the treasure chest lid and treasure patterns.
3. To make the treasure chest, fold the lid cutout along the bold lines. Place it over the top of the brown cube so that the two folded ends hang over opposite sides. Then glue the short end in place, creating a "lid" that opens and closes over the box.
4. Open the lid and put the treasure cutouts into the treasure chest.

Using the Props

Use the props and poem to practice recognizing and counting sets of two objects. First, ask children to place all the treasure cards faceup on the table. Have them count the number of items on each card. Then, as they recite the poem, have children place the card for each named treasure in their treasure chest.

My Treasure Chest

I have a special treasure chest,
I'll open it up wide.
Here is all the treasure
That I'll put inside.

Two gold coins,
Two diamond rings,
Two gold crowns—
These are my special things!

Two gold cups,
Two golden shoes,
Two gold forks—
All my treasure comes in twos!

■ MATH ■

Numbers & Counting

Three Little Airplanes

Children practice counting to three with these lively little airplanes.

Meeting the Standards: Math

Understands and applies basic and advanced properties of the concepts of numbers:

- Counts by ones to ten or higher
- Understands one-to-one correspondence
- Knows the written numerals 0–9

Materials (per child)

- airplane patterns (page 140)
- crayons
- scissors
- glue stick
- paper lunch bag

Making the Puppets and Prop

1. Color each airplane pattern a different color and then cut out each one.
2. Fold each cutout on the center lines. Overlap and glue the folded ends together where indicated to create an open-ended finger puppet.
3. To use, slip your finger through the back opening of the airplane puppet.
4. To make an airplane hangar, open the paper bag and lay it on its side.

Using the Puppets and Prop

Use the puppets and prop to reinforce one-to-one correspondence, counting, and recognizing numerals. First, ask children to place their hangars on the table. Then have them put the three airplane finger puppets on their fingers and recite the poem. As each airplane is named in the poem, have children move the corresponding finger puppet. On the last verse, ask them to "park" their airplanes in the hangar.

Three Little Airplanes

Three little airplanes flew through the air.
Plane Number One said,
"Look down there!"
Plane Number Two said,
"What do you see?"
"I see an airport!"
said Plane Number Three.

Three little airplanes flew in a row,
Plane Number One said, "I'll land low."
Plane Number Two said, "I'll land fast."
Plane Number Three said, "I'll land last!"

Three little airplanes now on the ground.
Plane Number One said,
"Look what I found!"
Plane Number Two said,
"What do you see?"
"I see a hangar,"
said Plane Number Three.

They rolled into the hangar, and said
"Good night!"
Then three little airplanes had sweet
dreams of flight.

Four Ants

Children explore the number four with these busy ants.

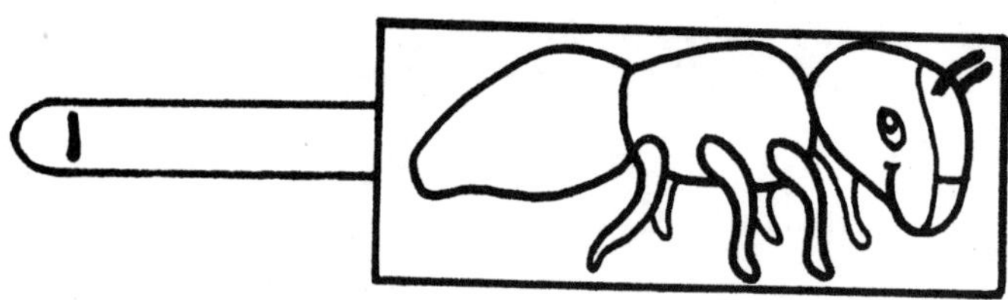

Meeting the Standards: Math

Understands and applies basic and advanced properties of the concepts of numbers:

- Counts by ones to ten or higher
- Understands one-to-one correspondence
- Knows the written numerals 0–9

Materials (per child)

- ant patterns (page 143)
- crayons
- scissors
- 4 jumbo craft sticks
- glue stick
- black crayon

Making the Puppets

1. Color and cut out the ant patterns. Fold each cutout in half along the line.
2. To make a handle for each ant puppet, glue a craft stick between the folded sides. Make sure the stick extends about 1½ inches from the tail end of the ant.
3. Use the black crayon to write a different numeral from 1–4 on each puppet handle.

Using the Puppets

Use the puppets and poem to give children practice in one-to-one correspondence, numeral recognition, and counting to four. To begin, ask children to line up their ants on the table or floor. Then, as they say each number in the poem, have them move the corresponding ant forward to "perform" the action.

Four Ants

One, two, three, four.
Four ants ready to explore!

One, two, three, four.
Four ants crawl under the door.

One, two, three, four.
Four ants march across the store.

One, two, three, four.
Four ants find crumbs on the floor.

One, two, three, four.
Four ants eat, and eat some more.

One, two, three, four.
Time to rest. Now four ants snore!

MATH

Numbers & Counting

Five in the Hive

Children count to five doing the honeybee jive with this hive full of dancing bees.

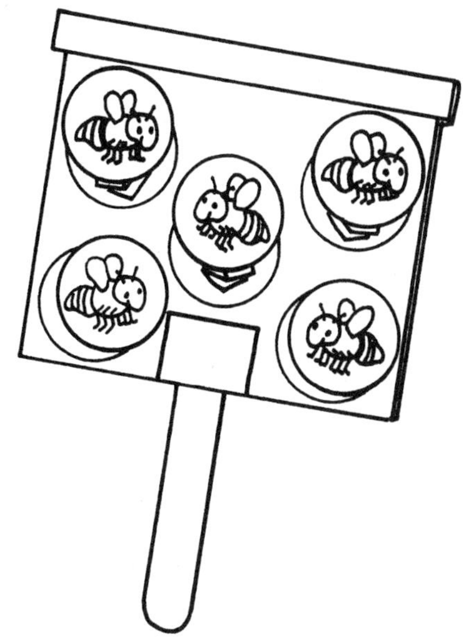

Meeting the Standards: Math

Understands and applies basic and advanced properties of the concepts of numbers:

- Counts by ones to ten or higher
- Understands one-to-one correspondence
- Knows the written numerals 0–9

Materials (per child)

- beehive and honeybee patterns (page 144)
- crayons
- scissors
- five ½- by 2-inch strips of construction paper
- glue stick
- jumbo craft stick

Making the Prop

1. Color and cut out the hive and bee patterns.
2. Accordion-fold the five 2-inch strips of construction paper. Glue one end of each strip to the center of a circle on the hive. Then glue a bee to the loose end of each strip.
3. Fold the hive in half along the line. Glue the front and back of the hive together, sandwiching the craft stick between the sides to create a handle.

Using the Prop

Use the prop and poem to provide practice in one-to-one correspondence, numeral recognition, and counting to five. As children recite the poem, ask them to wiggle the bee corresponding to each named number. On the last line of the first and last verses, have children bounce their hives to make all five bees do the honeybee jive.

Five in the Hive

How many honeybees in the hive
Dance and buzz to the honeybee jive?
One, two, three. Four and five.
Five little honeybees in the hive.

Says Honeybee One, "This is fun."
Honeybee Two says, "I'm with you!"
Honeybee Three says, "I agree!"
Honeybee Four says, "Let's dance more!"
Honeybee Five says, "Jive, jive, jive!"

How many honeybees in the hive
Dance and buzz to the honeybee jive?
One, two, three. Four and five.
Five little honeybees in the hive.

Six Chicks

Children count Mother Hen's eggs and chicks as they sing this lively tune.

Meeting the Standards: Math

Understands and applies basic and advanced properties of the concepts of numbers:

- Counts by ones to ten or higher
- Understands one-to-one correspondence
- Understands symbolic, concrete, and pictorial representations of numbers (e.g., written numbers, objects in sets, number lines)

Materials (per child)

- hen pattern (page 145)
- crayons
- scissors
- glue stick
- 6 small plastic pull-apart eggs
- 6 yellow pom-poms

Making the Props

1. Color and cut out the hen pattern.
2. Fold the cutout along the two fold lines, bringing the two ends of the cutout toward each other. Glue the top edges together to create a stand-up hen.
3. Open each egg, put a pom-pom "chick" inside, and close the egg.

Using the Props

Use the props and song to reinforce one-to-one correspondence and counting to six. Ask children to stand their hen on the table and then line up the six eggs in front of it. Have them sing the song, touching each egg in turn as they sing the last line of the first verse. During the second verse, have children "hatch" their eggs by opening each one. Ask them to count each pom-pom chick as they sing the last line of the second verse.

Six Chicks

(to the tune of "Mary Had a Little Lamb")

Mother Hen laid six little eggs,
Six little eggs, six little eggs.
Mother Hen laid six little eggs,
One, two, three, four, five, six!

From the eggs hatched six little chicks,
Six little chicks, six little chicks.
From the eggs hatched six little chicks.
One, two, three, four, five, six!

MATH

Numbers & Counting

Seven Feathers

Children help Rooster find and count seven feathers for his tail.

Meeting the Standards: Math

Understands and applies basic and advanced properties of the concepts of numbers:

- Counts by ones to ten or higher
- Understands one-to-one correspondence
- Knows the written numerals 0–9

Materials (per child)

- rooster, pockets, and feather patterns (page 146)
- crayons
- scissors
- glue stick
- wiggle eye
- jumbo craft stick

Making the Puppet

1. Color and cut out the rooster, pockets, and feather patterns.
2. Glue each pocket onto the rooster where indicated. Be sure to glue only the edges of the bottom and two short sides of the pocket to the rooster, leaving the top edge open.
3. Glue the wiggle eye over the rooster's eye.
4. Glue the craft stick to the back of the rooster to create a handle.
5. Insert four feathers in the long pocket and three feathers in the short pocket.

Using the Puppet

Use the puppet and song to provide practice in one-to-one correspondence, counting, and numeral recognition. To begin, ask children to remove the feathers from the rooster's pockets. Then as they sing the song, have them place one feather at a time in the rooster's pockets, starting at 1 and ending at 7. After singing the last line, have children count the feathers from 1 to 7, pointing to the feather behind each number as it is named.

Seven Feathers

(to the tune of "If You're Happy and You Know It")

Rooster needs seven feathers for his tail.
Rooster needs seven feathers for his tail.
Seven feathers, count them now,
It's not hard if you know how.
Rooster needs seven feathers for his tail.
One, two, three, four, five, six, seven!

■ MATH ■

Numbers & Counting

Let's Shake Hands!

This unique octopus puppet makes a handy counting buddy for children.

Meeting the Standards: Math

Understands and applies basic and advanced properties of the concepts of numbers:

- Counts by ones to ten or higher
- Understands one-to-one correspondence
- Knows the written numerals 0–9

Materials (per child)

- 8-ounce paper cup
- gray tempera paint
- paintbrush
- octopus tentacle patterns (page 147)
- crayons
- scissors
- glue
- 2 large wiggle eyes

Making the Puppet

1. Paint the paper cup gray. Set it aside to dry.
2. Color and cut out the tentacle patterns.
3. Glue the tentacles in numerical order around the rim of the cup.
4. Glue the wiggle eyes to the cup about one inch above tentacles 1 and 8.

Using the Puppet

Use the puppet and poem to reinforce counting to eight and numeral recognition. Ask children to place the puppet on one hand. Then, as they recite the poem, have them "shake" the octopus's tentacle for each number as it is named. During the last verse, invite children to choose a tentacle to shake.

Let's Shake Hands!

I've come here to shake your hand
And to say, "How do you do?"
But I'm an octopus, and I can't decide
Which tentacle I should use!

Should I use tentacle one or two?
Or should I use three or four?
Maybe five? Six? Seven or eight?
I'm glad I don't have more!

So help me choose a tentacle to use,
To shake your hand and say,
"It's lovely to see you, my good friend,
And how are you today?"

MATH

Numbers & Counting

Have You Ever Seen a Gator?

Children count and feed nine little fish to a hungry gator.

Meeting the Standards: Math

Understands and applies basic and advanced properties of the concepts of numbers:

- Counts by ones to ten or higher
- Understands one-to-one correspondence
- Knows the written numerals 0–9

Materials (per child)

- paper towel tube
- green tempera paint
- paintbrush
- gator and fish patterns (page 148)
- crayons
- scissors
- glue stick
- 2 wiggle eyes
- 30-inch length of yarn

Making the Prop

1. Paint the paper towel tube green. Set it aside to dry.
2. Color and cut out the gator and fish patterns.
3. Glue the gator head to one end of the tube and the tail to the other end. Glue on the wiggle eyes.
4. Fold each leg along the fold line. Glue two legs on each side of the gator's body.
5. Fold the fish strip in half along the horizontal line. Center and glue the strip to the length of yarn, trapping the yarn between the two folded sides of the strip.
6. To make the fish strip more flexible, fold and then unfold the strip along the lines between the fish. Thread the yarn through the gator's body, making sure fish 1 enters the gator's mouth first. Tie the ends of the yarn together.

Using the Prop

Use the prop and song to reinforce one-to-one correspondence, counting to nine, and numeral recognition. As children sing the song, have them pull one fish at a time through the gator's mouth so that it appears to "eat" each fish as its number is named.

Have You Ever Seen a Gator?

(to the tune of "Have You Ever Seen a Lassie?")

Have you ever seen a gator, a gator,
a gator,
Have you ever seen a gator eat nine
little fish?

Oh, one fish and two fish and three
fish—such good fish!
Have you ever seen a gator eat nine
little fish?

Oh, four fish and five fish and six fish—
such good fish!
Have you ever seen a gator eat nine
little fish?

Oh, seven fish and eight fish and nine
fish—such good fish!
Have you ever seen a gator eat nine
little fish?

■ MATH ■

Numbers & Counting

Ten Little Apples

Children count and pick ten pom-pom apples from the apple tree to put into their buckets.

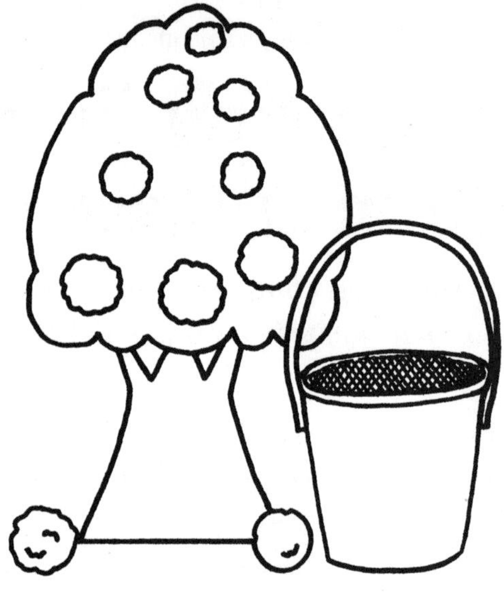

Meeting the Standards: Math

Understands and applies basic and advanced properties of the concepts of numbers:

- Understands that numbers represent the quantity of objects
- Counts by ones to ten or higher
- Understands one-to-one correspondence

Materials (per child)

- tree pattern (page 149)
- crayons
- scissors
- 6-ounce paper cup
- 6-inch length of pipe cleaner
- hole punch
- 10 red pom-poms

Making the Props

1. Color and cut out the tree.
2. For the bucket, punch a hole near the rim of the cup. Then punch another hole opposite the first hole. To create a handle, attach each end of the pipe cleaner to a hole in the cup. Twist each end tightly against the pipe cleaner to avoid exposing the sharp wire tip. (Note to teacher: An adult should complete this step.)

Using the Props

Use the props and song to provide practice in one-to-one correspondence and counting to ten. First, lay the tree flat and ask children to place ten pom-poms on it. While singing the first verse of the song, have them point to an apple for each number named. During the second verse, invite children to pick an apple for each number and place it in the bucket.

Ten Little Apples

(to the tune of "Ten Little Indians")

One little, two little, three little apples,
Four little, five little, six little apples,
Seven little, eight little, nine little apples.
Ten little apples in the tree!

One little, two little, three little apples,
Four little, five little, six little apples,
Seven little, eight little, nine little apples.
Ten little apples for me!

Friends on a Fence

Children learn about ordinal numbers as they help a lonely fence find some friends.

Meeting the Standards: Math

Understands and applies basic and advanced properties of the concepts of numbers:

- Understands the concept of position in a sequence (e.g., first, last)
- Counts whole numbers (i.e., both cardinal and ordinal numbers)

Materials (per child)

- birds on a fence pattern (page 149)
- crayons
- scissors

Making the Prop

1. Color and cut out the birds on a fence pattern. Be sure to color the fence brown. Cut along the dotted lines between the birds.
2. Fold the bird flaps down behind the fence.
3. To make a base, fold back the bottom section of the fence along the line. Stand the fence on a table.
4. To "sit" a bird on the fence, flip each flap up so that the bird appears to be sitting on the fence.

Using the Prop

Use the prop and song to practice counting with ordinal numbers. To begin, ask children to fold the bird flaps behind the fence and stand the fence on the table. When they reach the second verse, have children flip up the bird on the left side of the fence so that it appears to be sitting on the fence. Have them flip up the next bird on the third verse. Then have them repeat the third verse three times, replacing the word "second" with "third," "fourth," and then "fifth," in that order. Each time, have them flip up the corresponding bird to sit on the fence.

Friends on a Fence

(to the tune of "I'm a Little Teapot")

I'm a little brown fence, here I stand.
I have a rail where birds can land.
I wish a little bird would visit me,
Then I'd have some company.

Along came a bird and sat right down.
"I am your first friend, don't you frown!
I am here to keep you company,
We'll laugh, and sing, and be happy!"

Along came the next bird and
sat right down.
"I am your *second* friend, don't you
frown!
I am here to keep you company,
We'll laugh, and sing, and be happy!"

■ MATH ■

Numbers & Counting

My Socks

Children count by twos while hanging and removing pairs of socks from a clothesline.

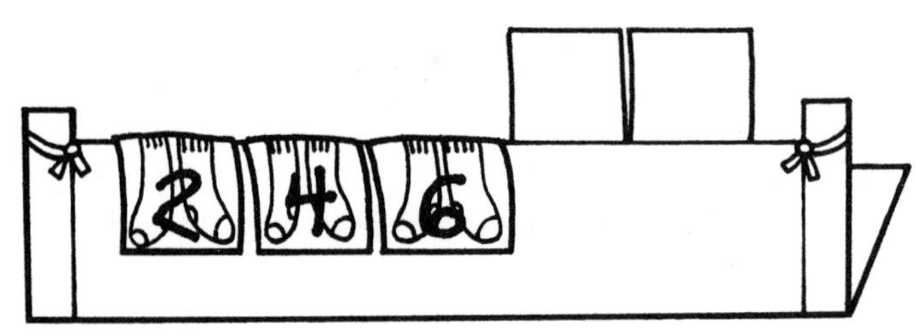

Meeting the Standards: Math

Understands and applies basic and advanced properties of the concepts of numbers:

- Counts whole numbers (i.e., both cardinal and ordinal numbers)
- Understands symbolic, concrete, and pictorial representations of numbers (e.g., written numbers, objects in sets, number lines)

Materials (per child)

- clothesline and sock patterns (page 150)
- crayons
- scissors
- glue stick

Making the Prop

1. Color and cut out the clothesline and sock patterns. Cut along the dotted lines between the pair of socks.
2. Glue the back of the socks strip to the top back of the clothesline. Fold the sock flaps down behind the clothesline.
3. To make a base, fold back the bottom section of the clothesline along the line. Stand the clothesline on a table.
4. To "hang" a pair of socks, flip each sock flap over the top of the clothesline and forward so that the socks appear to be hanging on the line.

Using the Prop

Use the prop and poem to reinforce counting by twos and numeral recognition. To begin, ask children to fold all the sock flaps behind the clothesline. Have them recite the first verse, flipping each flap over to "hang" the socks on the clothesline as they say the corresponding number in the last line of the verse. When they reach the last line of the second verse, have them "remove" each pair of socks in numerical order by folding each flap back behind the clothesline.

My Socks

My socks are clean, my socks are wet.
I know just what I'll do.
I'll hang my socks on the line to dry.
I'll hang them two by two.
Two, four, six, eight, ten.

My socks are clean, my socks are dry.
I know just what I'll do.
I'll take them off the line, so dry.
I'll count them two by two.
Two, four, six, eight, ten.

Counting Nickels

Children practice counting by fives using nickels from these handy wallets.

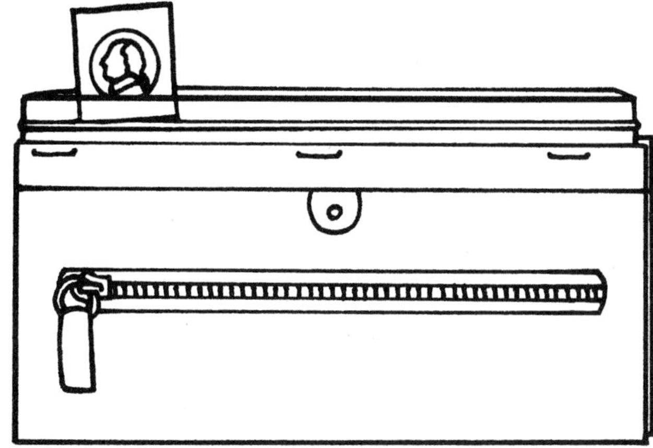

Meeting the Standards: Math

Understands and applies basic and advanced properties of the concepts of numbers:

- Counts whole numbers (i.e., both cardinal and ordinal numbers)
- Understands symbolic, concrete, and pictorial representations of numbers (e.g., written numbers, objects in sets, number lines)

Materials (per child)

- wallet patterns and nickel cards (page 151)
- crayons
- scissors
- snack-size resealable plastic bag
- stapler

Making the Props

1. Color and cut out the wallet patterns and nickel cards.
2. Staple a wallet cutout to each side of a snack-size plastic bag, attaching it just below the zipper. (Slide the stapler over the open edge of the bag.)
3. Place the nickels in the wallet and zip the zipper.

Using the Props

Use the props and poem to give children practice in counting by fives. Before reciting the poem, instruct children to remove a specific number of nickels from their wallet. Then, after they recite the poem, have children count their nickels by fives to find out how much money they have. Each time you repeat the activity, ask children to remove a different number of nickels from their wallet.

Counting Nickels

I'll count my nickels.
I'll count by fives.
Do I have a little or a lot?

I'll count my nickels.
I'll count by fives.
How much money have I got?

I Love Raisin Cookies

Counting by ten is delicious fun when children count the raisins in their cookies.

Meeting the Standards: Math

Understands and applies basic and advanced properties of the concepts of numbers:

- Counts whole numbers (i.e., both cardinal and ordinal numbers)
- Understands symbolic, concrete, and pictorial representations of numbers (e.g., written numbers, objects in sets, number lines)

Materials (per child)

- cookie jar and cookie patterns (page 152)
- crayons
- scissors
- snack-size resealable plastic bag
- stapler

Making the Props

1. Color and cut out the cookie jar and cookie patterns.
2. Staple the cookie jar cutout to one side of a snack-size plastic bag, attaching it just below the zipper. (Slide the stapler over the open edge of the bag.)
3. Place the cookies in the cookie jar and zip the zipper.

Using the Props

Use the props and poem to give children practice in counting by tens. To begin, ask children to remove two cookies from their cookie jar. Have them place the cookies faceup on the table. After they recite the poem, have children count the raisins in their two cookies by tens. Each time you repeat the activity, ask children to remove a different number of cookies from their cookie jar. Then replace "two" in the second verse with the corresponding number, such as three, five, or nine.

I Love Raisin Cookies

I love raisin cookies,
They're my favorite ones, you see.
Each cookie has ten raisins,
Ten raisins all for me!

I'll take two cookies from my jar.
Two cookies for a treat.
And when I eat my cookies,
How many raisins will I eat?

Each cookie has ten raisins,
I'll count them ten by ten.
Then I'll eat my raisin cookies,
Take some more, and count again!

Three Little Race Cars

Ready. Set. Go! Children are off to the races to learn about ordinal numbers with these cute little cars.

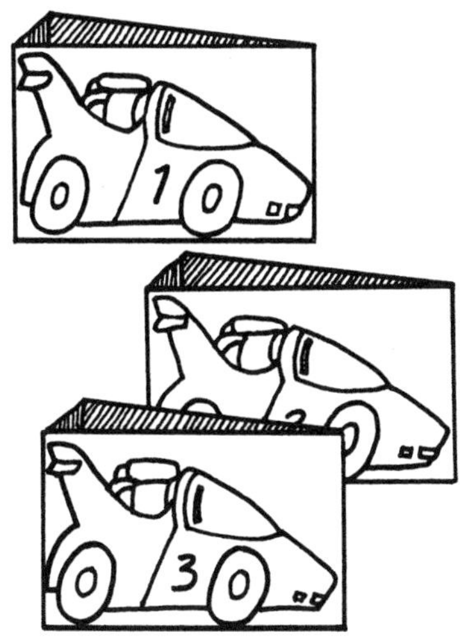

Meeting the Standards: Math

Understands and applies basic and advanced properties of the concepts of numbers:

- Understands the concept of position in a sequence (e.g., first, last)
- Knows the written numerals 0–9
- Counts whole numbers (i.e., both cardinal and ordinal numbers)

Materials (per child)

- race car patterns (page 153)
- crayons
- scissors
- glue stick

Making the Props

1. Color and cut out the race car patterns. Be sure to color each car a different color.
2. Fold each car cutout along the lines. Glue the folded end to the back of the car on the opposite end of the cutout. Stand the cars on a table.

Using the Props

Use the props and poem to reinforce numeral recognition and ordinal numbers. First, ask children to line up the race cars behind a real or imaginary Start line. Then point out a real or imaginary Finish line. As children recite the poem, have them move each car toward the Finish line as it is mentioned until all the cars cross the line.

Three Little Race Cars

Three little cars lined up in a row,
Ready for a race. Get set. Let's go!

Car Number One is in the lead,
Car Number Two picks up speed.

Car Number Three is catching up fast.
Which will be first? Which will be last?

The first to finish will win the race.
Car Number One wins first place!

The second to finish is Car Number Two.
Car Three is third—the race is through!

■ MATH ■

Geometry

Around and 'Round

Children use this merry-go-round to explore circles and colors.

Meeting the Standards: Math

Understands and applies basic and advanced properties of the concepts of geometry:

- Knows basic geometric language for naming shapes (e.g., circle, triangle, square, rectangle)
- Understands basic properties of (e.g., number of sides, corners, square corners) and similarities and differences between simple geometric shapes

Materials (per child)

- merry-go-round horse patterns (page 154)
- crayons
- scissors
- glue stick
- two 9-inch paper plates
- paper brad

Making the Prop

1. Color one merry-go-round horse pattern brown, one red, one blue, and one green. Cut out the patterns.
2. Fold each cutout along the fold lines, bringing the ends toward each other. Glue the top edges together to create a stand-up merry-go-round horse.
3. Glue each horse to the bottom of the paper plate to create a merry-go-round.
4. To attach the merry-go-round to the bottom of the other paper plate, poke the paper brad through the middle of both plates. Make sure the merry-go-round turns freely. (Note to teacher: An adult should complete this step.)

Using the Prop

Use the prop and song to reinforce children's understanding of a circle. First, ask children to position the brown horse directly in front of them. Have them spin the merry-go-round as they sing the first verse, making the brown horse circle completely around. Have children repeat the action for the other verses, starting with the color of horse named in each verse.

Around and 'Round

(to the tune of "Where, Oh Where Has My Little Dog Gone?")

Around and 'round goes the merry-go-round,
It makes a circle, you see.
Around and 'round goes
the little brown horse,
It circles right back to me.

Around and 'round goes the merry-go-round,
It makes a circle, you see.
Around and 'round goes the little red horse,
It circles right back to me.

Around and 'round goes the merry-go-round,
It makes a circle, you see.
Around and 'round goes the little blue horse,
It circles right back to me.

Around and 'round goes the merry-go-round,
It makes a circle, you see.
Around and 'round goes
the little green horse,
It circles right back to me.

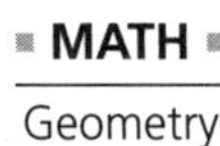

MATH

Geometry

Square Robot

This geometric robot has a lot to teach children about squares.

Meeting the Standards: Math

Understands and applies basic and advanced properties of the concepts of geometry:

- Knows basic geometric language for naming shapes (e.g., circle, triangle, square, rectangle)
- Understands basic properties of (e.g., number of sides, corners, square corners) and similarities and differences between simple geometric shapes

Materials (per child)

- single-serving cereal boxes
- tempera paint (in child's choice of color)
- paintbrush
- robot patterns (page 154)
- crayons
- scissors
- glue stick
- four ¾- by 5-inch strips of black construction paper
- two 1-inch squares of construction paper
- two 1½-inch squares of construction paper

Making the Prop

1. Paint the cereal box and set it aside to dry.
2. Color and cut out the robot patterns. Fold the head cutout where indicated and glue the folded section to the top of the box. Glue the control panel to the front of the box.
3. Accordion-fold each of the four strips of paper. Glue two strips to the bottom of the box to create legs. Glue the other two strips to the side of the box for arms.
4. To make hands, glue a 1-inch paper square to the end of each arm. For feet, glue a 1½-inch paper square to the end of each leg.

Using the Prop

Use the prop and poem to help children identify squares. To begin, ask children to sit their robots with the legs hanging over the edge of the table. Then have them point to each square feature on the robot as it is named in the poem. Invite children to call out the answer to the question at the end of each verse.

Square Robot

Square head, square mouth,
Square eyes and ears.
If ever I should want to cry,
What shape would be my tears?

Square hands, square feet,
Square buttons on my box.
If ever should my feet get cold,
What shape would be my socks?

Squares here, squares there,
Square robot, yes indeed!
If ever you should make my twin,
What shapes would you need?

What Shape Is This?

Children use this shape cube to discover rectangles all around them.

Meeting the Standards: Math

Understands and applies basic and advanced properties of the concepts of geometry:

- Knows basic geometric language for naming shapes (e.g., circle, triangle, square, rectangle)
- Understands basic properties of (e.g., number of sides, corners, square corners) and similarities and differences between simple geometric shapes
- Understands that geometric shapes are useful for representing and describing real world situations

Materials (per child)

- rectangle pictures (page 155)
- crayons
- scissors
- facial tissue cube
- glue stick

Making the Prop

1. Color and cut out the rectangle picture patterns.
2. Place the tissue cube with the hole side down on the table. Glue a different rectangle cutout to each side of the cube.

Using the Prop

Use the prop and poem to help children learn about the properties of rectangles. To begin, ask children to slip their hand inside the opening of the cube. Before saying each verse, have them turn their cube to the picture of the object named in the verse. Then, while reciting the verse, have children point to the sides and corners of the shape as each feature is mentioned.

What Shape Is This?

Two short sides, two long sides,
Four corners that I see.
What shape is this door?
It's a rectangle, yes sirree!

Two short sides, two long sides,
Four corners that I see.
What shape is this window?
It's a rectangle, yes sirree!

Two short sides, two long sides,
Four corners that I see.
What shape is this frame?
It's a rectangle, yes sirree!

Two short sides, two long sides,
Four corners that I see.
What shape is this envelope?
It's a rectangle, yes sirree!

My Triangle Hat

Children use this clever little captain to shape up their knowledge of triangles.

Meeting the Standards: Math

Understands and applies basic and advanced properties of the concepts of geometry:

- Knows basic geometric language for naming shapes (e.g., circle, triangle, square, rectangle)
- Understands basic properties of (e.g., number of sides, corners, square corners) and similarities and differences between simple geometric shapes
- Understands that geometric shapes are useful for representing and describing real world situations

Materials (per child)

- ship captain and hat patterns (page 156)
- crayons
- scissors
- glue stick
- 4½-inch length of paper towel tube
- stapler
- 2 wiggle eyes

Making the Puppet

1. Color and cut out the ship captain and hat patterns.
2. Fold the hat on the line. Glue together the short angled sides opposite the fold, leaving the longer bottom edge open.
3. Flatten one end of the 4½-inch tube and staple it closed.
4. Glue the ship captain to the tube, with the head at the stapled end. Add wiggle eyes. Then slip the hat over the captain's head.

Using the Puppet

Use the puppet and song to help children learn about the properties of triangles. To begin, ask children to take the hat off their puppet and place the puppet on their hand. Then have them sing the song, making up actions with their puppet to go along with the words.

My Triangle Hat

(to the tune of "Where, Oh Where Has My Little Dog Gone?")

Oh where, oh where is my triangle hat?
Oh where, oh where can it be?
It has three sides and three corners, too,
Oh where, oh where can it be?

Ahoy, now here is my triangle hat—
The perfect hat shape for me.
When I put my hat upon my head,
It's a perfect fit, you see.

I'll count three sides of my triangle hat,
I'll count three corners, too.
Then I'll sail away in my triangle hat
To cross the ocean so blue.

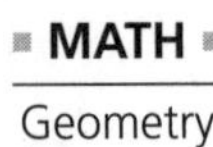

MATH

Geometry

Presto! Change-O!

Children use this puppet to perform a bit of magic with triangles and diamonds.

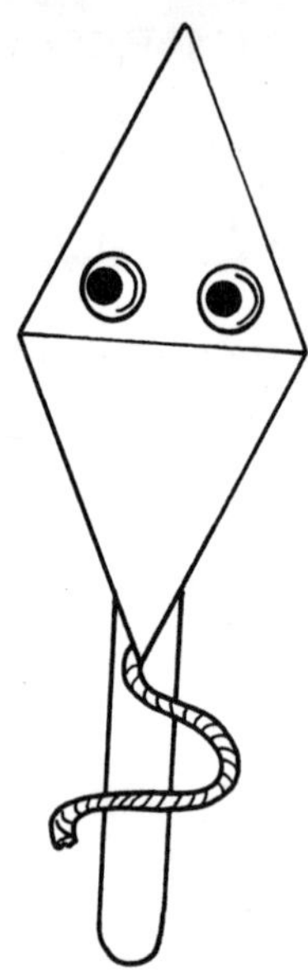

Meeting the Standards: Math

Understands and applies basic and advanced properties of the concepts of geometry:

- Knows basic geometric language for naming shapes (e.g., circle, triangle, square, rectangle)
- Knows that geometric shapes can be put together or taken apart to form other shapes
- Understands basic properties of (e.g., number of sides, corners, square corners) and similarities and differences between simple geometric shapes

Materials (per child)

- diamond pattern (page 156)
- crayons
- scissors
- glue stick
- jumbo craft stick
- 2 wiggle eyes
- 7-inch length of yarn

Making the Puppet

1. Cut out the diamond pattern. Flip the cutout over and color the back of the shape in the color of your choice.
2. To make a handle, glue the craft stick to the shape where indicated.
3. Fold the cutout on the line with the colored side on the inside. Unfold the cutout and glue the wiggle eyes on the colored side about ½ inch above the fold.
4. To make the puppet resemble a kite, glue one end of the yarn to the bottom corner of the shape.

Using the Puppet

Use the puppet and poem to help children discover the similarities and differences between triangles and diamonds. To begin, ask children to fold down the top half of the puppet to create a triangle. Then, as they recite the poem, have them point to the different features of the shape as they are named. When they reach the next to last line, invite children to unfold their puppet to reveal a diamond-shaped kite. Afterward, compare the features of triangles and diamonds.

Presto! Change-O!

This is a triangle, how do I know?
Three lines and three corners tell me so.
But I can make magic with this shape,
you see,
Presto! Change-O!
A diamond for me!

MATH

Measurement

The Three Bears

Children create three bear puppets to explore size concepts.

Meeting the Standards: Math

Understands and applies basic and advanced properties of the concepts of measurement:

- Orders objects qualitatively by measurable attribute (e.g., smallest to largest, lightest to heaviest, shortest to longest)
- Knows the common language of measurement (e.g., "big," "little," "long," "short," "light," "heavy")

Materials (per child)

- large, medium, and small bear patterns (page 157)
- crayons
- scissors
- paper towel tubes cut to each length: 4¾ inches, 4½ inches, and 2½ inches
- stapler
- glue stick

Making the Puppets

1. Color and cut out the large, medium, and small bear patterns.
2. Flatten one end of each of the paper towel tubes and staple that end closed.
3. Glue the large bear to the 4¾-inch tube, with the bear's head at the stapled end of the tube. Then glue the medium bear to the 4½-inch tube and the small bear to the 2½-inch tube.

Using the Puppets

Use the puppets and song to reinforce recognizing, comparing, and sequencing sizes. To begin, ask children to place their puppets on the table in any order. As they sing each verse of the song, have them dance the corresponding bear around on the table. At the end of the song, ask children to sequence their bears by size, from largest to smallest. Later, you might mix up the verses to give children additional practice in listening and finding the corresponding puppet.

The Three Bears

(to the tune of "A-Tisket, A-Tasket")

A large bear, a large bear.
Oh, Papa is a large bear.
He has a large head, body, and feet.
Oh, Papa is a large bear.

A medium bear, a medium bear.
Oh, Mama is a medium bear.
She has a medium head, body, and feet.
Oh, Mama is a medium bear.

A small bear, a small bear.
Oh, Baby is a small bear.
He has a small head, body, and feet.
Oh, Baby is a small bear.

▪ MATH ▪

Pre-Algebra

Moving Day

Children create a pattern of boxes to load onto a moving truck.

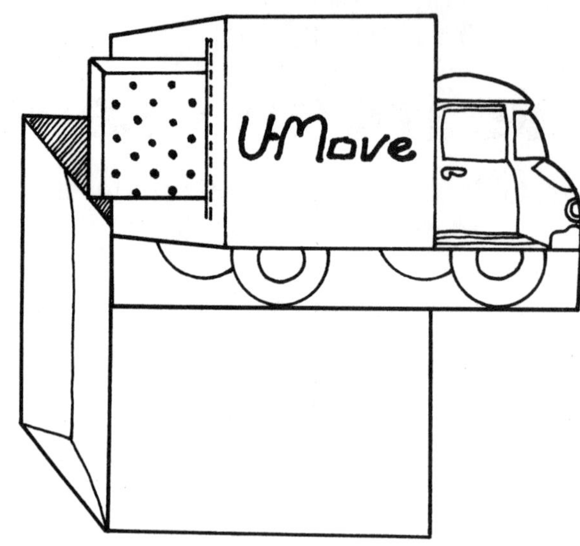

Meeting the Standards: Math

Understands and applies basic and advanced properties of functions and algebra:

- Understands simple patterns (e.g., boy-girl-boy-girl)
- Repeats simple patterns

Materials (per child)

- moving truck and box patterns (page 158)
- crayons
- scissors
- glue
- brown paper lunch bag trimmed to 4 inches high

Making the Props

1. Color and cut out the truck and box patterns. Be sure to color each matching box the same color.
2. Cut a slit along the dotted line on the truck. (Note to teacher: An adult should complete this step.)
3. Glue the truck to the paper bag so that the left edge of the truck lines up with the left edge of the bag and the bottom of the slit is just above the top edge of the bag. Open the bag and stand it on the table.
4. To load the truck, insert each box through the slit (the box will drop into the bag).

Using the Props

Use the props and song to reinforce patterning skills. First, ask children to stand their truck on the table and remove the boxes. Then have them place their boxes faceup on the table. While singing the first verse, have children arrange the boxes in a repeating pattern in front of their truck. During the second verse, ask them to "load" each box onto the truck, inserting the boxes in the sequence of their pattern.

Moving Day

(to the tune of "Have You Ever Seen a Lassie?")

We are packing up our boxes, our boxes,
our boxes.
We are packing up our boxes. Now it's
time to pack.
Pack this box and that box and this box
and that box.
Pack our boxes in a pattern to put on
the truck.

We are loading up our boxes, our boxes,
our boxes.
We are loading up our boxes. Now load
up the truck!
Load this box and that box and this box
and that box.
Load our boxes in a pattern to fill up
the truck.

Searching for Vowels

Children search for vowels in this special homemade alphabet soup.

Meeting the Standards: Language Arts

Demonstrates competence in the general skills and strategies of the reading process.

- Knows some letters of the alphabet, such as those in the student's own name

Materials (per child)

- letter cards (page 157)
- scissors
- twelve 2-inch red construction paper squares
- glue stick
- large paper bowl
- crinkled paper strips
- plastic spoon

Making the Props

1. Cut out the letter cards.
2. Paste each card onto a red paper square.
3. Half-fill the bowl with crinkled paper strips. Mix in the letter cards.
4. Use the spoon to stir the "soup" and scoop out letters.

Using the Props

Use the props and song to reinforce children's letter recognition skills and help them identify vowels. As they sing the first verse of the song, ask children to gently stir their alphabet soup with the spoon. During the second verse, have them find and scoop out the *A* card. Invite them to repeat the song several more times, each time replacing the *A* in the last verse with a different vowel and then finding and scooping out that vowel from the bowl.

Searching for Vowels

(to the tune of "I've Been Working on the Railroad")

I am searching for some vowels,
A, E, I, O, U.
I am searching for some vowels,
Not *B, L,* or *W.*
I'll stir and search my soup for vowels,
They're special letters, you see.
Five vowels hiding in my soup bowl,
Oh, where can each one be?

I'm searching for an *A*, searching for an *A*,
Searching for the vowel *A, A, A*!
Searching for an *A*, searching for an *A*,
I'm searching for the vowel *A*!

Letter Sounds

Children create and use this lift-the-flap letter box to share their knowledge of letter sounds.

Meeting the Standards: Language Arts

Uses the general skills and strategies of the reading process:

- Knows some letters of the alphabet, such as those in the student's own name

Uses listening and speaking strategies for different purposes:

- Discriminates among the sounds of spoken language

Materials (per child)

- letter box patterns (page 159)
- crayons
- scissors
- facial tissue cube
- glue stick
- small photo of self

Making the Prop

1. Write the first letter of your name on the blank letter box pattern. Color and cut out all the letter box patterns.
2. Turn the tissue cube upside down (with the hole at the bottom). Glue your photo to the top of the cube and an animal cutout onto each side of the cube.
3. Center and glue the letter cutout labeled with your initial over your picture on the box, gluing only along the top edge. Glue each of the other letter cutouts over the picture that begins with that letter.
4. Fold back each flap to reveal the picture under it.

Using the Prop

Use the prop and song to reinforce recognition of beginning sounds. First, ask children to place their hand in the hole in their prop. Have them turn the cube so that *D* faces them. Then, as they sing the song, have children point to *D*. When they sing "Now show it!" invite them to lift the flap to reveal the picture that begins with *D*. Repeat the song three times, each time replacing *D* with a different letter on the cube and inserting the name of the corresponding picture. Then sing the song once more, having children use their initial and name in the song.

Letter Sounds

(to the tune of "If You're Happy and You Know It")

Here's the letter *D*,
The letter sounds like this: /d/, /d/.

Here's the letter *D*,
The letter sounds like this: /d/, /d/.

Here's the letter *D*, you know it.
Donkey starts with *D*. Now show it!
The beginning sound of *donkey* sounds
like this: /d/, /d/.

It's Vacation Time!

Children create a map and car to use for a vacation road trip filled with straight and curvy roads.

Meeting the Standards: Language Arts

Uses listening and speaking strategies for different purposes:

- Uses descriptive language (e.g., color words; size words, such as *bigger, smaller;* shape words)
- Creates or acts out familiar stories, songs, rhymes, and plays in play activities

Materials (per child)

- map and car patterns (page 160)
- crayons
- scissors
- glue stick

Making the Props

1. Color and cut out the map and car patterns.
2. To make a stand-up car, fold the car cutout on the lines. Then glue the short folded section to the back of the car on the opposite end of the cutout.
3. Move the car along the road on the map.

Using the Props

Use the props and song to reinforce children's knowledge of opposites. First, ask children to place their car on the road next to the house. As they sing the song, have them move their car along the road, keeping it on the section of road mentioned in each verse.

It's Vacation Time!

(to the tune of "The Wheels on the Bus")

Let's ride in the car on the long
straight road, long straight road,
long straight road.
Let's ride in the car on the long,
straight road.
It's vacation time!

Let's ride in the car on the curvy road,
curvy road, curvy road.
Let's ride in the car on the curvy road.
It's vacation time!

Let's ride in the car on the short
straight road, short straight road,
short straight road.
Let's ride in the car on the short,
straight road.
It's vacation time!

The Race Is On!

Children learn about opposites while racing a tortoise and hare on this unique racetrack.

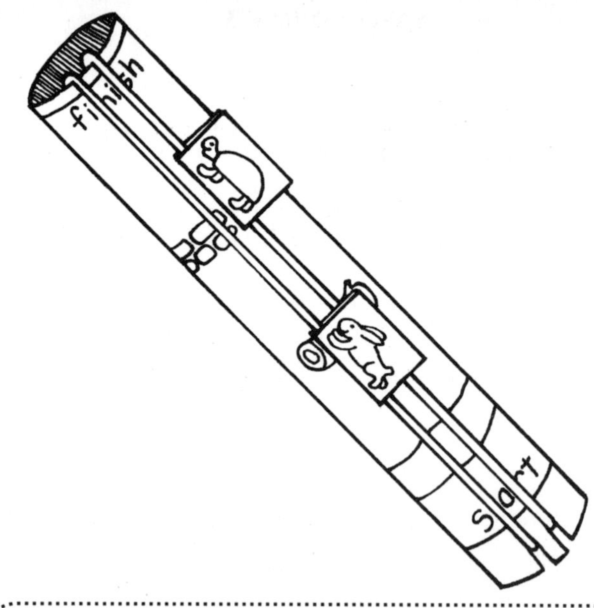

Meeting the Standards: Language Arts

Uses listening and speaking strategies for different purposes:

- Uses descriptive language (e.g., color words; size words, such as *bigger*, *smaller*; shape words)
- Creates or acts out familiar stories, songs, rhymes, and plays in play activities

Materials (per child)

- racecourse, hare, and tortoise patterns (page 161)
- crayons
- scissors
- paper towel tube
- glue stick
- two 12-inch lengths of yarn

Making the Prop

1. Color and cut out the racecourse, hare, and tortoise patterns.
2. Glue the racecourse cutout along the length of the tube, lining up the "Finish" end with the edge of the tube.
3. Cut two short slits in the "Start" end of the tube, spacing the slits about 1¼ inches apart. (Note to teacher: An adult should complete steps 3, 4, and 5.)
4. Fold the hare and tortoise cutouts along the line. Center and glue each animal on a length of yarn, gluing the yarn between the two folded sides.
5. Thread each length of yarn through the tube. Slip the yarn into one of the slits in the tube. Then tie the ends together, making sure the yarn is taut but can still be pulled around and through the tube.
6. Gently pull the yarn to move the hare and tortoise along the racecourse.

Using the Prop

Use the prop and poem to reinforce the opposite concepts of *fast* and *slow*. To begin, ask children to position the hare and tortoise at "Start" on the racecourse. Then have them move each animal along the racecourse to go along with the words in the poem.

The Race Is On!

Time for the race. Get set and go!
Hare goes fast. Tortoise goes slow.

Hare hops to the stream and stops to rest.
Tortoise goes slow. He does his best.

Watch them race, watch them go!
Hare goes fast. Tortoise goes slow.

Hare hops to the log and stops to sleep.
Tortoise goes slow. Watch him creep.

Watch them race, watch them go!
Hare goes fast. Tortoise goes slow.

Hare hops to the path and stops to nap.
Tortoise wins the race. Everyone clap!

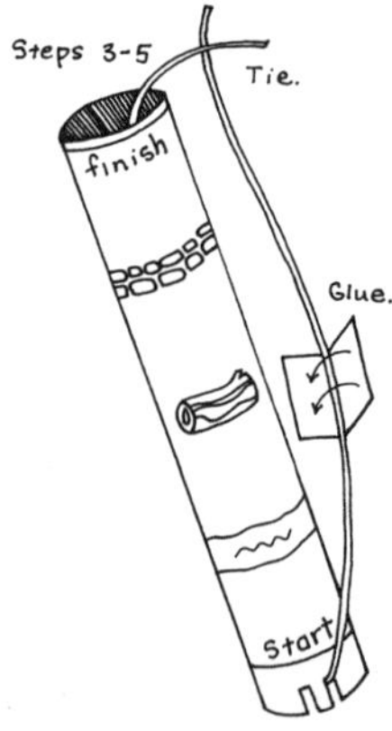

Inchworm Shrinks and Grows

Children explore length with this stretchable and shrinkable inchworm.

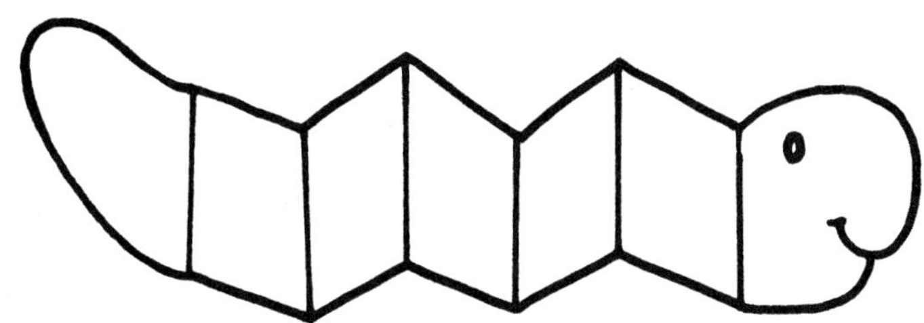

Meeting the Standards: Math

Understands and applies basic and advanced properties of the concept of measurement:

- Knows the common language of measurement (e.g., "big," "little," "long," "short," "light," "heavy")

Materials (per child)

- inchworm pattern (page 161)
- crayons
- scissors

Making the Prop

1. Color and cut out the inchworm pattern.
2. Accordion-fold the inchworm cutout between the lines.
3. Press the folds together to make the inchworm short. Stretch the folds apart to make the inchworm long.

Using the Prop

Use the prop and poem to reinforce children's understanding of *short* and *long*. Before reciting the poem, have children practice making their inchworms shrink and grow by squeezing and stretching the accordion-folded section of its body. Then, as they recite the poem, have children squeeze or stretch their inchworm to go along with the words.

Inchworm Shrinks and Grows

Inchworm moves along the ground,
Changing as he goes.

First he's short and then he's long.
He shrinks and then he grows.

Short and long, short and long,
That's how Inchworm goes.

First he's short and then he's long,
Inchworm shrinks and grows.

Iguana on a Log

Children help a little critter on and off its log to do the things iguanas do all day.

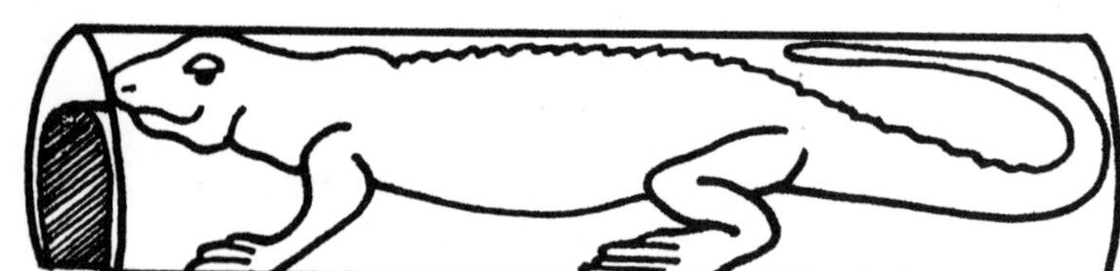

Meeting the Standards: Math

Understands and applies basic and advanced properties of the concepts of geometry:

- Understands the common language used to describe position and location (e.g., "up," "down," "below," "above," "beside," "inside," "outside")

Materials (per child)

- paper towel tube
- scissors
- iguana pattern (page 162)
- crayons
- glue stick

Making the Puppet

1. Cut away a one-inch-wide section from the length of the paper towel tube.
2. Color and cut out the iguana pattern.
3. Fold the iguana cutout along the line. Glue each long edge of the iguana along a cut edge of the tube. Trim the ends of the tube to fit the length of the iguana.
4. To put the iguana on a "log," spread the open ends of the tube and fit it onto your arm. When you remove the iguana from the log, you can place the stand-up critter on a table or other flat surface.

Using the Puppet

Use the puppet and poem to demonstrate understanding of the concepts of *on* and *off*. Tell children they will use their arm as the iguana's log. Then ask them to slip the puppet onto its log and recite the poem. Have children move the iguana on and off the log to follow the actions mentioned in the poem.

Iguana on a Log

I am an iguana on a log.
I hop off to get a drink.

I climb back on to take a nap.
Time to eat! I'm off in a blink.

I climb back on to sleep some more,
Then hop off when I want to play.

I'm a busy little iguana,
On and off my log all day!

The Little Goat

Children move a goat across, around, and through an obstacle to help it reach the grass so green.

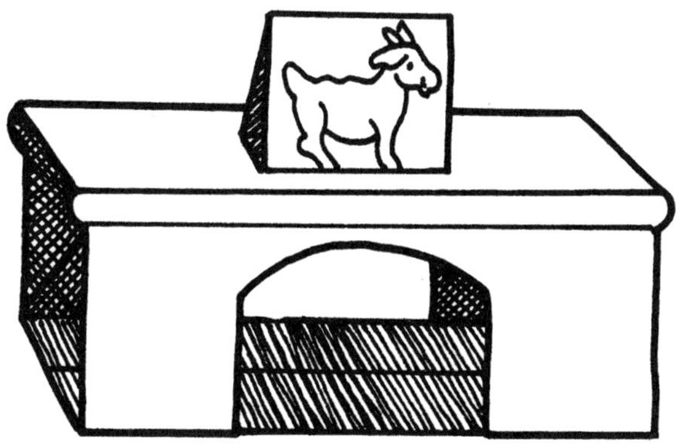

Meeting the Standards: Math

Understands and applies basic and advanced properties of the concepts of geometry:

- Understands the common language of spatial sense (e.g., "left," "right," "horizontal," "in front of")

Materials (per child)

- bridge and goat patterns (pages 162–163)
- crayons
- scissors
- tape
- glue stick

Making the Props

1. Color and cut out the bridge and goat patterns.
2. Cut out the openings on the bridge cutout. (Note to teacher: An adult should complete steps 2 and 3.)
3. Fold the bridge along the gray lines and the bottom fold lines, bringing the edges of the two folded bottom sections toward each other. Tape the edges together to form the bottom of the bridge. Stand the bridge on the table.
4. Fold the goat cutout along the lines, bringing the two ends of the cutout toward each other. Glue the edges together to create a stand-up goat.

Using the Props

Use the props and song to help children demonstrate their understanding of the spatial concepts *across*, *around*, and *through*. First, ask children to stand their bridge on a table or other flat surface. While singing the first verse, have them walk their goat across the top of the bridge. During the second verse, have children walk their goat around one end of the bridge. Ask them to walk their goat through the bridge tunnel as they sing the last verse.

The Little Goat

(to the tune of "The Wheels on the Bus")

The little goat walks across the bridge,
across the bridge, across the bridge.
The little goat walks across the bridge
To reach the grass so green.

The little goat walks around the bridge,
around the bridge, around the bridge.
The little goat walks around the bridge
To reach the grass so green.

The little goat walks through the tunnel,
through the tunnel, through the tunnel.
The little goat walks through the tunnel
To reach the grass so green.

Where Is Joey?

Children help a joey in and out of its mom's pouch.

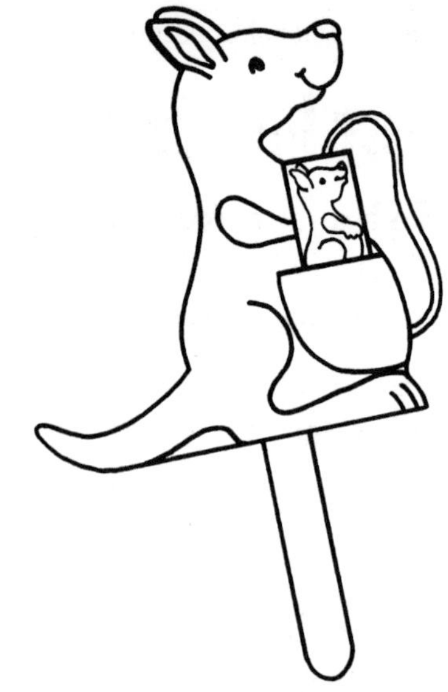

Meeting the Standards: Math

Understands and applies basic and advanced properties of the concepts of geometry:

- Understands the common language used to describe position and location (e.g., "up," "down," "below," "above," "beside," "inside," "outside")

Materials (per child)

- kangaroo, joey, and pouch patterns (page 164)
- crayons
- scissors
- glue stick
- 12-inch length of yarn
- jumbo craft stick

Making the Puppet

1. Color and cut out the kangaroo, joey, and pouch patterns.
2. Glue the pouch cutout to the kangaroo along the curved lines, leaving the straight top edge open to form a pocket.
3. Fold the joey cutout along the line. Glue the two folded sides together, trapping one end of the yarn between the top edges.
4. Glue the other end of the yarn to the back of the kangaroo.
5. To make a handle, glue the craft stick to the back of the kangaroo.

Using the Puppet

Use the puppet and song to demonstrate understanding of the concepts of *in* and *out*. While singing the first line of each of the song's verses, have children "hide" the joey behind the kangaroo. Then have them use the joey and kangaroo to act out the rest of the lines in each verse.

Where Is Joey?

(to the tune of "Where Is Thumbkin?")

Where is Joey? Where is Joey?
In Mom's pouch. In Mom's pouch.
Cuddling, hiding, peeping.
Eating, resting, sleeping.
In Mom's pouch. In Mom's pouch.

Where is Joey? Where is Joey?
Out of Mom's pouch. Out of Mom's pouch.
Jumping, leaping, hopping.
Moving without stopping.
Out of Mom's pouch. Out of Mom's pouch.

▪ EARLY CONCEPTS ▪

Directional & Positional Concepts

Little Gray Dolphin

Children create this little dolphin to take for a swim over and under the waves.

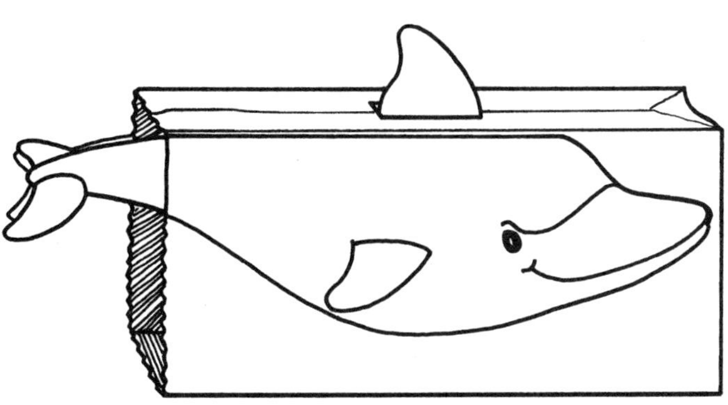

Meeting the Standards: Math

Understands and applies basic and advanced properties of the concepts of geometry:

- Understands the common language used to describe position and location (e.g., "up," "down," "below," "above," "beside," "inside," "outside")

Materials (per child)

- dolphin, tail, and fin patterns (page 165)
- crayons
- scissors
- paper lunch bag
- glue stick

Making the Puppet

1. Color and cut out the dolphin patterns.
2. Open the paper bag and glue a body cutout to each side of the bag.
3. Fold each tail cutout along the line and glue it to a dolphin body.
4. Fold the fin cutout along the line. Glue the fin to the top of the bag above the dolphin's flippers.

Using the Puppet

Use the puppet and song to reinforce children's understanding of *over* and *under*. To begin, ask children to slip their dominant hand into the dolphin puppet. Then have them hold out their free arm to represent waves. As they sing the song, have children move the dolphin over or under the "waves" to act out the words in the song.

Little Gray Dolphin

(to the tune of "The Wheels on the Bus")

The little gray dolphin leaps
over the waves, over the waves,
over the waves.
The little gray dolphin leaps
over the waves,
Then dives into the sea.

The little gray dolphin dives
under the waves, under the waves,
under the waves.
The little gray dolphin dives
under the waves,
Then leaps out of the sea.

Up the Ladder

Children move this brave firefighter up and down the ladder to fight a fire.

Meeting the Standards: Math

Understands and applies basic and advanced properties of the concepts of geometry:

- Understands the common language used to describe position and location (e.g., "up," "down," "below," "above," "beside," "inside," "outside")

Materials (per child)

- ladder and firefighter patterns (page 166)
- crayons
- scissors
- paper towel tube
- glue stick
- 12-inch length of yarn

Making the Prop

1. Color and cut out the ladder and firefighter patterns.
2. Glue the ladder cutout along the length of the tube.
3. Cut a short slit in the bottom end of the tube just under the ladder rung. (Note to teacher: An adult should complete steps 3, 4, and 5.)
4. Fold the firefighter cutout along the line. Center and glue the cutout to the length of yarn, trapping the yarn between the two folded sides.
5. Thread the yarn through the tube, slipping it into the slit in the end of the tube. Then tie the ends together, making sure the yarn is taut but can still be pulled around and through the tube.
6. Gently pull the yarn to move the firefighter up and down the ladder.

Using the Prop

Use the prop and poem to reinforce the concepts of *up* and *down*. To begin, ask children to position the firefighter at the bottom of the ladder. Then have them move the firefighter up or down the ladder to go along with the words in the poem.

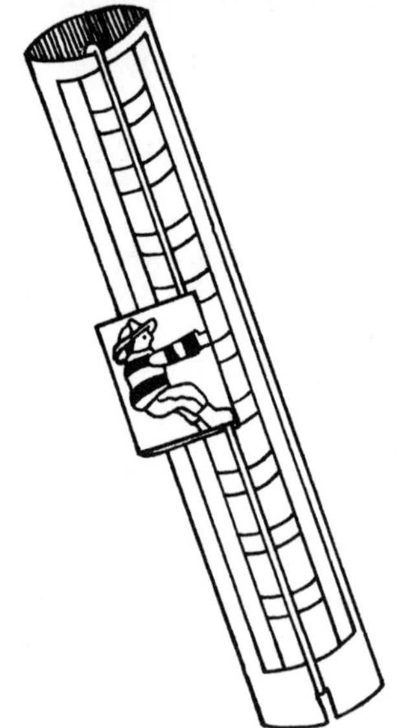

Up the Ladder

(to the tune of "London Bridge")

Up the ladder. Up, up, up.
Up, up, up. Up, up, up.
Up the ladder to the top.
Put out the fire!

Down the ladder. Down, down, down.
Down, down, down. Down, down, down.
Down the ladder to the ground.
Brave firefighter!

TEACHING TIP

This activity provides a good opportunity to discuss fire safety with students.

■ EARLY CONCEPTS ■

Directional & Positional Concepts

Tag, You're It!

Children move different critters forward and backward to help them play a friendly game of tag.

Meeting the Standards: Math

Understands and applies basic and advanced properties of the concepts of geometry:

- Understands the common language of spatial sense (e.g., "left," "right," "horizontal," "in front of")

Materials (per child)

- bird, bee, and beetle patterns (page 166)
- crayons
- scissors
- glue stick
- paper bowl
- turtle patterns (page 167)

Making the Props

1. Color and cut out the bird, bee, and beetle patterns. Fold each cutout along the lines and glue the top edges together to create a stand-up critter.
2. Color the turtle patterns and bowl green. Cut out the turtle patterns.
3. Glue the turtle head and legs around the rim of the bowl to create a turtle.

Using the Props

Use the props and poem to help children demonstrate their understanding of *forward* and *backward*. To begin, ask them to place the three critters about a foot away from the turtle, with all the critters facing the turtle. Then invite children to recite the poem, moving the bird and turtle to act out the words. Have them repeat the poem two more times, replacing "Bird" with "Bee" and then "Beetle" and moving the corresponding critter to go along with the words.

Tag, You're It!

Bird and Turtle like to play tag,
Backward and forward they go.
Bird tags Turtle, then Turtle tags Bird.
Going back and forth just so.

Bird runs forward. "Tag, you're it!"
Then moves backward to run away.
Turtle runs forward. "Tag, you're it!"
They play tag like this all day!

A Spider on Her Web

Children help a spider move to her favorite high and low spots on her web.

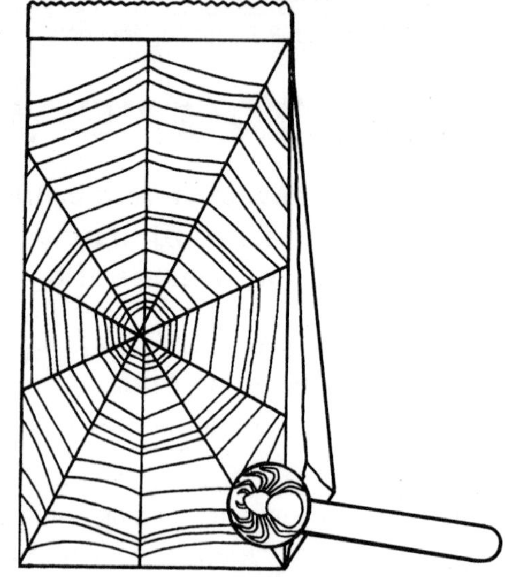

Meeting the Standards: Math

Understands and applies basic and advanced properties of the concepts of geometry:

- Understands the common language used to describe position and location (e.g., "up," "down," "below," "above," "beside," "inside," "outside")

Materials (per child)

- spider and web patterns (page 167)
- crayons
- scissors
- glue stick
- paper lunch bag
- craft stick

Making the Puppet and Prop

1. Color and cut out the spider and web patterns.
2. Glue the craft stick to the back of the spider cutout.
3. Glue the web cutout to the lunch bag. Open the bag and glue the top edges together to make a freestanding web.

Using the Puppet and Prop

Use the puppet, prop, and song to reinforce the concepts of *high* and *low*. First, ask children to stand their paper-bag web on the table. Then, as they sing the song, have children move their puppet to a high or low spot on the web to go along with the words in the song.

A Spider on Her Web

(to the tune of "The Itsy Bitsy Spider")

A spider on her web climbs
high and low all day.
High up at the top is where she likes
to play.
Down low at the bottom is where she
goes to rest.
Climbing high and low all day,
a spider's life is best!

Catch a Fly!

Children open and close this hungry frog's mouth to help it catch a fly.

Meeting the Standards: Math

Understands and applies basic and advanced properties of the concepts of geometry:

- Understands the common language used to describe position and location (e.g., "up," "down," "below," "above," "beside," "inside," "outside")

Materials (per child)

- 6-inch paper plate
- green tempera paint
- paintbrush
- frog head, legs, and tongue patterns (page 168)
- green and red crayons
- scissors
- glue
- 2 large wiggle eyes
- small black pom-pom

Making the Puppet

1. Paint the top of the paper plate green. Allow the paint to dry.
2. Color the frog head and leg patterns green and the tongue pattern red. Cut out all the patterns.
3. Fold the paper plate in half with the painted side on the inside. Glue the head cutout to one side of the folded plate, leaving the straight edge open to create a pocket. Fold up each eye flap and glue a wiggle eye onto it.
4. Glue a back leg to each side of the frog near the top straight edge. Glue the front legs along the bottom curve. Be sure to glue all the legs to the unpainted side of the folded plate.
5. Open the frog's mouth and glue one end of the tongue along the fold on the inside, leaving the other end free to move about.

Using the Puppet

Use the prop and song to reinforce children's understanding of *open* and *close*. Tell children they will use the small pom-pom to represent a fly. Then have them place the frog puppet on their hand. As they sing, encourage children to act out the words by moving the fly around the frog and opening and closing the frog's mouth to go along with the actions in the song.

Catch a Fly!

(to the tune of "Here We Go 'Round the Mulberry Bush")

Open Frog's mouth to catch a fly,
catch a fly, catch a fly.
Open Frog's mouth to catch a fly.
Buzz-buzz, buzz-buzz, buzz-buzz!

Close Frog's mouth to swallow a fly,
swallow a fly, swallow a fly.
Close Frog's mouth to swallow a fly.
Gulp-gulp, gulp-gulp, gulp-gulp!

Open Wide!

Children use this big-mouth puppet to explore the kind of work a dentist does.

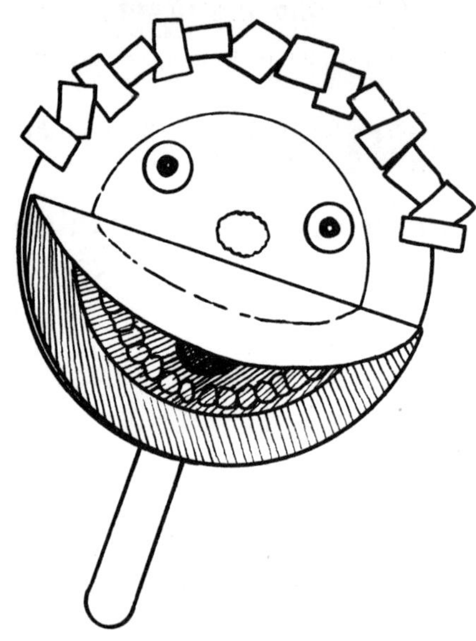

Meeting the Standards: Health

Knows the availability and effective use of health services, products, and information:

- Knows community health service providers and their roles (e.g., paramedics, dentists, nurses, physicians, sanitarians, dietitians)

Materials (per child)

- two 6-inch paper plates
- red and pink crayons
- mouth pattern (page 169)
- scissors
- glue
- flesh-tone crayons
- 2 large wiggle eyes
- pom-pom
- crinkle paper strips or yarn
- jumbo craft stick

Making the Puppet

1. Color the rim of one paper plate dark red. Fold the plate with the colored side on the inside.
2. Color the mouth pattern pink, making sure you leave the teeth white. Color the tongue on the pattern dark red. Then cut out the pattern.
3. Fold and glue the mouth cutout to the inside of the folded plate.
4. Color the other paper plate with a flesh-tone crayon. Nest and glue the folded plate onto this plate, leaving the teeth-only side free to open and close.

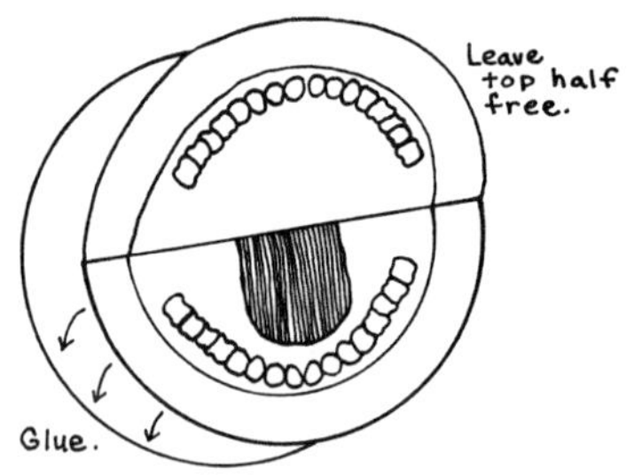

5. Close the mouth and glue the wiggle eyes and a pom-pom nose above the fold. Add crinkle paper strips or yarn to create hair for the puppet.
6. For a handle, glue the craft stick to the back of the puppet.

Using the Puppet

Use the puppet and song to reinforce the job a dentist does. As children sing the song, have them open their puppet's mouth and pretend to be a dentist by acting out the words in the song.

Open Wide!

(to the tune of "Take Me Out to the Ball Game")

"Open wide," says the dentist.
"Let me look at your teeth.
I'll check your top teeth and bottom, too.
Open wide and I soon will be through!"

"Then I'll count and clean all your toothies,
And floss the tooth plaque away.
I'll give you a toothbrush to use
Each and every day."

SOCIAL STUDIES

Community Awareness

Firefighter Wears a Coat

Children create and use this puppet to learn about the special gear worn by a firefighter.

Meeting the Standards: Health

Knows essential concepts and practices concerning injury prevention and safety:

- Knows how to recognize emergencies and respond appropriately (e.g., identifies and obtains help from police officers, firefighters, and medical personnel)

Materials (per child)

- firefighter and mask patterns (page 169)
- crayons
- scissors
- glue stick
- jumbo craft stick

Making the Puppet

1. Color and cut out the firefighter and mask patterns.
2. Glue the mask to the firefighter where indicated. Fold the mask along the line to make a flap that opens and closes.
3. To make a handle, glue the craft stick to the back of the firefighter.

Using the Puppet

Use the puppet and song to reinforce children's knowledge of what a firefighter wears to fight fires. To begin, ask children to fold the mask back away from the firefighter's face. Then, as they sing the song, have children point to each piece of the firefighter's equipment as it is named. Have them fold the mask over the firefighter's face when they sing the last verse.

This activity provides a good opportunity to discuss fire safety with students.

Firefighter Wears a Coat

(to the tune of "The Farmer in the Dell")

Firefighter wears a coat.
Firefighter wears a coat.
When it's time to fight a fire,
Firefighter wears a coat.

Firefighter wears two gloves.
Firefighter wears two gloves.
When it's time to fight a fire,
Firefighter wears two gloves.

Firefighter wears a helmet.
Firefighter wears a helmet.
When it's time to fight a fire,
Firefighter wears a helmet.

Firefighter wears a mask.
Firefighter wears a mask.
When it's time to fight a fire,
Firefighter wears a mask.

▪ SOCIAL STUDIES ▪

Community Awareness

The Farmer's Barn

Children spin the wheel and open the door to see which animals the farmer keeps in the barn.

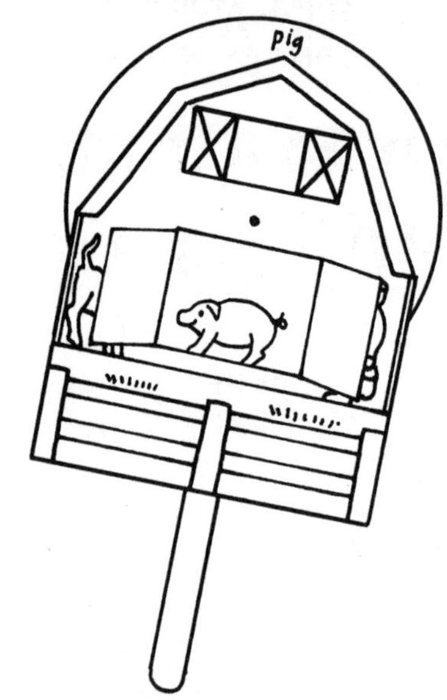

Meeting the Standards: Language Arts

Uses the general skills and strategies of the reading process:

- Knows some familiar words in print
- Uses basic elements of phonetic analysis (e.g., common letter/sound relationships, beginning and ending consonants, vowel sounds, blends, word patterns) to decode unknown words

Materials (per child)

- barn and animal wheel patterns (pages 170–171)
- crayons
- scissors
- paper brad

Making the Prop

1. Color and cut out the barn and animal wheel patterns.
2. Carefully cut along the dotted lines around the barn doors. (Note to teacher: An adult should complete steps 2 and 3.)
3. Place the wheel cutout behind the barn and poke the paper brad through the center of both pieces. Turn the wheel to make sure it moves freely.
4. Glue the craft stick to the back of the barn.
5. Fold and unfold the barn doors to open and close them.

Using the Prop

Use the prop and poem to help children recognize and read the names of animals a farmer might keep in the barn. Before singing each verse, ask children to turn the wheel so that the name of the animal in that verse appears above the barn. Have them read the animal name and then sing the verse. On the last line, invite children to open the barn door so that the named animal appears in the doorway.

The Farmer's Barn

(to the tune of "Row, Row, Row Your Boat")

"Oink, oink," says the pig.
It oinks so merrily.
The farmer's pig lives in the barn.
Open the door and see.

"Maa, maa," says the goat.
It maas so merrily.
The farmer's goat lives in the barn.
Open the door and see.

"Baa, baa," says the sheep.
It baas so merrily.
The farmer's sheep lives in the barn.
Open the door and see.

"Cluck, cluck," says the hen.
It clucks so merrily.
The farmer's hen lives in the barn.
Open the door and see.

SOCIAL STUDIES
Community Awareness

I'm a Doctor

Children create and use a doctor puppet to learn about a doctor's job.

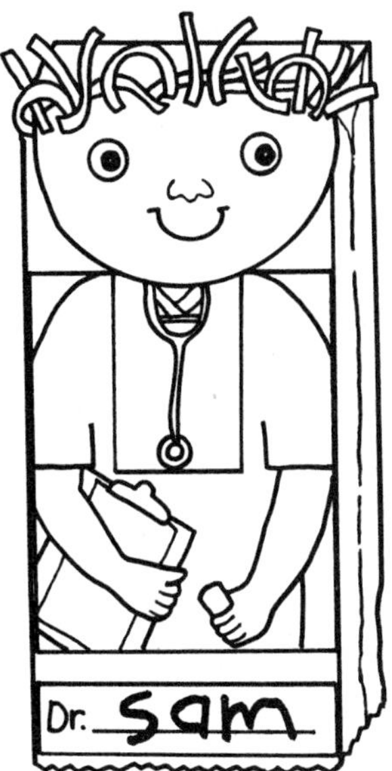

Meeting the Standards: Health

Knows the availability and effective use of health services, products, and information:

- Knows community health service providers and their roles (e.g., paramedics, dentists, nurses, physicians, sanitarians, dietitians)

Materials (per child)

- doctor's head, body, stethoscope, and name tag patterns (page 172)
- crayons
- scissors
- paper lunch bag
- glue stick
- 2 wiggle eyes
- crinkle paper strips or yarn

Making the Puppet

1. Write your name on the name tag pattern. Then color and cut out the head, body, stethoscope, and name tag patterns.
2. Glue the head cutout to the bottom of the bag. Glue on the wiggle eyes, draw a mouth, and add crinkle paper strips or yarn to create hair.
3. Glue the body cutout to the bag just below the head. Then glue the stethoscope cutout onto the body where indicated.
4. Glue the name tag near the bottom edge of the bag.

Using the Puppet

Use the puppet and song to help reinforce children's knowledge of what a doctor does. First, ask children to slip their hand into their puppet. Then invite them to move their puppet to act out the words to the song.

I'm a Doctor

(to the tune of "Yankee Doodle")

I'm a doctor. I'm your friend.
I'll help you get well quick.
Come to my office to see me
When you get hurt or sick.

I'm a doctor. I'm your friend.
I'll check your throat and ears.
I'll listen to your heart and lungs.
I'm here to help all year!

Put It in the Mailbox

Children fill a mailbox with different kinds of mail for the postal worker to collect.

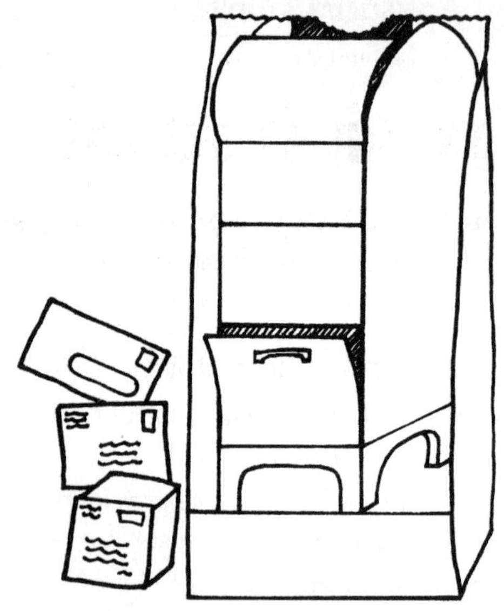

Meeting the Standards: Language Arts

Uses listening and speaking strategies for different purposes:

- Creates or acts out familiar stories, songs, rhymes, and plays in play activities

Materials (per child)

- mailbox and mail patterns (page 173)
- crayons
- scissors
- paper lunch bag
- glue stick

Making the Props

1. Color and cut out the mailbox and mail patterns. Glue the mailbox cutout to the front of the paper bag, lining up the top of the cutout with the top of the bag.
2. Open the paper-bag mailbox and stand it on the table. Cut along the curved dotted lines near the top of the mailbox to create a fold-down door.
3. Cut along the dotted lines on the bottom door of the mailbox to create another fold-down door. (Note to teacher: You may want to do this step for the child.)
4. Glue the top edges of the bag together, making sure the fold-down door is left free to open and close.
5. Open the top door on the mailbox to deposit the letter, bill, or package. Open the bottom door to remove the mail.

Using the Props

Use the props and song to teach about the job of a postal worker. Ask children to stand their mailbox on the table. As each piece of mail is mentioned in the first verse, have children deposit it in the top door of the mailbox. Have them remove the mail from the bottom door during the second verse.

Put It in the Mailbox

(to the tune of "Ten Little Indians")

Write a letter, stamp the letter,
put it in the mailbox.
Pay a bill, stamp the bill,
put it in the mailbox.
Wrap a package, stamp the package,
put it in the mailbox.
Put your mail into the box!

Postal worker comes along and
takes the letter.
Postal worker comes along and
takes the bill.
Postal worker comes along and
takes the package.
And sends your mail on its way!

SOCIAL STUDIES

Community Awareness

Shopping at the Grocery Store

Students pretend to buy food at the grocery store to match the items on their shopping list.

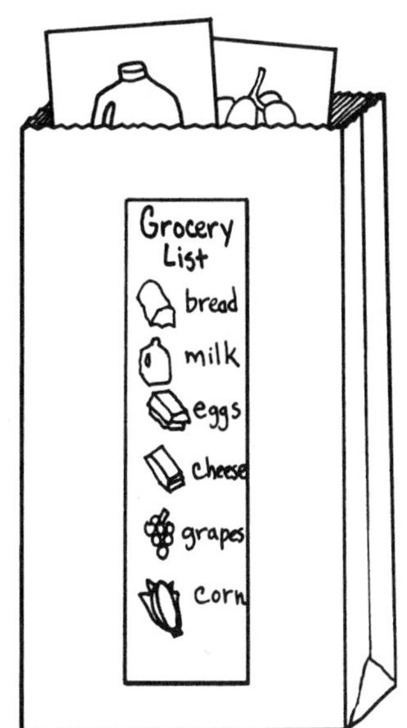

Meeting the Standards: Economics

Understands basic features of market structures and exchanges:

- Understands basic concepts of buying, selling, and trading

Materials (per child)

- food cards and grocery list pattern (page 174)
- crayons
- scissors
- paper lunch bag

Making the Props

1. Color and cut out the food cards and shopping list.
2. Glue the shopping list to the front of the paper bag.
3. Place the food cards one at a time into the bag in the order shown on the list.

Using the Props

Use the props and song to help children understand the concept of shopping for and buying food at the grocery store. Ask children to stand their bag on the table and spread the food cards faceup in front of the bag. As they sing the first verse, have them point to the bread on the shopping list. During the second verse, invite them to find the card with the loaf of bread, pretend to buy the bread, and place it in the bag. Repeat the song five times, each time pointing to the next item on the list and using the name of that food in the second verse. The food names to use in the song are: *jug of milk, dozen eggs, block of cheese, bunch of grapes,* and *ear of corn.*

Shopping at the Grocery Store

(to the tune of "Do You Know the Muffin Man?")

Shopping at the grocery store,
The grocery store, the grocery store.
Check my list at the grocery store
To buy just what I need.

I will buy a loaf of bread,
A loaf of bread, a loaf of bread.
I will buy a loaf of bread
And put it in the bag.

SOCIAL STUDIES

Health and Safety

I Have Feelings

Children use this puppet to demonstrate how their feelings can change.

Meeting the Standards: Health

Knows how to maintain mental and emotional health:

- Identifies and shares feelings in appropriate ways

Materials (per child)

- four faces and shirt patterns (page 175)
- crayons
- scissors
- glue stick
- paper bathroom cup
- 8-ounce foam cup
- paper brad

Making the Puppet

1. Color and cut out the four faces and shirt patterns.
2. Glue the four faces pattern around the paper bathroom cup, overlapping and gluing the ends together where indicated.
3. Glue the shirt cutout to the 8-ounce foam cup, leaving the arms free to extend out from the sides of the cup or be folded toward the shirt.
4. To connect the cups, poke the paper brad through the bottom of the small cup and then through the bottom of the larger cup. Spread the ends of the brad to hold it in place. Make sure the small cup spins freely on top of the large cup. (Note to teacher: An adult should complete this step.)

Using the Puppet

Use the puppet and song to reinforce children's understanding of different emotions and how emotions can change. Ask children to place their hand inside the large cup and turn the puppet's shirt to face them. Then have them use their other hand to spin the head until the happy face rests above the shirt. As they sing each verse, have children turn the puppet's head so that the face corresponding to the named feeling rests above the shirt.

I Have Feelings

(to the tune of "Clementine")

I have feelings, different feelings
That can change from day to day.
Sometimes I have happy feelings.
I don't always feel one way.

I have feelings, different feelings
That can change from day to day.
Sometimes I have angry feelings.
I don't always feel one way.

I have feelings, different feelings
That can change from day to day.
Sometimes I have sad feelings.
I don't always feel one way.

I have feelings, different feelings
That can change from day to day.
Sometimes I have scared feelings.
I don't always feel one way.

Wash Your Hands

Use this personalized puppet to teach children about proper hand-washing practices.

Meeting the Standards: Health

Knows how to maintain and promote personal health:

- Performs personal hygiene skills independently (e.g., uses toilet, brushes teeth, washes hands, blows nose)
- Knows basic personal hygiene habits required to maintain health (e.g., caring for teeth, gums, eyes, ears, nose, skin, hair, nails)

Materials (per child)

- towel, soap, and puppet patterns (pages 175–176)
- crayons
- scissors
- glue stick
- crinkle paper strips or yarn
- two 9- by 12-inch sheets of white construction paper
- paper lunch bag

Making the Puppet and Props

1. Draw your own facial features on the puppet pattern. Then color and cut out the towel, soap, and puppet patterns.
2. Add crinkle paper strips or yarn to your puppet to create hair.
3. Trace your left and right hands and forearms on the white construction paper. (You might ask a friend to help you trace your writing arm and hand.) Color and cut out the outlines.
4. Glue an arm to each sleeve on your puppet.
5. Glue your puppet to the flat side of the paper bag.
6. Store the soap and towel cutout inside your bag puppet until you're ready to use them.

Using the Puppet and Props

Use the puppet, props, and song to reinforce the proper way to wash hands. Ask children to set the soap and towel faceup on the table and then slip their hand into their puppet. While singing the song, have them act out the words with the puppet, using the soap and towel as they are mentioned in the verses. Remind children to have the puppet wash and dry its hands thoroughly, including its wrists, palms, back of hands, and fingers.

Wash Your Hands

(to the tune of "Here We Go 'Round the Mulberry Bush")

Wash your hands to get them clean,
Get them clean, get them clean.
Wash your hands to get them clean
To wash the germs away.

Water and soap are what you need,
What you need, what you need.
Water and soap are what you need
To wash the germs away.

Lather your hands and count to ten,
Count to ten, count to ten.
Lather your hands and count to ten
To wash the germs away.

Rinse your hands and wipe them dry,
Wipe them dry, wipe them dry.
Rinse your hands and wipe them dry.
You washed the germs away!

■ SOCIAL STUDIES ■

Health and Safety

Brush Your Teeth

Children demonstrate how to brush their teeth with these special props.

Meeting the Standards: Health

Knows how to maintain and promote personal health:

- Performs personal hygiene skills independently (e.g., uses toilet, brushes teeth, washes hands, blows nose)
- Knows basic personal hygiene habits required to maintain health (e.g., caring for teeth, gums, eyes, ears, nose, skin, hair, nails)

Materials (per child)

- toothbrush, toothpaste tube, and cap patterns (page 177)
- crayons
- scissors
- jumbo craft stick
- glue stick
- plastic drinking straw

Making the Props

1. Color and cut out the toothbrush, toothpaste, and cap patterns.
2. For the toothbrush, color the craft stick to match the handle on the toothbrush cutout. Fold the cutout along the center line. Then glue the craft stick between the two sides of the cutout.
3. To make the tube of toothpaste, fold the tube cutout along the center line. Glue together the short angled edges on the folded side. Then glue together all the edges on the opposite side of the tube. Be sure to leave the top and bottom edges open.
4. Glue the cap cutout to the top of the tube where indicated. Fold the cap along the line to "put the cap on" the tube.
5. Insert the straw through the bottom of the tube. Fold back the cap to "open" the tube. Then, to "squeeze" toothpaste out of the tube, push the straw through the tube until it extends from the top.

Using the Props

Use the props and song to reinforce good toothbrushing habits. As children sing the song, invite them to use their toothbrush and toothpaste tube to act out the words.

Brush Your Teeth

(to the tune of "The Hokey Pokey")

You take your toothbrush out,
You put your toothpaste on,
You put it in your mouth,
And you move it all about.
You brush and brush your teeth,
Then you rinse your whole mouth out.
That's how you brush your teeth!

You brush your bottom teeth,
You brush your top ones, too.
You brush the back and front
So they sparkle like brand-new.
You brush and brush your teeth,
Then you rinse your whole mouth out.
That's how you brush your teeth!

School Rules

Children don a personalized cap and name tag as they review some important school rules.

Meeting the Standards: Health

Knows essential concepts and practices concerning injury prevention and safety:

- Knows safe behaviors in the classroom (e.g., walks indoors) and on the playground (e.g., participates safely in activities)
- Knows the safe and proper use of classroom materials

Materials (per child)

- cap, cap bill, and name tag patterns (page 178)
- crayons
- scissors
- 2- by 24-inch strip of construction paper
- glue stick
- tape
- double-sided tape

Making the Props

1. Write your name on the name tag pattern and the bottom section of the cap pattern. Color and cut out the cap, cap bill, and name tag patterns.
2. Glue the cap cutout to the middle of the construction-paper strip.
3. Tape the ends of the strip together to make a hatband. Be sure to fit the hatband to your head and trim the ends as needed.
4. Glue the tabs of the cap bill to the inside of the hatband. Fold the bill up.
5. Use double-sided tape to attach the name tag to the front of your shirt.

Using the Props

Use the props and poem to reinforce important rules to follow while in school. Ask children to put on their caps and name tags. Then, as they recite the poem, have them fill in their names in the first line and make up actions to go along with each of the other lines.

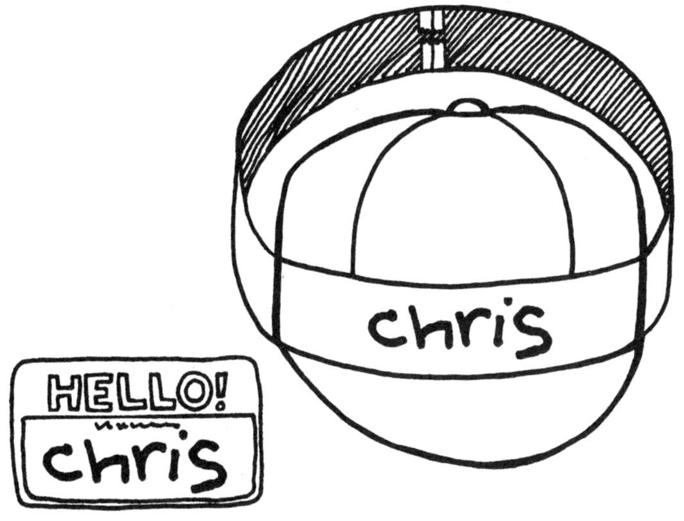

School Rules

I'm __________, and how do you do?
There's something I want to tell you.
Each day when I go to school,
I try to mind every rule.

I wait until my turn to talk.
When indoors, I always walk.
I keep my hands to myself,
And put things back on the shelf.

I put my book bag away.
I'm careful when I go out to play.
I'm a friend to everyone.
See, rules make school safe and fun!

School Bus Safety

Children make this personalized puppet to share about safety practices on the school bus.

Meeting the Standards: Health

Knows essential concepts and practices concerning injury prevention and safety:

- Knows rules for traffic and pedestrian safety (e.g., crossing the street safely, safety around vehicles)
- Knows basic fire, traffic, water, and recreation safety practices

Materials (per child)

- puppet pattern (page 176)
- crayons
- scissors
- glue stick
- crinkle paper strips or yarn
- scraps of colored construction paper, including flesh tones
- four 7-inch lengths of crepe paper streamer
- paper lunch bag

Making the Puppet

1. Draw your own facial features on the puppet pattern. Color the rest of the pattern and cut it out. Add crinkle paper strips or yarn to create hair.
2. Cut out two hands from scraps of flesh-toned construction paper. Then cut out two shoes from construction paper scraps in the color of your choice.
3. For arms and legs, glue a hand or shoe cutout to one end of each 7-inch length of crepe paper streamer. Glue the arms and legs to your puppet.
4. Glue your puppet to the flat side of the paper bag.

Using the Puppet

Use the puppet and poem to reinforce bus safety practices. Ask children to open their puppets and set them on the edge of a table so that the legs bend and drape over the edge. As they recite the poem, invite children to move the arms and legs of their puppet to act out the words.

School Bus Safety

School bus safety is a snap!
I face front with my hands in my lap.

Feet in the aisle? No sirree!
I keep my feet in front of me.

I talk quietly and stay in my seat.
School bus safety can't be beat!

Crossing the Street

Children use this pedestrian signal to learn about crossing a street safely.

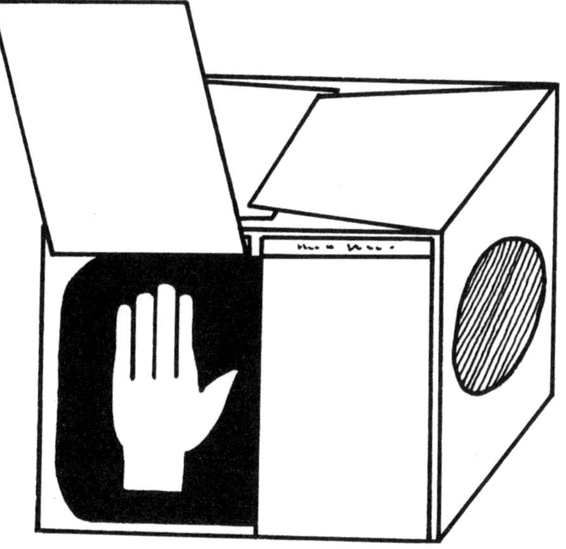

Meeting the Standards: Health

Knows essential concepts and practices concerning injury prevention and safety:

- Knows rules for traffic and pedestrian safety
- Knows basic fire, traffic, water, and recreation safety practices

Materials (per child)

- facial tissue cube
- yellow tempera paint
- paintbrush
- pedestrian signal and flap patterns (page 179)
- orange crayon
- scissors
- glue stick

Making the Prop

1. Paint the facial tissue cube yellow. Set it aside to dry.
2. Color the hand on the pedestrian signal pattern orange. Leave the walking person white. Color the flap patterns yellow. Cut out all the patterns.
3. Place the tissue cube with the hole end facing left or right. Glue the pedestrian signal to one side of the cube.
4. Glue the top edge of each flap onto the pedestrian signal where indicated.
5. Fold each flap back to expose the signal under it.

Using the Prop

Use the prop and poem to reinforce safely crossing a street following pedestrian signals. Explain that these signals are often found in cities and at busy street corners. Then ask children to close the flaps on their pedestrian signal and slip their hand into the opening. While reciting the second verse of the poem, invite them to fold back the flap on the left to expose the hand signal. Have children close the flap at the end of the verse. During the last verse, ask them to open the right flap to uncover the walking person and then pretend to cross the street.

Crossing the Street

When you cross a busy street,
There's a light that lets you know
When it's time to stop
And when it's time to go.

Just look up at the light.
What signal do you see?
A hand means "Don't Walk."
Be as safe as you can be!

When the walking person lights,
This is the "Walk" signal you see.
Look both ways before you cross,
And be as safe as you can be!

SOCIAL STUDIES

Health and Safety

Helmet On, Helmet Off

Children use this safety-conscious puppet to learn about wearing head safety gear.

Meeting the Standards: Life Skills

Considers risks:

- Knows potential safety hazards, and knows common strategies to avoid hazard or injury
- Applies preventative measures (e.g., the proper use of safety equipment) prior to a task to minimize security or safety problems

Materials (per child)

- 4½-inch length of paper towel tube
- 4½- by 5½-inch flesh-colored construction paper
- crayons
- scissors
- glue stick
- 2 wiggle eyes
- assorted craft materials (yarn, pom-poms, scraps of craft foam, and so on)
- half of a pull-apart plastic egg

Making the Puppet

1. Glue the 4½- by 5½-inch flesh-colored construction paper around the tube.
2. Glue on the wiggle eyes about one-third from the top of the tube. Use crayons to draw on other facial features, or cut out features from craft items to glue onto the tube (such as yarn hair, a pom-pom nose, and craft foam mouth).
3. Fit the plastic egg half on top of the puppet's head to serve as a helmet.

Using the Puppet

Use the puppet and poem to help children understand during which activities they should wear their safety helmets. To begin, ask children to put the puppet on their hand and remove the helmet from its head. As they recite the poem, have them put the helmet on the puppet or take it off according to the words in the verses.

Helmet On, Helmet Off

Helmet on to ride my bike.
Helmet off to read a book.

Helmet on to ride my skateboard.
Helmet off to help Dad cook.

Helmet on to roller blade.
Helmet off when I'm at school.

Helmet on protects my head.
I wear it as a safety rule.

Stop, Drop, and Roll

This clever puppet can be used to help children practice what they should do if their clothes catch on fire.

Meeting the Standards: Life Skills

Considers risks:

- Selects an appropriate course of action in an emergency
- Thinks clearly under stress

Materials (per child)

- clean plastic cap from laundry detergent bottle
- permanent marker
- scissors
- craft glue
- 2 wiggle eyes
- assorted craft materials (pom-poms, ribbon, yarn, scraps of craft foam, and so on)

Making the Puppet

1. Glue wiggle eyes near the top of the plastic cap.
2. Use the permanent marker to draw on other facial features, or cut out features from craft items to glue onto the cap (such as pom-pom hair, a button nose, and yarn mouth).
3. Add other decorations as desired, such as a colorful ribbon or craft foam shapes glued around the bottom border of the cap.

Using the Puppet

Use the puppet and poem to reinforce the concept of "Stop, drop, and roll." Explain to children that if their clothes ever catch on fire, the safe thing to do is to stop, drop, and roll. (Tell children that they should cover their face with their hands before rolling.) To emphasize this safety practice, demonstrate the entire procedure and have students practice it. Then ask children to place their puppet on their hand and recite the first verse. During the second and third verses, have them remove and use their puppets to act out the words, demonstrating how to stop, drop, and roll.

Stop, Drop, and Roll

If your clothes catch on fire,
Here's what you must do.
To put out the flames,
It's the safest thing for you:

Stop! Don't ever run.
Drop! Fall to the ground.
Roll! From side to side.
Just roll and roll around!

If your clothes catch on fire,
Here's what you must do:
Stop, drop, and roll.
It's the safest thing for you.

SCIENCE

All About Me

I Use My Eyes to See

Children make and use a pair of binoculars to describe what they see.

Meeting the Standards: Science

Understands the nature of scientific inquiry:

- Uses the senses to make observations about living things, nonliving objects, and events
- Asks questions about observations

Materials (per child)

- 2 paper bathroom cups
- scissors
- tape
- 36-inch length of yarn

Making the Prop

1. Cut out the bottom of each bathroom cup.
2. Place the cups with the two small open ends pushed together side by side. Tape the cups together near the small and large openings.
3. Tape each end of the length of yarn to the binoculars to create a strap.

Using the Prop

Use the prop and song to help children understand how they rely on sight to gather information about their surroundings. While singing the song, ask children to look around through their binoculars. At the end of the first verse, invite a few volunteers to describe something nearby that they see. At the end of the last verse, have volunteers describe something far away that can be viewed through the binoculars.

I Use My Eyes to See

(to the tune of "The Farmer in the Dell")

I use my eyes to see,
I use my eyes to see.
What do I see that's near to me?
I use my eyes to see.

I use my eyes to see,
I use my eyes to see.
What do I see that's far from me?
I use my eyes to see.

Listen!

Children use a pair of oversized ears to accentuate their sense of hearing.

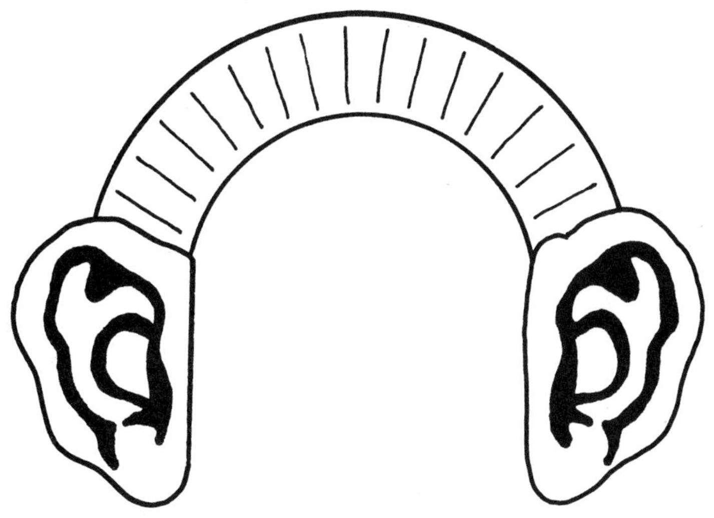

Meeting the Standards: Science

Understands the nature of scientific inquiry:

- Uses the senses to make observations about living things, nonliving objects, and events
- Asks questions about observations

Materials (per child)

- ear patterns (page 180)
- crayons
- scissors
- half of a 9-inch paper plate
- glue stick

Making the Prop

1. Color and cut out the ear patterns.
2. Cut the rim from the paper plate half. Discard the interior part of the plate and keep the rim to use as a headband.
3. Glue an ear cutout near each end of the headband to make a giant-size pair of ears.
4. Put on the headband so that the ears rest on each side of your head.

Using the Prop

Use the prop and song to help children understand how they use their sense of hearing. Before beginning the activity, collect a few rhythm instruments—such as a bell, drum, and shaker—and hide them behind a screen. Then ask children to put on their headband. As children sing the song, play one of the instruments, keeping it hidden behind the screen. Have them fill in the name of the instrument they think they heard in the last line. Afterward, show children the instrument so they can check their guess. Repeat the song several times, each time playing a different instrument for children to guess.

Listen!

Listen!
Listen!
What do I hear?

Listen!
Listen!
It sounds so clear.

Listen!
Listen!
I'll use my ears.

A __________ is what
I think I hear!

Use Your Nose

Children use this unique puppet to explore their sense of smell.

Meeting the Standards: Behavioral Studies

Understands that interactions among learning, inheritance, and physical development affect human behavior:

- Knows that people use their senses to find out about their surroundings and themselves and that different senses provide different information

Materials (per child)

- scent cards and nose pattern (page 180)
- crayons
- scissors
- foam cup
- glue stick
- 2 wiggle eyes
- crinkle paper strips

Making the Puppet

1. Color and cut out the picture cards and nose pattern.
2. Turn the cup upside down. Fold the nose cutout along the line and glue it to the cup just above the rim.
3. Glue a wiggle eye to the cup on each side of the nose.
4. Glue crinkle paper strips to the top of the cup to create hair.

Using the Puppet

Use the puppet and song to reinforce children's understanding of their use of smell. First, have children place the cards faceup on the table. Then have them slip their hand into the puppet. As they sing the song, ask children to find the picture named in the verse. Then have them use that picture and the puppet to act out the verse.

Use Your Nose

(to the tune of "Mary Had a Little Lamb")

Use your nose to smell a pie,
smell a pie, smell a pie.
Use your nose to smell a pie.
Just smell it with your nose.

Use your nose to smell a skunk,
smell a skunk, smell a skunk.
Use your nose to smell a skunk.
Just smell it with your nose.

Use your nose to smell a rose,
smell a rose, smell a rose.
Use your nose to smell a rose.
Just smell it with your nose.

Use your nose to smell the trash,
smell the trash, smell the trash.
Use your nose to smell the trash.
Just smell it with your nose.

I Touch With My Hands

Children use their sense of touch to distinguish between the textures on this special flip puppet.

Meeting the Standards: Behavioral Studies

Understands that interactions among learning, inheritance, and physical development affect human behavior:

- Knows that people use their senses to find out about their surroundings and themselves and that different senses provide different information

Materials (per child)

- flip puppet pattern (page 181)
- crayons
- scissors
- glue
- jumbo craft stick
- cotton ball
- several large pasta shells

Making the Puppet

1. Color and cut out the flip puppet pattern.
2. Fold the puppet cutout along the line. Glue the two sides of the puppet together, sandwiching the craft stick between them.
3. Glue a cotton ball to the bunny's tail. Flip the puppet over and glue the pasta shells on the sand in the pail.

Using the Puppet

Use the puppet and song to help children use their sense of touch to identify different textures. While singing the first verse, ask children to feel the cotton-ball tail on the bunny side of the puppet. Then have them flip the puppet and feel the pasta shells on the sand pail.

I Touch With My Hands

(to the tune of "He's Got the Whole World in His Hands")

I touch a soft bunny with my hands.
I touch a soft bunny with my hands.
I touch a soft bunny with my hands.
The bunny feels so soft to me.

I touch a hard seashell with my hands.
I touch a hard seashell with my hands.
I touch a hard seashell with my hands.
The seashell feels so hard to me.

Three Tastes

With the help of this paper-bag puppet, children identify foods that taste sour, sweet, and salty.

Meeting the Standards: Behavioral Studies

Understands that interactions among learning, inheritance, and physical development affect human behavior:

- Knows that people use their senses to find out about their surroundings and themselves and that different senses provide different information

Materials (per child)

- food cards and mouth pattern (page 181)
- crayons
- scissors
- paper lunch bag
- glue stick
- 2 large wiggle eyes
- pom-pom
- scraps of brown construction paper

Making the Puppet

1. Color and cut out the food cards and mouth pattern.
2. Glue the mouth cutout about two inches above the bottom of the paper bag.
3. Cut along the dotted lines to create an opening in the mouth. (Note to teacher: An adult should complete this step.)
4. To create a face on the bag, glue on the wiggle eyes and a pom-pom nose. Cut out ears from the brown paper scraps and glue them onto the bag.
5. To feed the paper-bag puppet, deposit the food cards into its mouth.

Using the Puppet

Use the puppet and song to help children identify foods that taste sour, sweet, or salty. To begin, ask them to place all their food cards faceup on the table and then stand their paper-bag puppet nearby. As they sing each verse of the song, invite children to find the named food and place that card into the puppet's mouth. After singing the entire song, repeat it, this time replacing the food names with *lemons*, *cherries*, and *popcorn*, in that order.

Three Tastes

(to the tune of "London Bridge")

Oh, how pickles taste so sour,
Taste so sour, taste so sour.
Oh, how pickles taste so sour.
Pickles taste sour.

Oh, how apples taste so sweet,
Taste so sweet, taste so sweet.
Oh, how apples taste so sweet.
Apples taste sweet.

Oh, how pretzels taste so salty,
Taste so salty, taste so salty.
Oh, how pretzels taste so salty.
Pretzels taste salty.

Mr. Wiggles

This handy puppet can be used to help children point out different parts of their body.

Meeting the Standards: Health

Understands the fundamental concepts of growth and development:

- Knows the names and locations of some body parts (e.g., head, eyes, eyebrows, nose, mouth, hair, arms, hands, legs, and feet)

Materials (per child)

- Mr. Wiggles patterns (page 182)
- crayons
- scissors
- glue stick
- 2 large wiggle eyes

Making the Puppet

1. Color and cut out the two Mr. Wiggles patterns.
2. Glue the wiggle eyes on the cutout that shows the folded fingers. Draw a mouth below the eyes.
3. Glue the two cutouts together along all but the straight edges. Leave the straight end open so that you can slip your hand into the puppet.

Using the Puppet

Use the puppet and song to help children identify different parts of their body. To begin, ask children to slip their left hand into their puppet. As they sing the song, have them point their puppet to the named body part and then begin to wiggle that body part. After singing the three printed verses, you can add more simply by replacing the named body parts in the song with different body parts. (You might continue moving up the body by naming *chest, shoulder, head,* and so on.)

Mr. Wiggles

(to the tune of "Pop, Goes the Weasel")

When Mr. Wiggles touches my foot,
It always starts to jiggle.
That part of me just has to move.
How it has to wiggle!

When Mr. Wiggles touches my knee,
It just begins to jiggle.
That part of me just has to move.
How it has to wiggle!

When Mr. Wiggles touches my hip,
It just begins to jiggle.
That part of me just has to move.
How it has to wiggle!

■ SCIENCE ■

Animals

Like All the Insects

Children use an ant, bee, and butterfly puppet to share their insect knowledge with others.

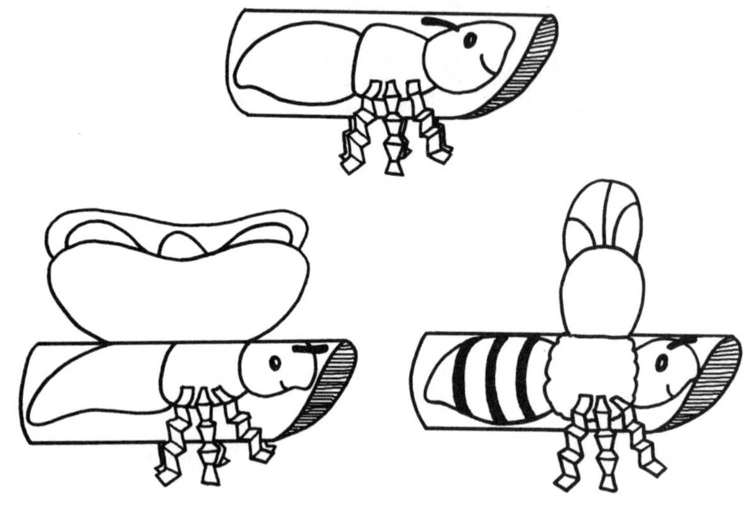

Meeting the Standards: Science

Understands biological evolution and the diversity of life:

- Knows simple ways that living things can be grouped (e.g., appearance, behavior, plant, animal)
- Knows that there are similarities and differences in the appearance and behavior of plants and animals

Materials (per child)

- ant, bee, and butterfly patterns and bee and butterfly wings (page 183)
- crayons
- scissors
- glue stick
- crinkle paper strips

Making the Puppets

1. Color and cut out all the insect patterns and wings.
2. Overlap and glue together the straight edges of each insect cutout to create a tube-shaped finger puppet.
3. Glue the bee wings to the bee puppet. Be sure to center the wings between the two bees and glue down only the middle part of the wings.
4. Repeat step 2 using the butterfly wings and butterfly puppet.
5. For legs, glue three crinkle paper strips to each side of each insect finger puppet.

Using the Puppets

Use the puppets and song to reinforce children's knowledge of insect characteristics. Ask children to put each insect puppet on their nondominant hand. Then, as they sing the song, encourage them to move the ant and point to each of its body parts as it is mentioned. Have them repeat the song twice, replacing *ant* with *bee* and then *butterfly*. Each time, ask children to move the named insect puppet and point to its body parts.

Like All the Insects

(to the tune of "Camptown Races")

I'm an ant. I have six legs.
Count 'em. Count 'em.
All my babies hatch from eggs
Like all the insects do.
Oh, I have a head
And a thorax, too.
And I have an abdomen
Like all the insects do.

Ant and Spider

Children use an ant and spider puppet to compare the two critters.

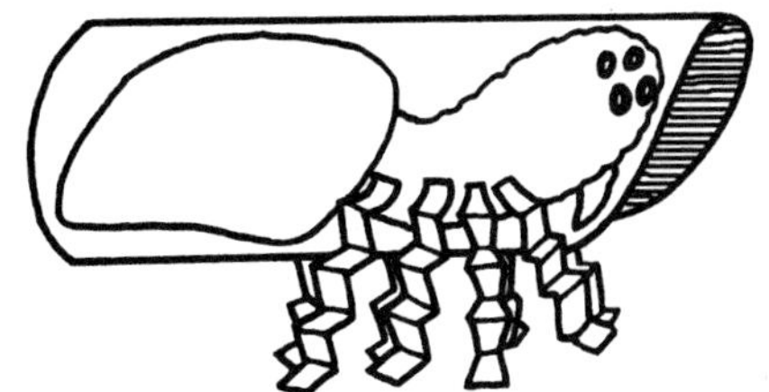

Meeting the Standards: Science

Understands biological evolution and the diversity of life:

- Knows simple ways that living things can be grouped (e.g., appearance, behavior, plant, animal)
- Knows that there are similarities and differences in the appearance and behavior of plants and animals

Materials (per child)

- ant and spider patterns (page 183)
- crayons
- scissors
- glue stick
- crinkle paper strips

Making the Puppets

1. Color and cut out the ant and spider patterns.
2. Overlap and glue together the straight edges of each cutout to create a tube-shaped finger puppet.
3. Glue three crinkle paper strips to each side of the ant finger puppet to create legs.
4. For the spider legs, glue four crinkle paper strips to each side of the spider finger puppet.

Using the Puppets

Use the puppets and poem to help children understand the difference between insects and spiders. To begin, ask children to put each puppet on their nondominant hand. As they recite the first two lines, encourage them to move the ant puppet and count its legs. Then have them move the spider puppet as they recite the rest of the poem, counting its legs and pointing to its body parts as they are mentioned in the poem.

Ant and Spider

I am an ant with six legs on me.
Six legs make me an insect, you see.

I am a spider with lots of legs, too.
But some things about me are *not* like you.

I'm an arachnid with eight legs on me,
And I have eight eyes to help me see.

I have only a head and abdomen,
But I catch bugs like you in the webs I spin!

This Is a Bird

Children make and use a bird puppet to share what they know about birds.

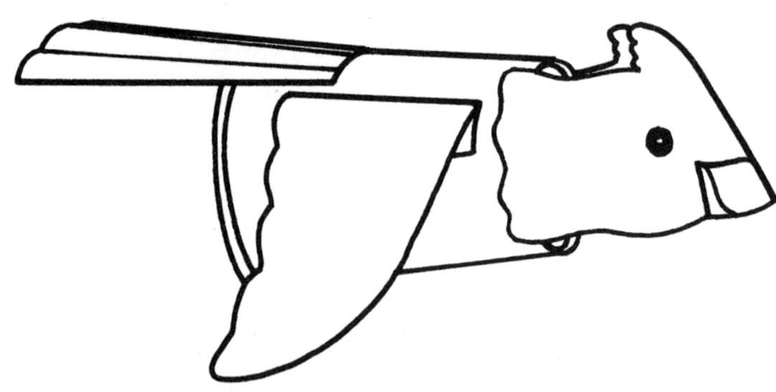

Meeting the Standards: Science

Understands the structure and function of cells and organisms:

- Knows that animals have features that help them live in different environments

Understands biological evolution and the diversity of life:

- Knows simple ways that living things can be grouped (e.g., appearance, behavior, plant, animal)

Materials (per child)

- paper bathroom cup
- red tempera paint
- paintbrush
- bird head, wing, and tail patterns (page 184)
- red crayon
- scissors
- glue stick

Making the Puppet

1. Paint the bathroom cup red. Set it aside to dry.
2. Color the bird head, wing, and tail patterns red. Cut out all the patterns.
3. Fold the head along the line and glue it to the bottom of the cup with each side opposite the other side.
4. Glue the wings and tail to the cup.

Using the Puppet

Use the puppet and poem to reinforce children's knowledge of the characteristics of birds. Ask children to slip their hand into the puppet. Then, as they recite the poem, have children point to each body part on the puppet as it is named in the poem. Invite them to also use the puppet to make up actions to go along with the words in the verses.

This Is a Bird

This is a bird. It's special, you see.
And it's quite different from you and me.

A bird has wings and a very fine tail
To help it fly and swoop and sail.

A bird has feathers and a beak that's strong.
It might eat seeds or bugs, or worms
that are long.

And when springtime comes, a bird builds
a nest
To lay its eggs in, and to sit in and rest.

Animals

It's a Fish!

Children use this swishy-tailed fish to learn about the different characteristics of a fish.

Meeting the Standards: Science

Understands the structure and function of cells and organisms:

- Knows that animals have features that help them live in different environments

Understands biological evolution and the diversity of life:

- Knows simple ways that living things can be grouped (e.g., appearance, behavior, plant, animal)

Materials (per child)

- fish and fin patterns (page 185)
- crayons
- scissors
- glitter glue pens
- glue stick
- jumbo craft stick

Making the Puppet

1. Color and cut out the fish and fin patterns.
2. Decorate the fish scales and fins with glitter glue. Allow the glue to dry.
3. Glue only the body sections of the two fish cutouts together, sandwiching the craft stick between them to create a handle. (Do not glue the tails together.)
4. Glue a fin to each side of the fish where indicated.
5. Fold each fin so that it extends out to the side of the fish. Spread the tail so that it swishes when you "swim" the puppet back and forth.

Using the Puppet

Use the puppet and song to help children understand the features that characterize a fish. As they sing the first two lines of the song, ask children to point to each named body part on their puppet. Then invite them to swim their fish around during the remaining lines of the song.

It's a Fish!

(to the tune of "Six Little Ducks")

What has fins and a swishy tail?
What has gills and is covered with scales?
What swims and glides around in the sea?
I know the answer—it's a fish, you see!
Fish, you see! Fish, you see!
I know the answer—it's a fish, you see!

Bear and Mouse

Children perform a dialogue between a bear and mouse to discover how the two critters are the same.

Meeting the Standards: Science

Understands biological evolution and the diversity of life:

- Knows simple ways that living things can be grouped (e.g., appearance, behavior, plant, animal)
- Knows that there are similarities and differences in the appearance and behavior of plants and animals

Materials (per child)

- bear and mouse patterns (page 186)
- crayons
- scissors
- glue stick
- 2 jumbo craft sticks

Making the Puppets

1. Color and cut out the bear and mouse patterns.
2. Fold each cutout on the line. Glue the two sides of the animal body together, sandwiching the craft stick between the sides to create a handle. Do not glue the legs together.
3. Spread out the legs on each puppet.

Using the Puppets

Use the puppets and poem to teach children about the common features of mammals. As children recite the poem, invite them to use their puppets to act out the dialogue in the verses.

Bear and Mouse

"You're big, I'm small," said little Mouse.
"But still we are the same."

"That's right," said Bear. "We're both
mammals,
Although we go by a different name."

Mouse said, "We are both covered
with fur.
And we both have lungs, you know."

"Our babies are born alive," said Bear.
"And we care for them as they grow."

"So we may be different in size and
shape," said Mouse.
"Still I'm a lot like you."

"I'm big. You're small," said big, big Bear.
"But we're both mammals, it's true!"

Animals

Spouting Whale

Children create a spouting whale to take for a lively swim "out in the sea."

Meeting the Standards: Science

Understands the structure and function of cells and organisms:

- Knows that animals have features that help them live in different environments

Understands biological evolution and the diversity of life:

- Knows simple ways that living things can be grouped (e.g., appearance, behavior, animal)

Materials (per child)

- whale tail, body, flipper, and spout patterns (pages 186–187)
- crayons
- scissors
- paper lunch bag
- glue stick

Making the Puppet

1. Color and cut out the whale tail, body, flipper, and spout patterns.
2. Open the paper bag and glue a whale body to each side of the bag.
3. Fold each tail cutout along the line and glue it to a whale body. Glue each flipper onto the whale puppet where indicated.
4. Fold the spout along the line. Then accordion-fold the column of the spout. Glue the spout to the top of the whale puppet, centering it over the eyes. Fold the spout down so that it lies flat on top of the puppet.

Using the Puppet

Use the puppet and song to reinforce children's whale knowledge. Have children slip their hands into their whale puppet and swim it around as they sing the first verse of the song. When they reach the last line, invite them to lift the whale's spout to its full height on the puppet. As they sing the last line of the next two verses, have children move the named body part on their puppet.

Spouting Whale

(to the tune of "Down by the Bay")

Out in the sea, where the little fishes go,
There is a mammal we all know.
She is a whale, big as can be!
Have you ever seen a whale
Blowing her spout, out in the sea?

Out in the sea, where the little fishes go,
There is a mammal we all know.
She is a whale, big as can be!
Have you ever seen a whale
Flipping her tail, out in the sea?

Out in the sea, where the little fishes go,
There is a mammal we all know.
She is a whale, big as can be!
Have you ever seen a whale
Waving her flipper, out in the sea?

Bats Are Flying Mammals

Children learn fun facts about flying mammals with this cute bat puppet.

Meeting the Standards: Science

Understands the structure and function of cells and organisms:

- Knows that animals have features that help them live in different environments

Understands biological evolution and the diversity of life:

- Knows simple ways that living things can be grouped (e.g., appearance, behavior, animal)

Materials (per child)

- bat and wing patterns (page 184)
- crayons
- scissors
- 4½-inch length of paper towel tube
- stapler
- glue stick
- paper lunch bag

Making the Puppet and Prop

1. Color and cut out the bat and wing patterns.
2. Flatten one end of the 4½-inch tube and staple it closed.
3. Glue the bat cutout to the tube, with the head at the stapled end.
4. Fold each wing along the fold line. Glue a wing to each side of the bat's body, gluing only the folded section to the tube.
5. To make a cave for your bat, open the paper bag and lay it on its side.

Using the Puppet and Prop

Use the puppet, prop, and poem to teach children about the features of a bat. To begin, ask children to place their paper-bag cave on the table. Then have them recite the poem, using the puppet and cave to act out the words.

Bats Are Flying Mammals

Bats are flying mammals.
They swoop and zoom about.
When the dark night comes,
The hungry bats come out!

Bats are insect eaters.
They catch bugs that crawl or fly.
Bats can catch their food
While they're flying through the sky!

Bats are furry mammals.
They have thin wings of skin.
And when the sun comes out,
The sleepy bats go in!

SCIENCE

Animals

A Turtle's a Reptile

Children create and use a turtle, lizard, and snake puppet to share what they know about reptiles.

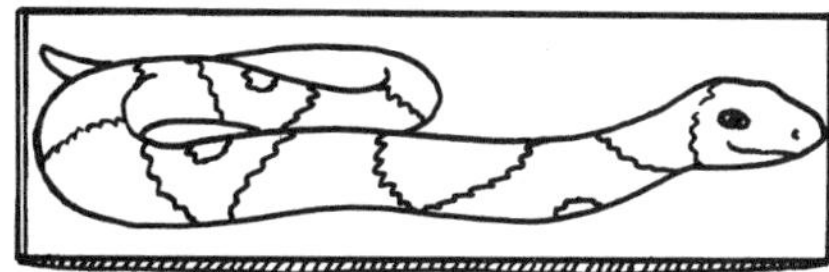

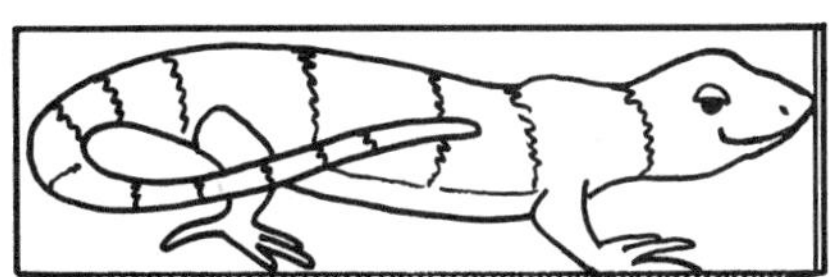

Meeting the Standards: Science

Understands biological evolution and the diversity of life:

- Knows simple ways that living things can be grouped (e.g., appearance, behavior, plant, animal)
- Knows that there are similarities and differences in the appearance and behavior of plants and animals

Materials (per child)

- lizard, turtle, and snake patterns (page 188)
- crayons
- scissors
- sealed legal-size envelope
- glue stick

Making the Puppets

1. Color and cut out the lizard, turtle, and snake patterns.
2. Cut away a 3-inch-wide section from one end of the envelope. Glue the turtle cutout onto this section, lining up the bottom of the cutout with the open edge of the section.
3. Cut the remaining section of the envelope in half lengthwise. Glue the short open end closed on each section, leaving the long end open to form a pocket.

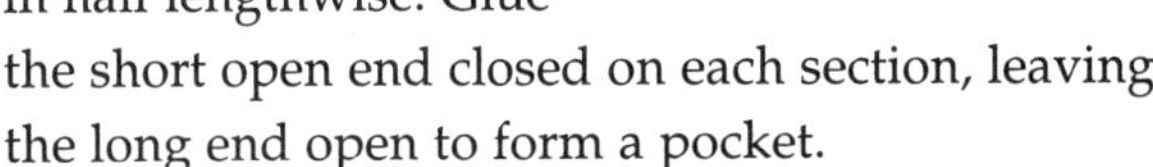

4. Glue the lizard on one of the envelope sections and the snake on the other, lining up the bottom of each cutout with the open edge of the "pocket."

Using the Puppets

Use the puppets and song to reinforce facts about reptiles. As children sing the song, have them place the turtle puppet on their fingers and move it around to the rhythm. Repeat the song twice, replacing *turtle* with *lizard* and then *snake*. Each time, have children use the corresponding puppet during the song.

A Turtle's a Reptile

(to the tune of "My Bonnie Lies Over the Ocean")

A turtle has skin that is scaly,
Bumpy or smooth it might be.
A turtle is hatched from a small egg.
A turtle's a reptile, you see.
A turtle. A turtle.
A turtle's a reptile, you see, you see.
A turtle. A turtle.
A turtle's a reptile, you see!

How a Frog Grows

Children use this special spinner to review the life cycle of a frog.

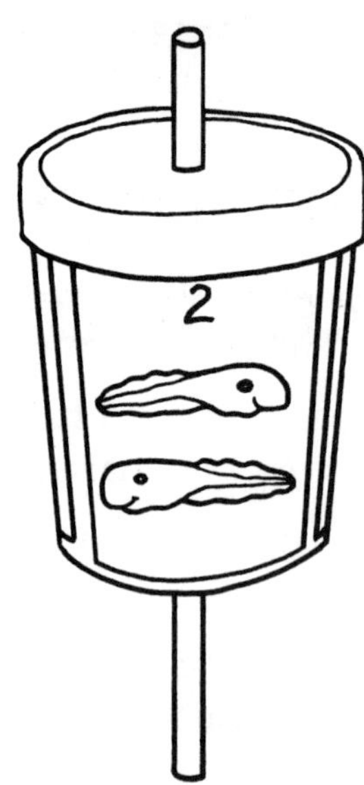

Meeting the Standards: Science

Understands the structure and function of cells and organisms:

- Knows that living things go through a process of growth and change

Materials (per child)

- pint-sized cardboard ice-cream canister (with lid)
- blue tempera paint
- paintbrush
- frog life cycle cards (page 188)
- crayons
- scissors
- glue
- pencil
- long plastic drinking straw

Making the Prop

1. Paint the ice-cream canister and lid blue. Set them aside to dry.
2. Color and cut out the frog life cycle patterns. Glue the cards in sequence around the painted canister.
3. Use the pointed end of the pencil to poke a hole in the center of the lid and the bottom of the canister. Push the straw through the lid and then through the canister. Snap the lid onto the canister so that the straw handle extends from the top and bottom. Make sure the canister spins easily on the handle. (Note to teacher: An adult should complete this step.)

Using the Prop

Use the prop and song to help children understand the stages in a frog's life cycle. Ask them to hold the spinner by the bottom handle. As they sing the song, have children rotate their spinner to find the frog's life stages that correspond to the words.

How a Frog Grows

(to the tune of "Baa, Baa, Black Sheep")

Here's how a frog's life cycle goes.
This is how a small frog grows.
It starts as an egg
And then hatches out.
It sprouts little legs
And swims about.
Now it's a tadpole
That grows and grows
Into a frog.
That's how it goes!

SCIENCE

Life Cycles

Butterfly Egg

Use this large leaf prop to highlight the stages in a butterfly's development.

Meeting the Standards: Science

Understands the structure and function of cells and organisms:

- Knows that living things go through a process of growth and change

Materials (per child)

- butterfly life cycle cards, label, and butterfly patterns (page 189)
- crayons
- scissors
- 9- by 12-inch green construction paper
- glue stick
- black marker

Making the Prop

1. Color and cut out the life cycle cards, label, and butterfly patterns.
2. Cut a large leaf shape from the green construction paper.
3. Glue the life cycle cards around the edges of the leaf, starting with card 1 at the top and spacing the other cards evenly and in order around the leaf.
4. Glue the label and butterfly to the center of the leaf. Be sure to glue only the center of the butterfly in place, leaving the wings free to flap back and forth.
5. Use the black marker to draw eyes and antennae on the butterfly.

Using the Prop

Use the prop and poem to help children understand the stages in a butterfly's life cycle. As children recite each line of the poem, have them find and point to the corresponding picture on their leaf. On the last line, invite them to "flap" the wings of the butterfly in the center of the leaf.

Butterfly Egg

This leaf holds a butterfly egg so small.
A caterpillar hatches out and starts
to crawl.

It eats and grows, and eats some more.
It makes a chrysalis. Changes are in store.

After days of waiting, there's some activity.
Out comes a butterfly to fly away free!

■ SCIENCE ■

Life Cycles

A Hen Lays an Egg

The pull-through strip in this nifty nest can be used to help children understand the life cycle of a chicken.

Meeting the Standards: Science

Understands the structure and function of cells and organisms:

- Knows that living things go through a process of growth and change

Materials (per child)

- 6-inch paper plate
- crayons
- scissors
- brown crinkle paper strips
- glue
- chicken life cycle patterns (page 190)

Making the Prop

1. To make a nest, color the paper plate brown.
2. Cut two 2½-inch-long slits in the center of the plate, spacing them 2½ inches apart. (Note to teacher: An adult should complete this step.)
3. Glue brown crinkle paper strips around the rim of the nest.
4. Color and cut out the chicken life cycle patterns.
5. To create a pull-through strip, glue the end of picture 2 to the back of picture 3 where indicated. Then thread the strip through the two slits in the nest and glue the end of picture 4 to the back of picture 1.
6. Gently pull the strip through the slits to display one picture at a time on the nest.

Using the Prop

Use the prop and poem to teach children about the stages of a chicken's life cycle. To begin, ask children to display the hen on their nest. As they recite the poem, have them pull the strip to the left to display the pictures that correspond to the words in the verses.

A Hen Lays an Egg

A hen sits on her nest.
A little egg she lays.

Crack! goes the egg
After 21 days.

The baby chick eats
And grows into a hen.

The hen lays an egg,
And the cycle starts again!

Plants

What a Plant Needs

Children learn about the needs of a plant with this special cube.

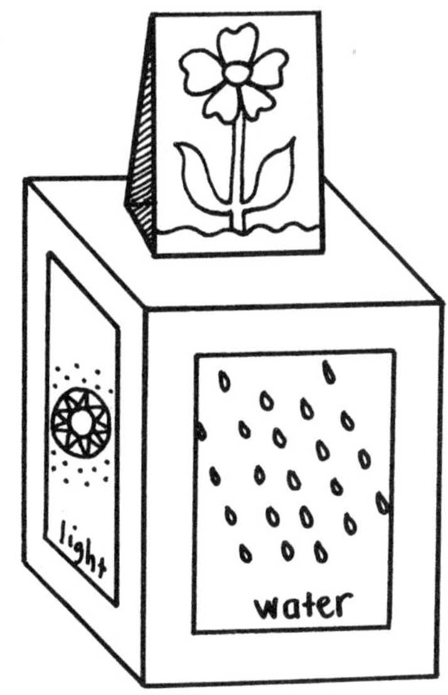

Meeting the Standards: Science

Understands the structure and function of cells and organisms:

- Knows the basic needs of plants and animals (e.g., air, water, nutrients, light or food, shelter)

Materials (per child)

- facial tissue cube
- white tempera paint
- paintbrush
- plant needs cards and flower pattern (page 191)
- crayons
- scissors
- glue

Making the Prop

1. Paint the facial tissue cube white. Set it aside to dry.
2. Color and cut out the plant needs cards and flower pattern.
3. To make the stand-up flower, fold the flower cutout on the lines. Then glue the short folded section to the back of the flower on the opposite end of the cutout.
4. Place the tissue cube with the hole side down on the table. Glue a plant needs card to each side of the cube, placing them in numerical order around the cube. Glue the stand-up flower to the top of the cube.

Using the Prop

Use the prop and song to reinforce children's knowledge of what plants need to grow. To begin, ask children to slip their hand inside the bottom opening of their plant needs cube. Then, as they sing the song, invite them to rotate the cube to find the picture that corresponds to the words in the verses. On the last line of the song, have children point to the flower at the top of the cube.

What a Plant Needs

(to the tune of "If You're Happy and You Know It")

Oh, a plant needs good, rich soil
so it can grow.
Oh, a plant needs water, too,
so it can grow.
Oh, a plant needs lots of light.
And it needs some warmth, you know.
Oh, a plant needs all these things
so it can grow.

■ SCIENCE ■

Plants

The Parts of a Plant

Use this flowering puppet to help children learn about the parts of a plant.

Meeting the Standards: Science

Understands the structure and function of cells and organisms:

- Knows that plants and animals have features that help them live in different environments

Materials (per child)

- stem and leaf patterns (page 190)
- crayons
- scissors
- 4½-inch length of paper towel tube
- glue stick
- two 8- by 10-inch sheets of tissue paper
- 2 wiggle eyes

Making the Puppet

1. Color and cut out the stem and leaf patterns.
2. Glue the stem cutout to the length of the 4½-inch tube. Glue the leaves along the plant stem.
3. To make the flower, stack the two sheets of tissue paper and fold them in half lengthwise. Gather the folded end of the tissue paper. Then glue the gathered end inside the top of the tube. Spread the tissue paper above the tube to form a flower.
4. Glue wiggle eyes on the flower.

Using the Puppet

Use the puppet and song to reinforce the parts of a plant. Invite children to place the puppet on their hand. Then have them point to each plant part on the puppet as it is named in the song.

The Parts of a Plant

(to the tune of "London Bridge")

Roots and stem and leaves and flower.
Leaves and flower, leaves and flower.
Roots and stem and leaves and flower
Are parts of a plant!

■ SCIENCE ■
Earth Science

The Water Cycle

Children learn about the ongoing process of the water cycle with this special cube.

Meeting the Standards: Science

Understands atmospheric processes and the water cycle:

- Knows that water can be a liquid or a solid and can be made to change from one form to the other, but the amount of water stays the same

Materials (per child)

- facial tissue cube
- green tempera paint
- paintbrush
- water cycle sign and cards (page 192)
- crayons
- scissors
- glue

Making the Prop

1. Paint the facial tissue cube green. Set it aside to dry.
2. Color and cut out the water cycle sign and cards.
3. To make the stand-up sign, fold the sign cutout on the lines. Then glue the short folded section to the back of the sign on the opposite end of the cutout.
4. Place the tissue cube with the hole side down on the table. Glue a water cycle card to each side of the cube, placing them in numerical order around the cube. Glue the stand-up sign to the top of the cube.

Using the Prop

Use the prop and song to introduce children to the water cycle. To begin, have children slip their hand inside the bottom opening of their water cycle cube. Then, as they sing the song, invite them to rotate the cube to find the picture that corresponds to the words in the verses. Repeat the song several times to emphasize the ongoing process of the water cycle.

The Water Cycle

(to the tune of "Skip to My Lou")

Raindrops falling down from a cloud.
Raindrops falling down from a cloud.
Raindrops falling down from a cloud.
Rain fills up the lakes and streams.

Water sitting in lakes and streams.
Water sitting in lakes and streams.
Water sitting in lakes and streams.
The bright sun warms the water.

Warm sun making the water rise.
Warm sun making the water rise.
Warm sun making the water rise.
The water turns to vapor.

Vapor gathering in the sky,
Vapor gathering in the sky,
Vapor gathering in the sky,
To form a brand-new rain cloud.

Sun and Moon

Children use a sun and moon puppet to show how the two take turns in the sky.

Meeting the Standards: Science

Understands the composition and structure of the universe and Earth's place in it:

- Knows basic patterns of the sun and moon (e.g., the sun appears every day and the moon appears sometimes at night and sometimes during the day; the sun and moon appear to move from east to west across the sky; the moon appears to change shape over the course of the month; the sun's position in the sky changes through the seasons)

Materials (per child)

- two 6-inch paper plates
- yellow and orange crayons
- yellow tissue paper
- glue stick
- black permanent marker
- scissors
- gray crayon
- plastic soda bottle lid
- gray tempera paint
- 2 jumbo craft sticks

Making the Puppets

1. To make the sun puppet, color one paper plate yellow. Glue torn pieces of tissue paper to the center of the plate.
2. Use the orange crayon to draw sunrays around the rim of the sun. Draw a face with the marker and then glue the sun to a craft stick.
3. For the moon puppet, cut off the rim of the other paper plate. Color the resulting circle gray. Use the soda bottle lid to paint-print a few gray circles onto the paper circle.
4. Use the marker to draw a face on the moon. Then glue it to a craft stick.

Using the Puppets

Use the puppets and poem to help children understand the daily pattern of the sun and moon. As they recite the poem, invite children to use their puppets to act out the verses.

Sun and Moon

"There's only one of me," says Sun.
"I shine throughout the day.
When nighttime comes I go to sleep,
And Moon comes out to play."

"There's only one of me," says Moon.
"I glow throughout the night.
When daytime comes I go to sleep,
So Sun can shine so bright."

Sun for day and Moon for night—
There's just one Moon and Sun.
Each one takes a turn to play
And make light for everyone.

Backpack and Apple Patterns

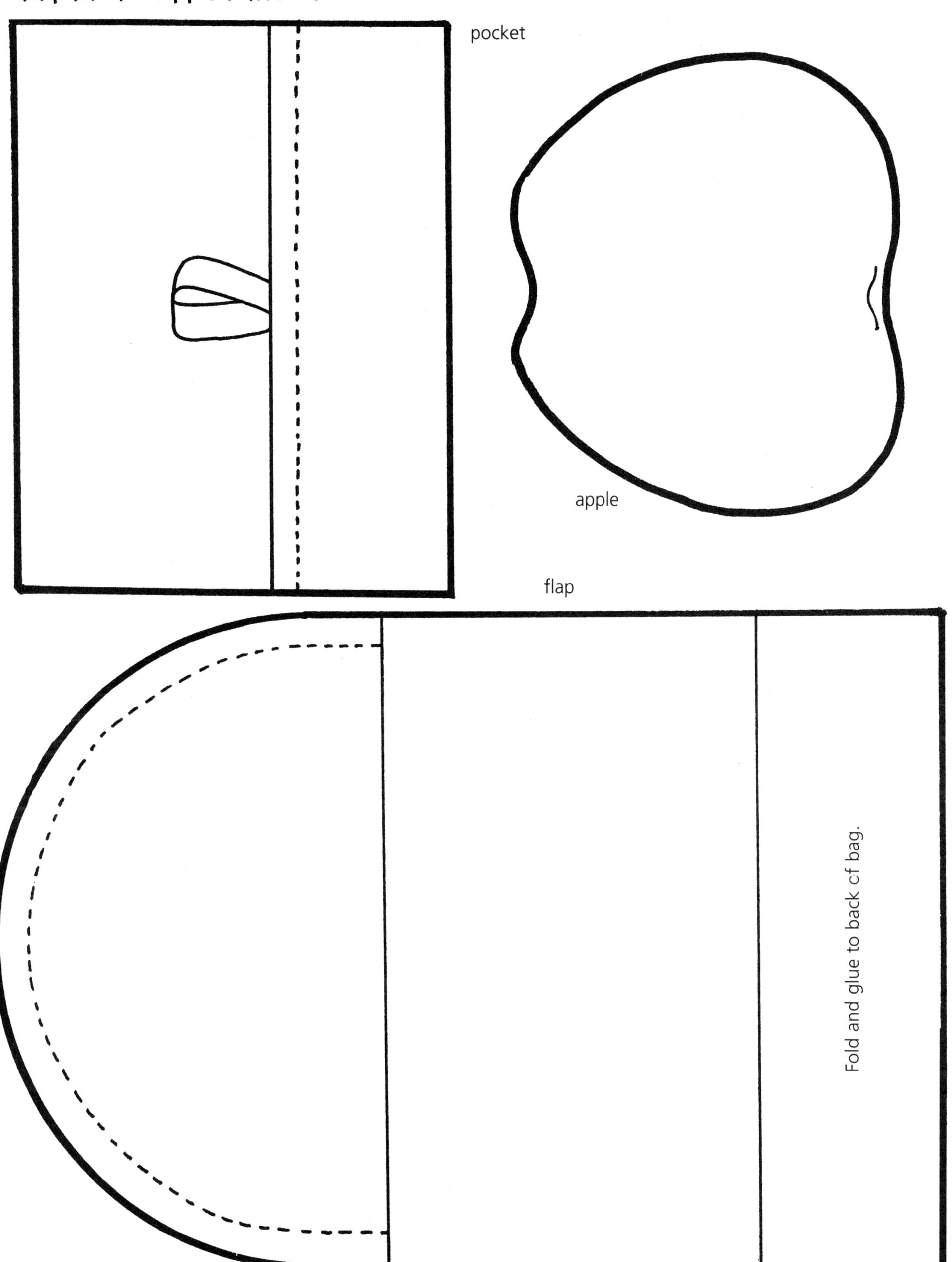

Birthday Cake, Tooth, and Tooth Fairy Patterns

Snake Pattern

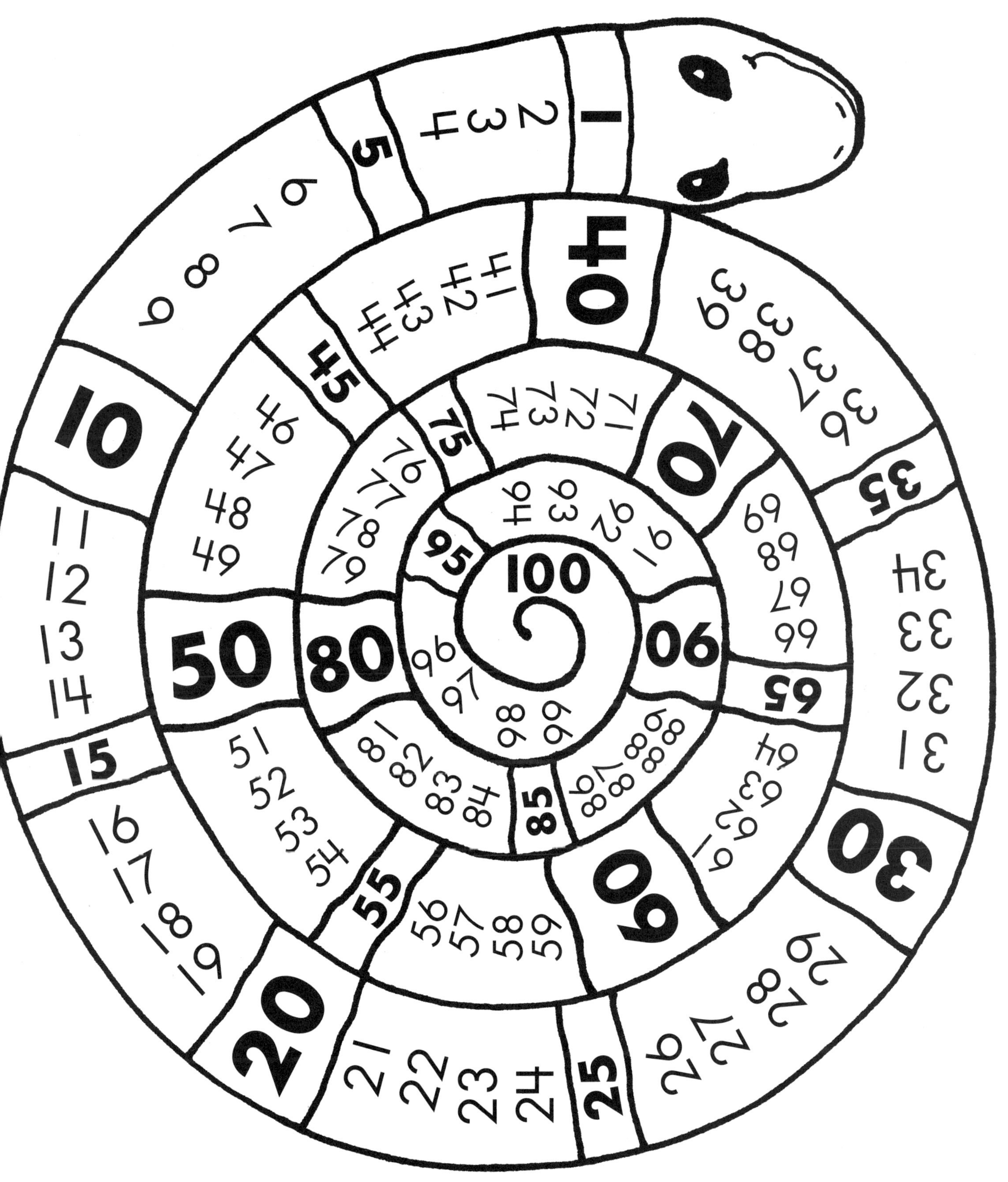

Apple and Treetop Patterns

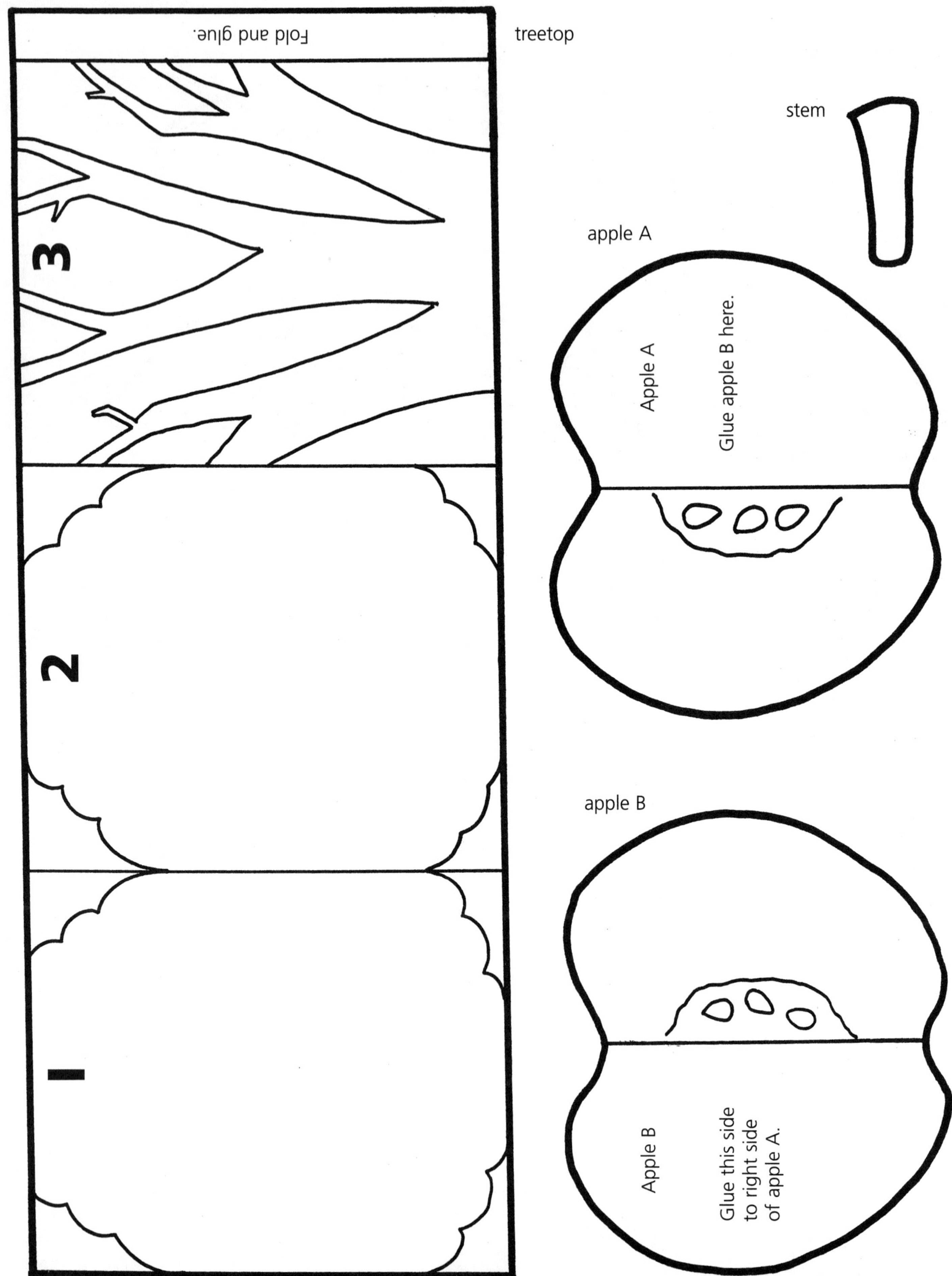

Squirrel, Columbus, and Ship Patterns

Owl Patterns and Thanksgiving Puppets

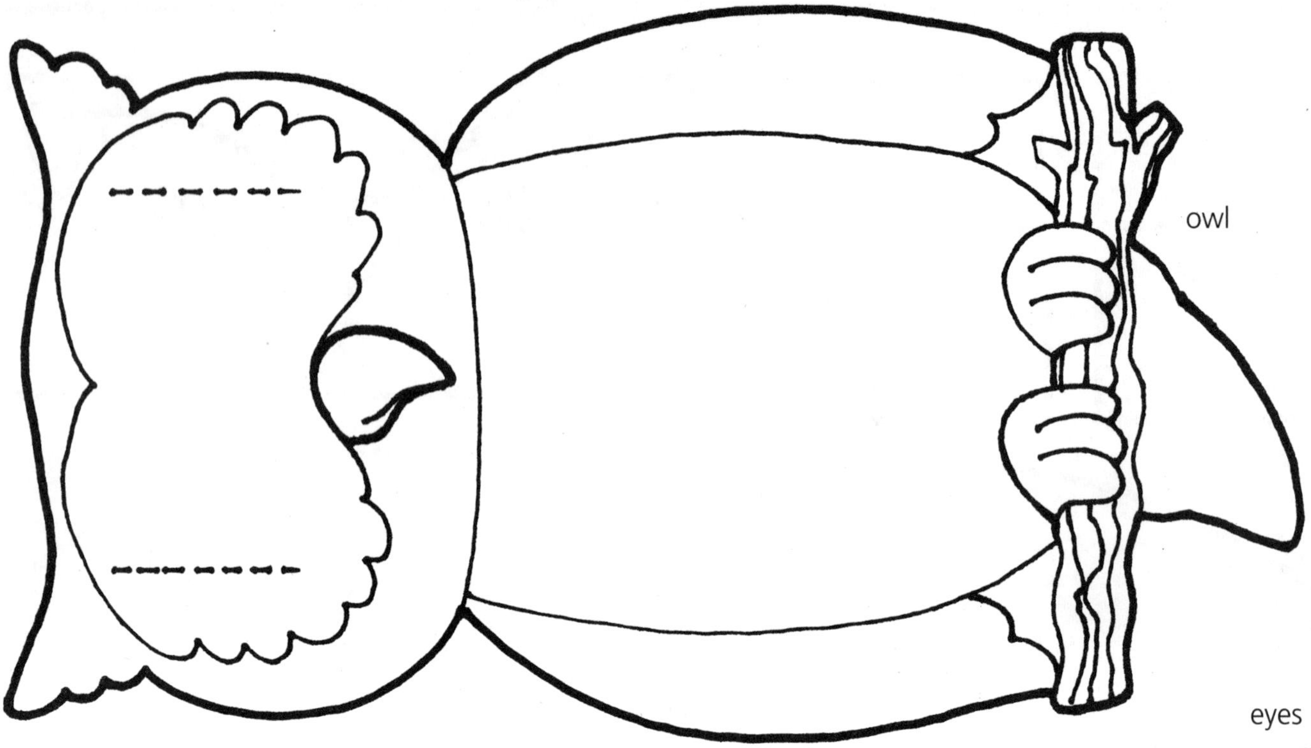

owl

eyes

Wampanoags

Pilgrims

Turkey and Warm Clothes Patterns

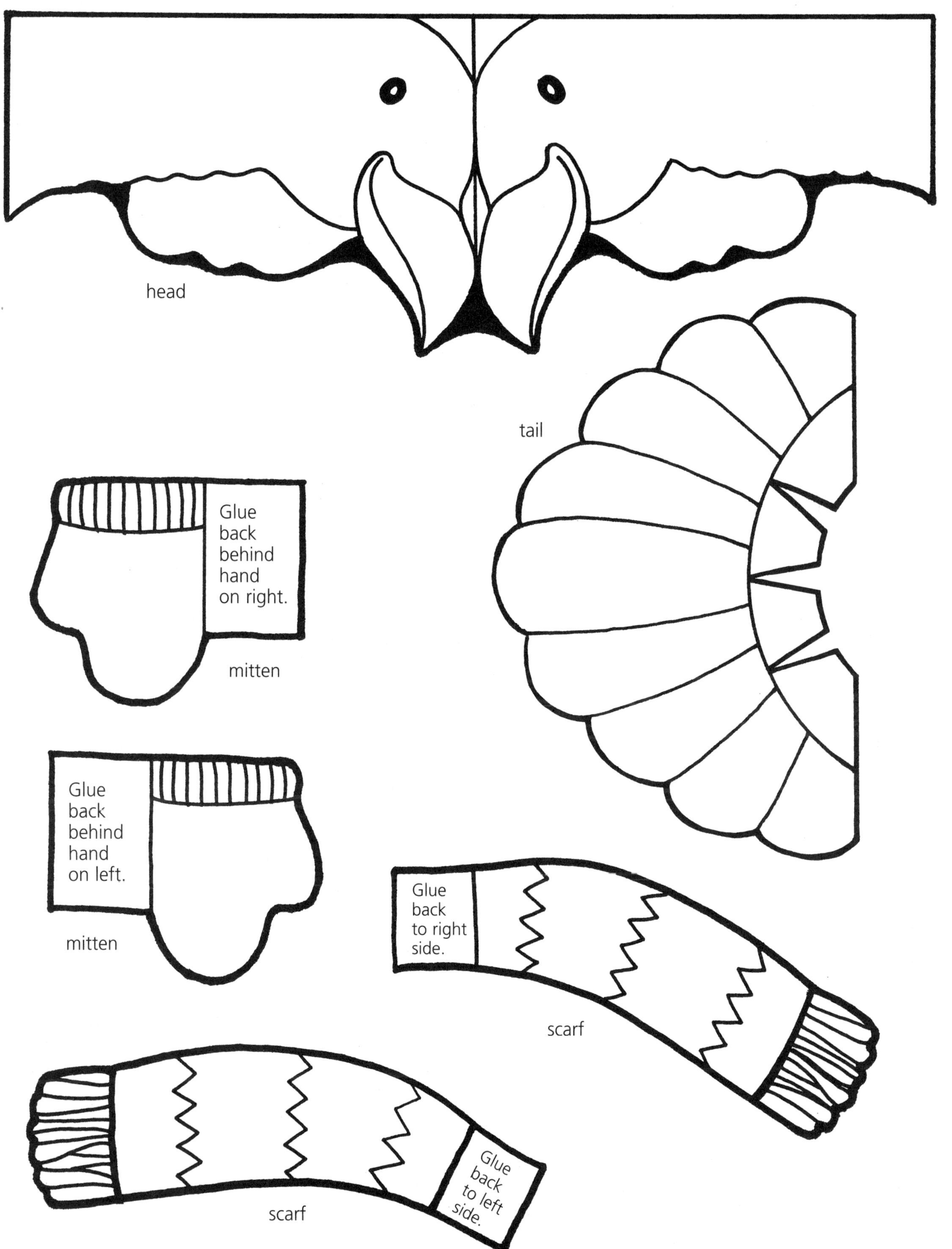

Warm Clothes Puppet

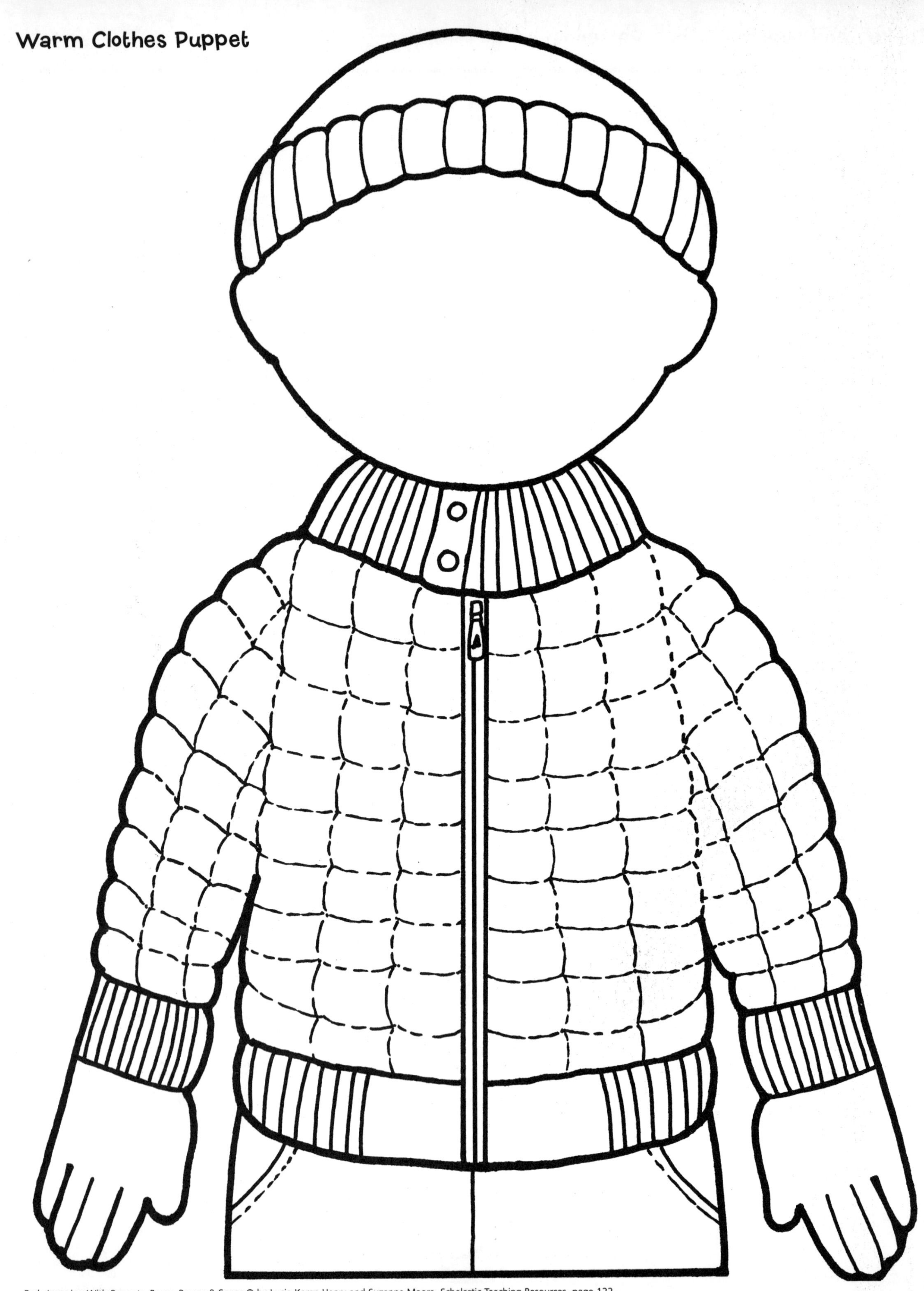

Snowman Patterns

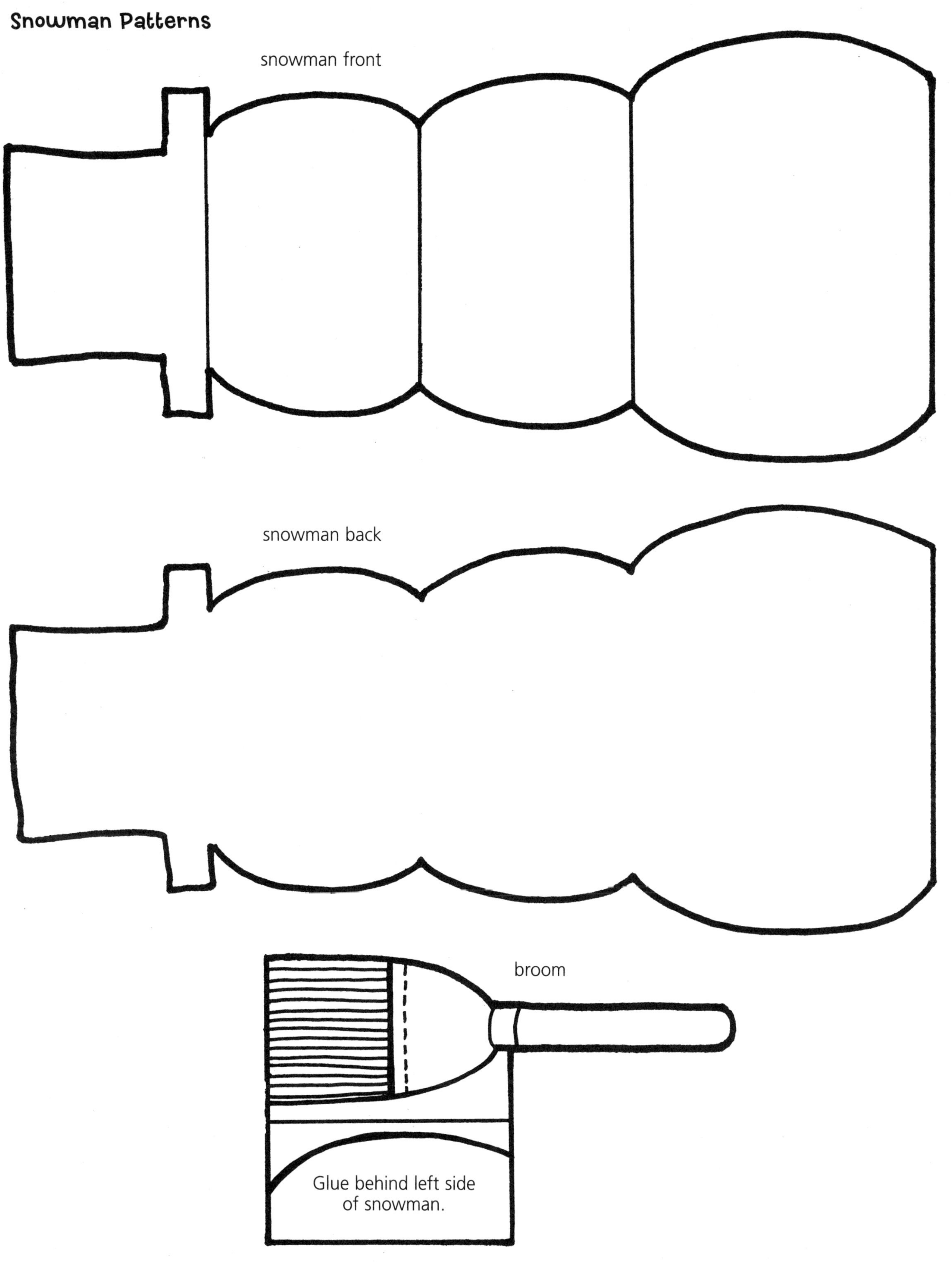

Luminaria Candle and Presidents Patterns

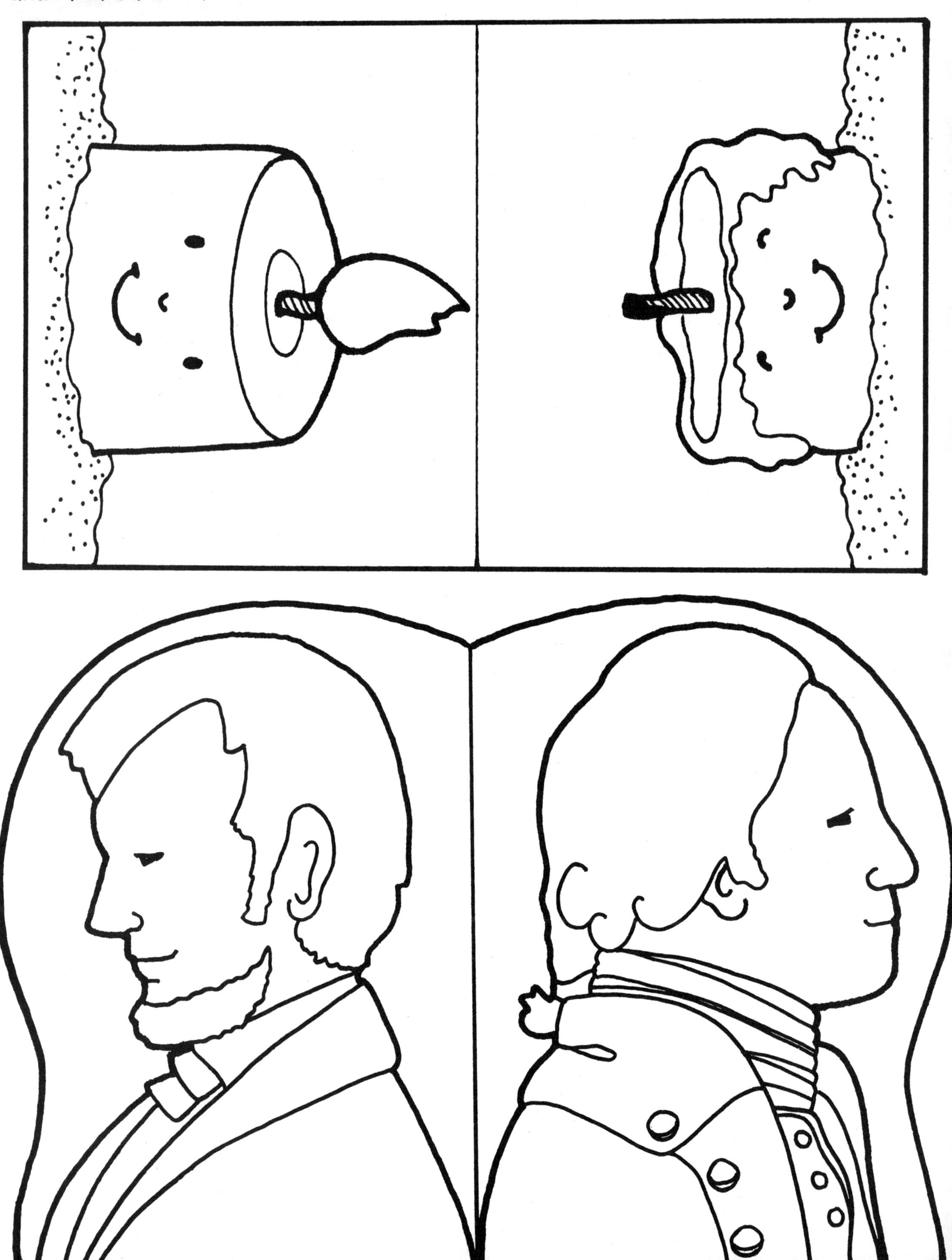

Menorah and Kwanzaa Candles

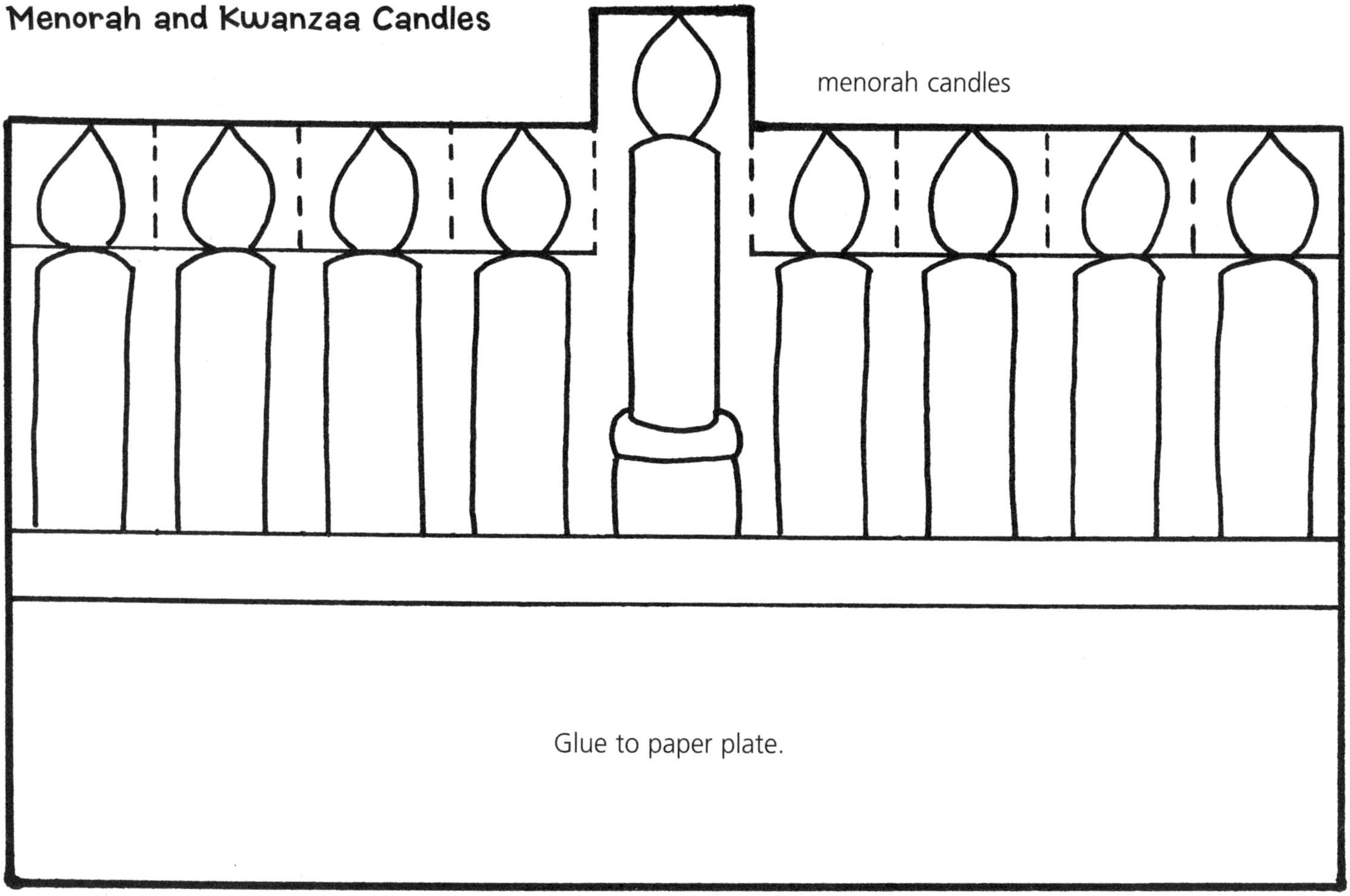

menorah candles

Glue to paper plate.

Kwanzaa candle

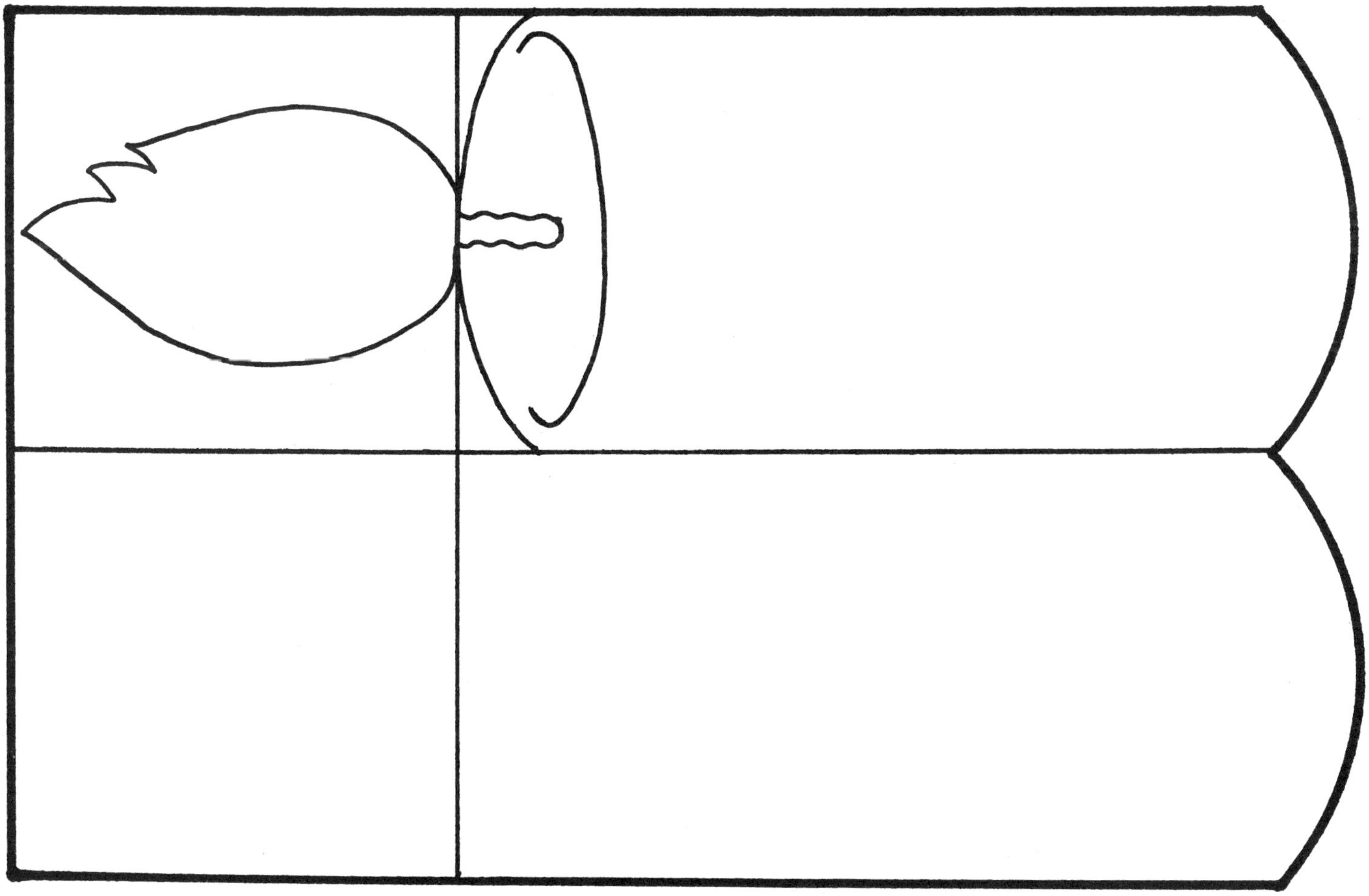

Fireplace and Stocking Patterns

stockings

Glue back behind top of fireplace.

fireplace

fold

base

New Year Flip Sign

10	9	8	7	6	5	4	3	2	1

fold

bottom

fold

Happy New Year!

____

year

Dragon Patterns

Dove Patterns

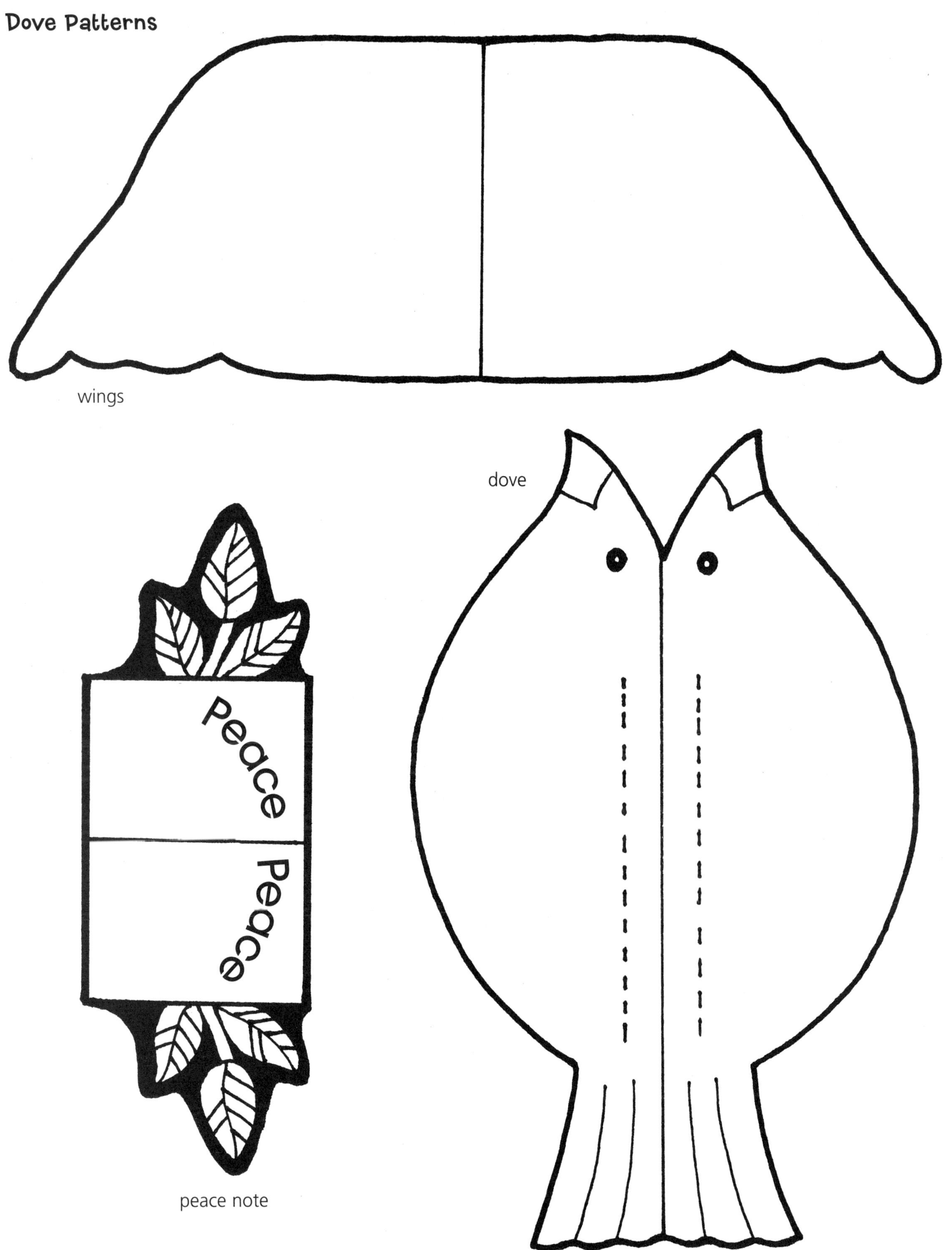

Valentine Finger Puppets and Groundhog Patterns

valentine finger puppets

groundhog

Plant and Leprechaun Patterns

Cloud Patterns

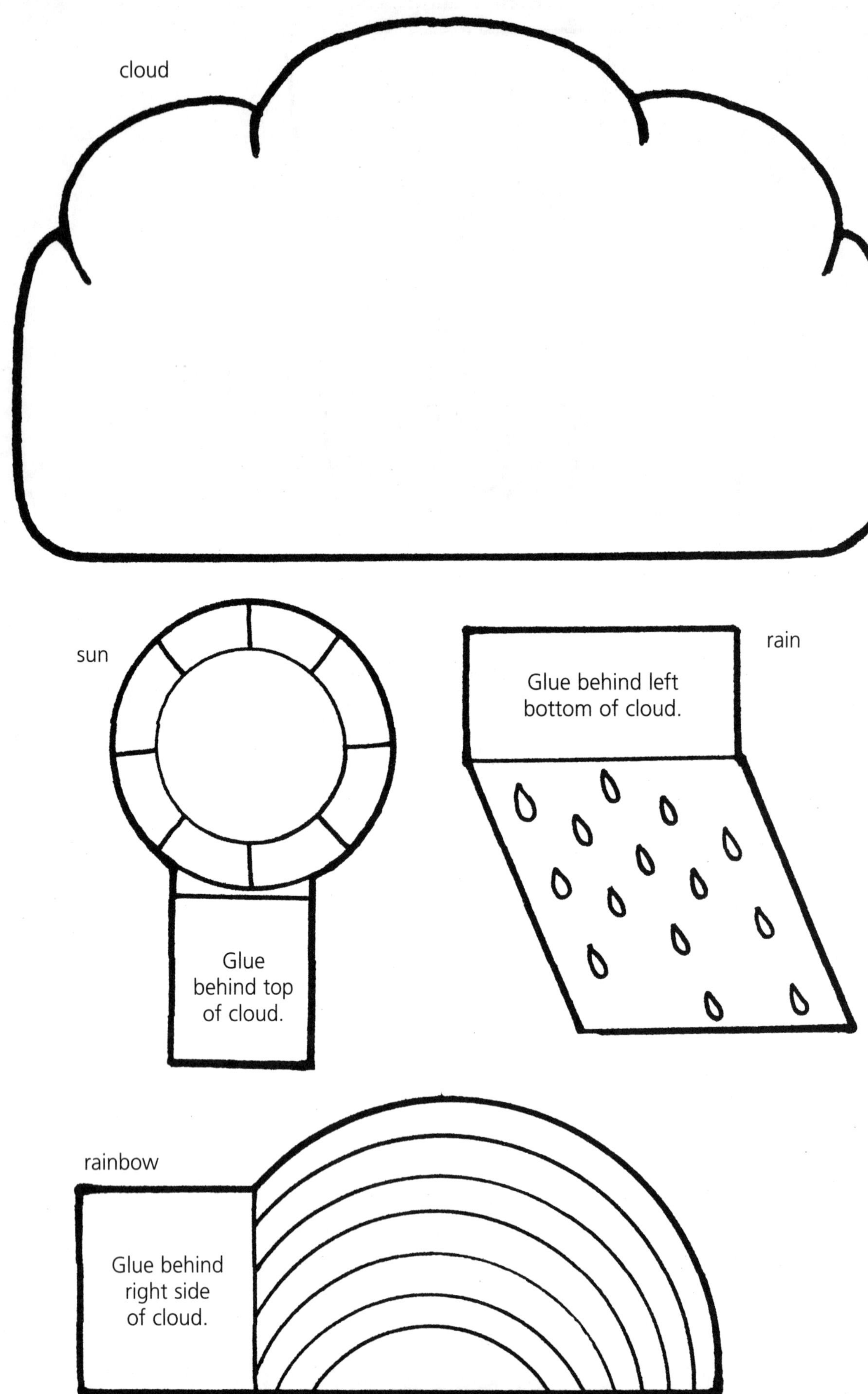

Tulip Garden and Flower Finger Puppet Patterns

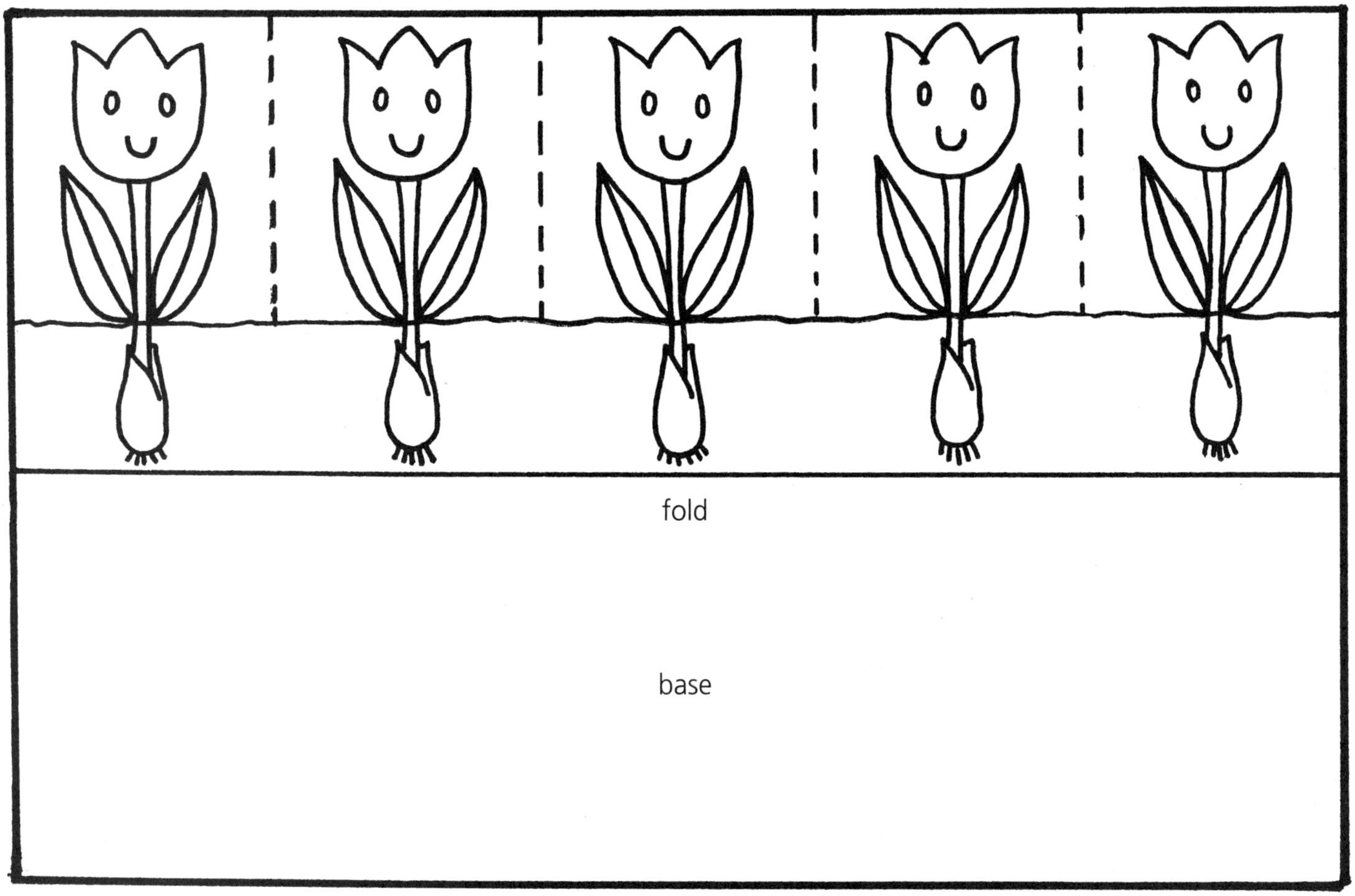

fold

base

tulip garden

flower finger puppets

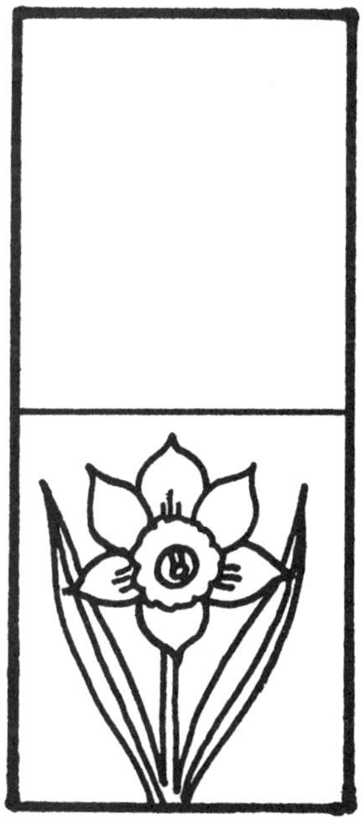

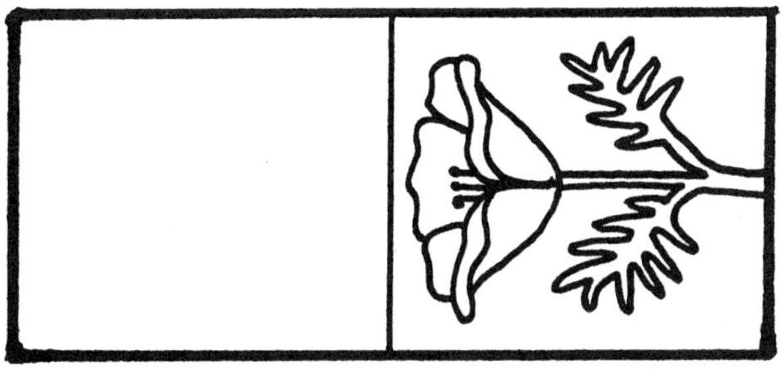

Recycle Wheel Patterns

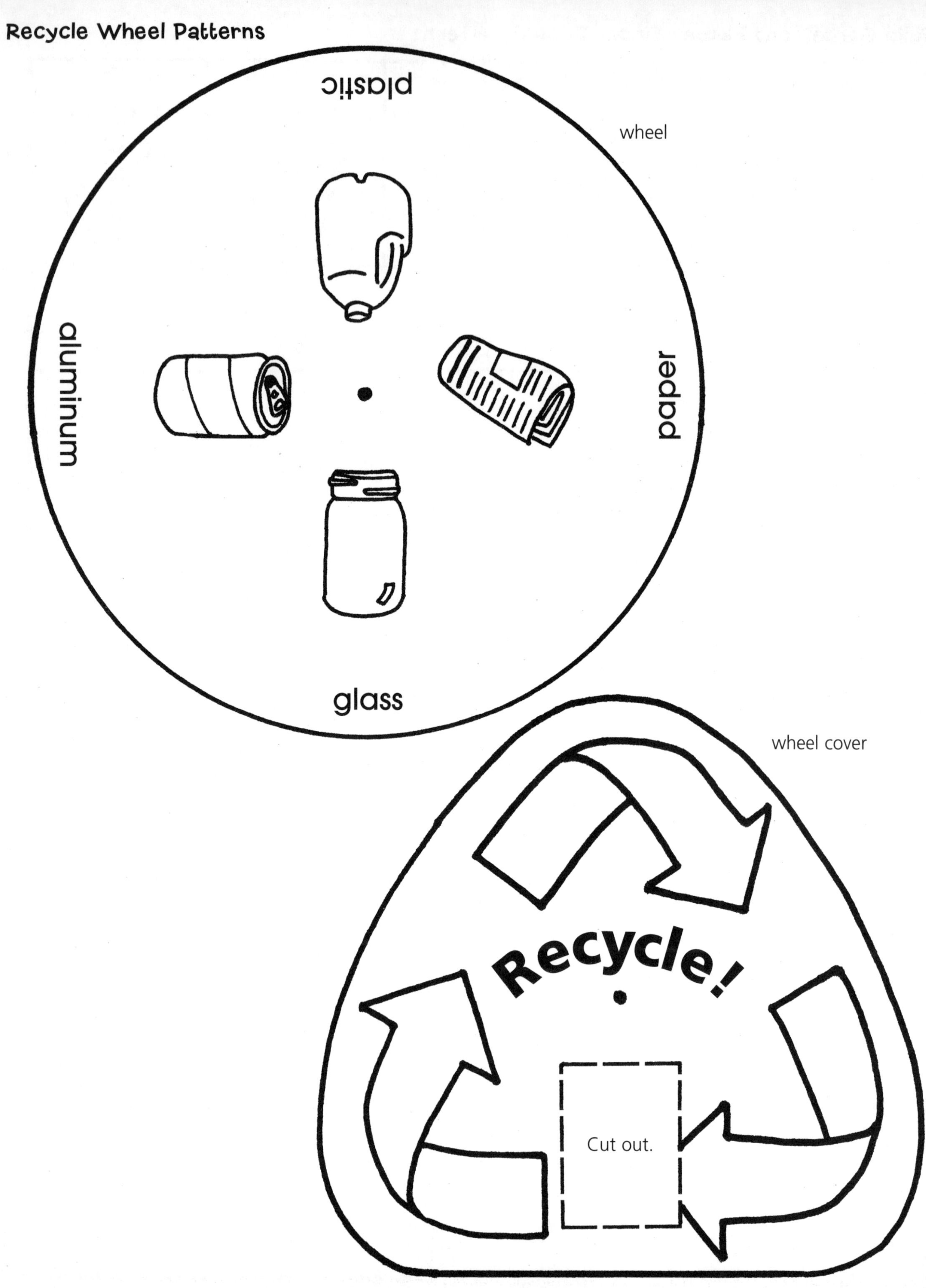

Piñata and Treat Patterns

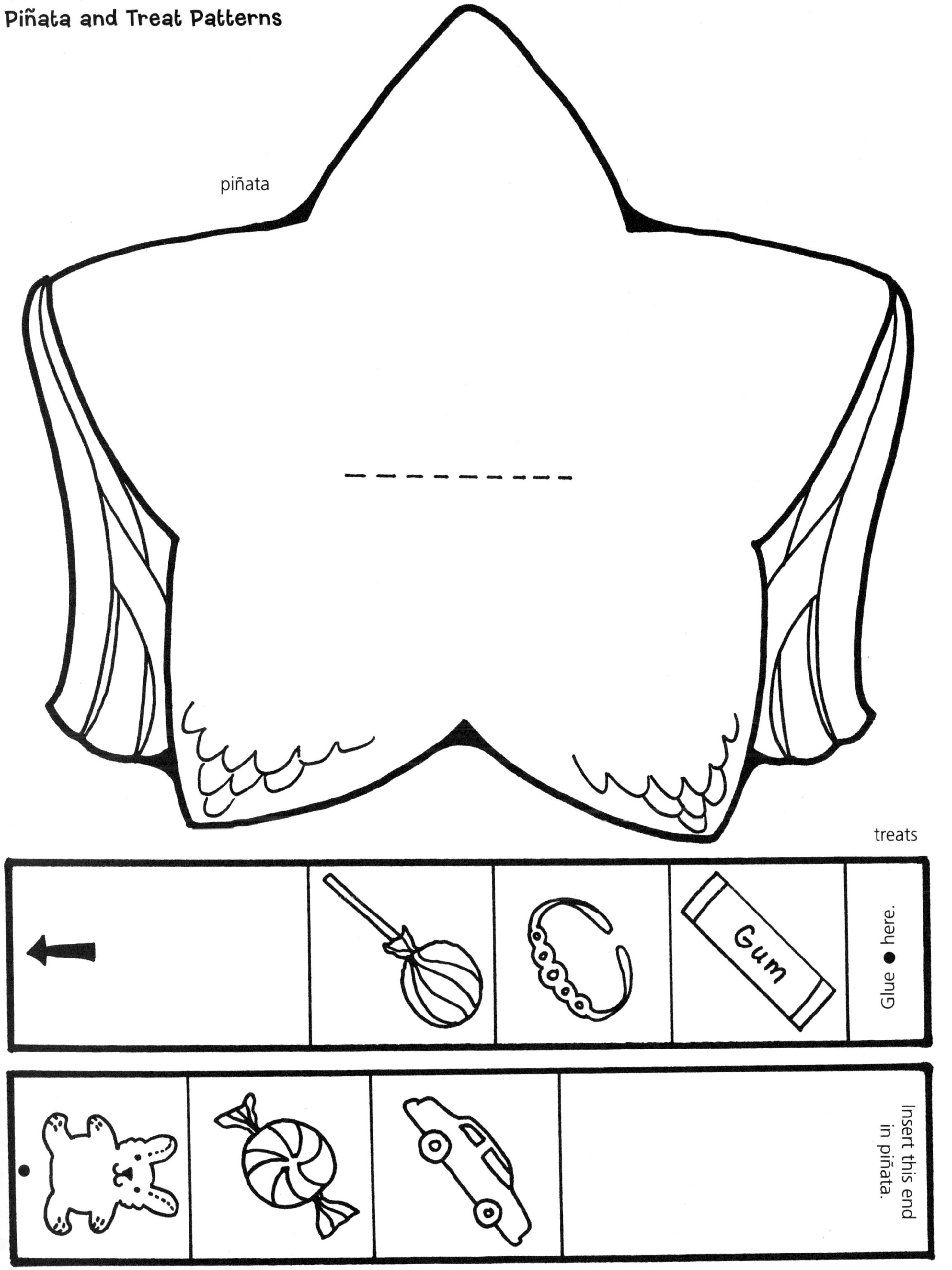

Picnic Patterns

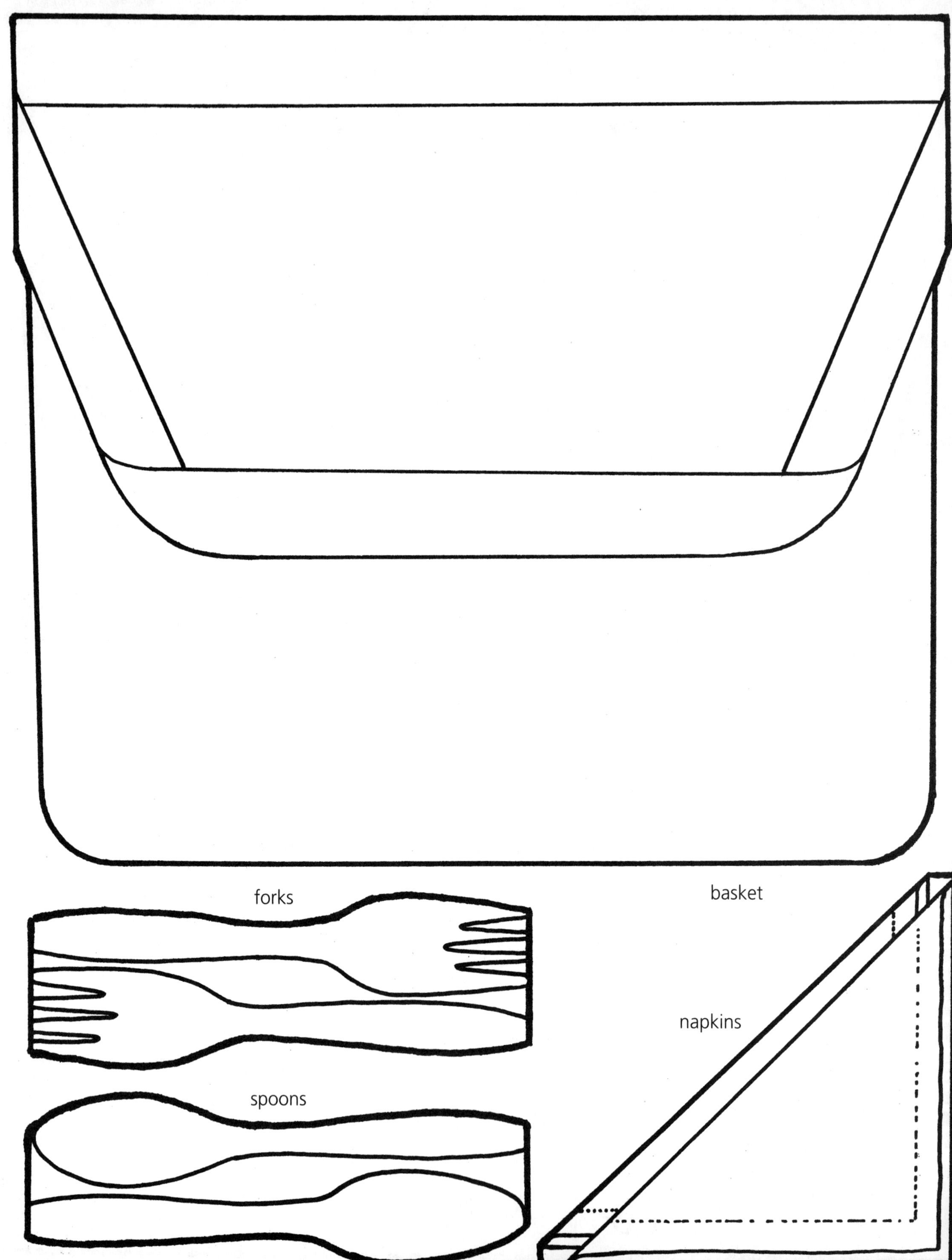

Picnic Patterns
plate
apples
chips
water
sandwiches

Summertime Puppet and Flag Pattern

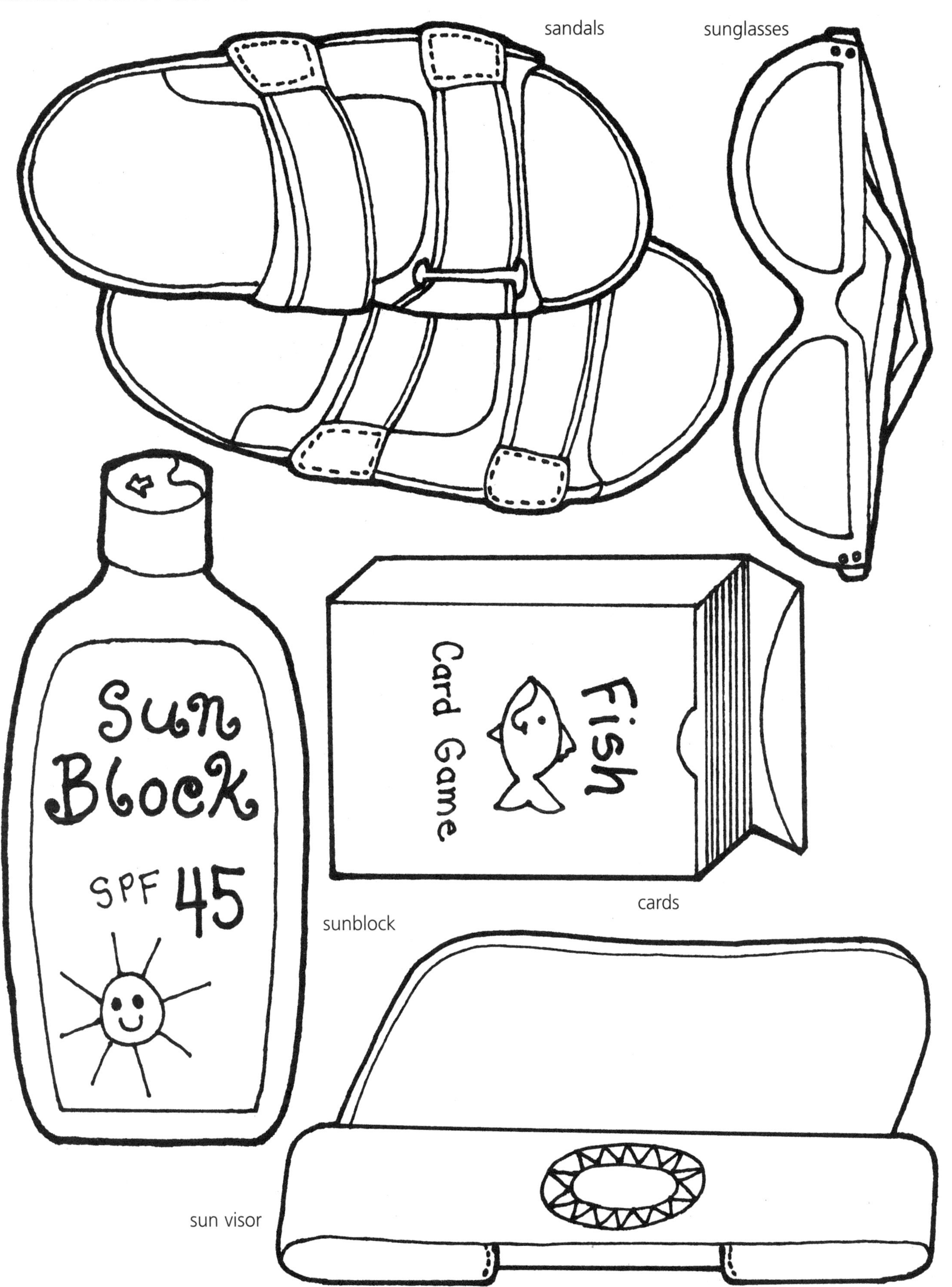
sandals
sunglasses
Sun
Block
SPF 45
Fish
Card Game
cards
sunblock
sun visor

Drum Major and Airplane Patterns

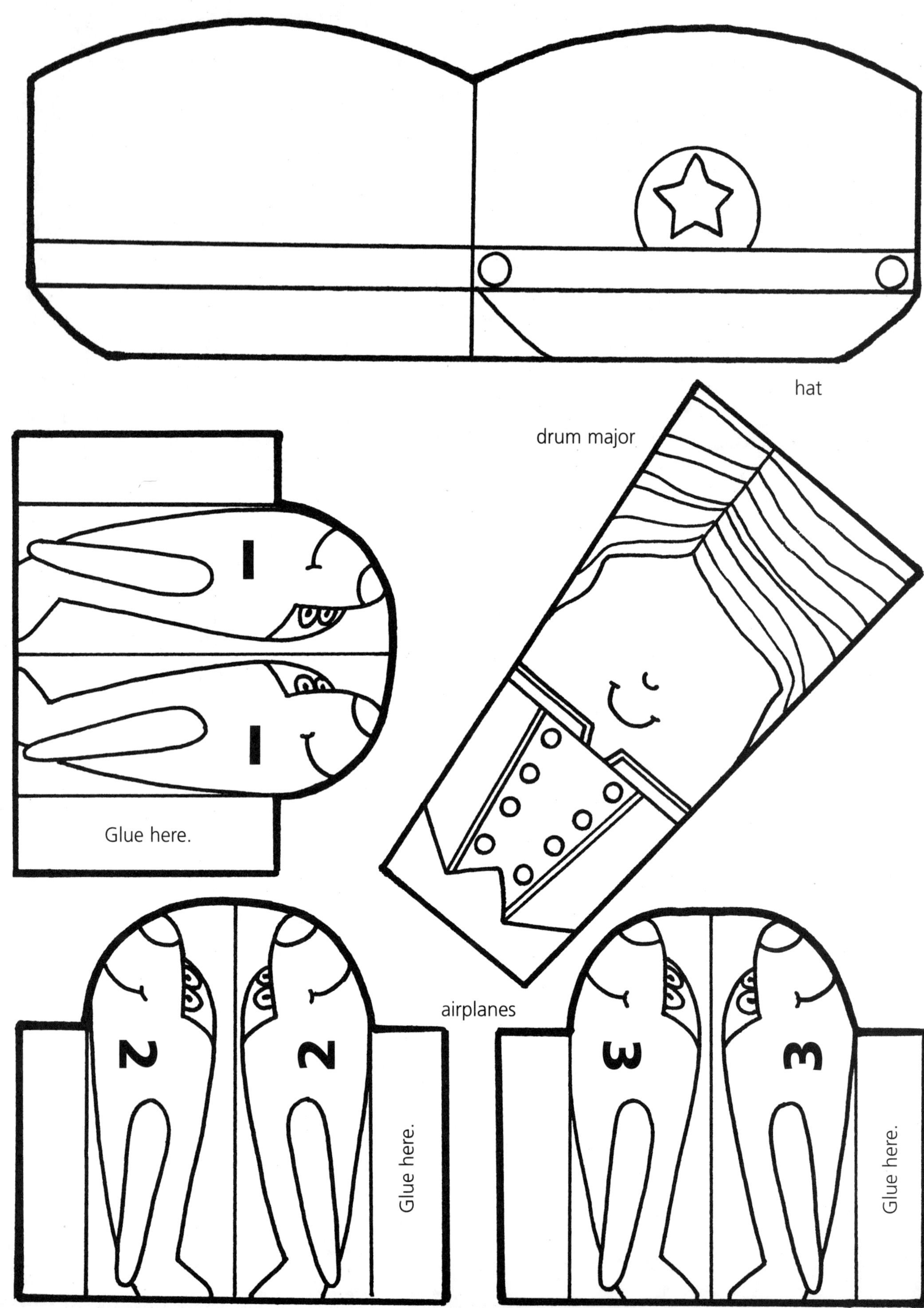

Monkey and Food Strip Patterns

Treasure Chest Lid and Treasure Cards

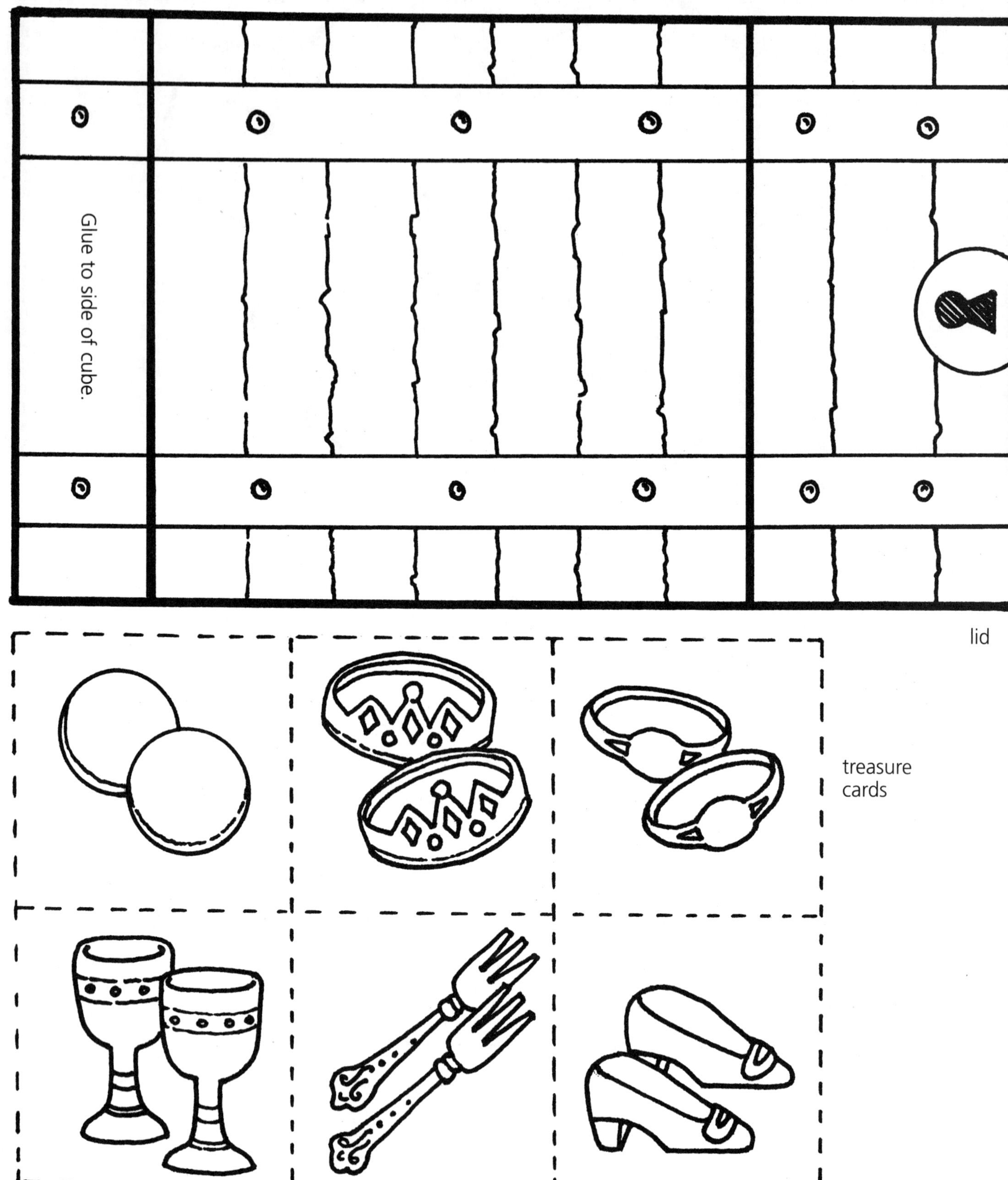

Ant Patterns

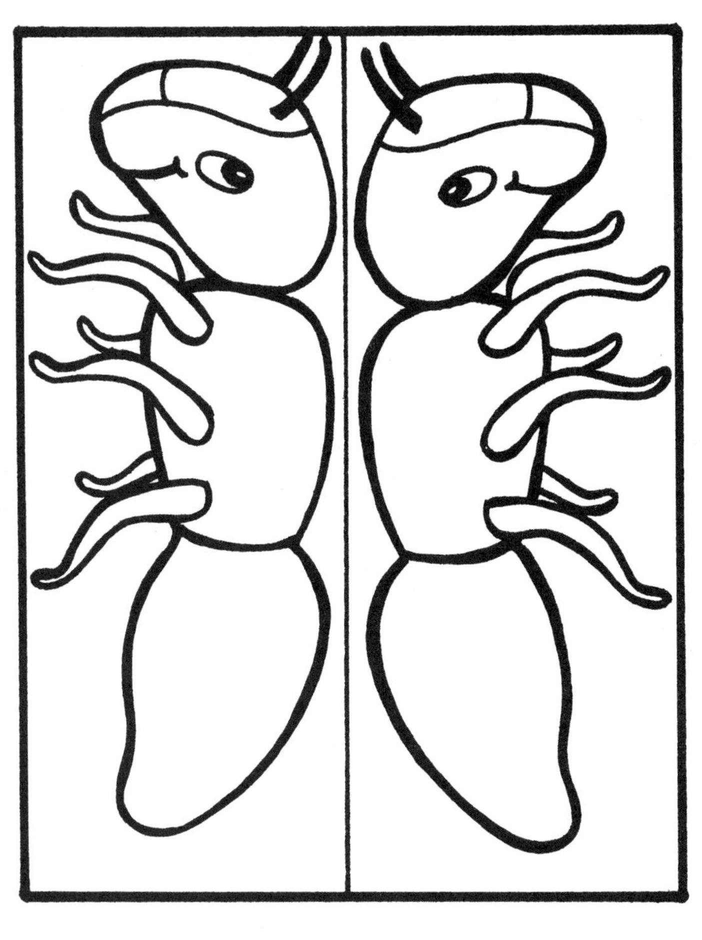

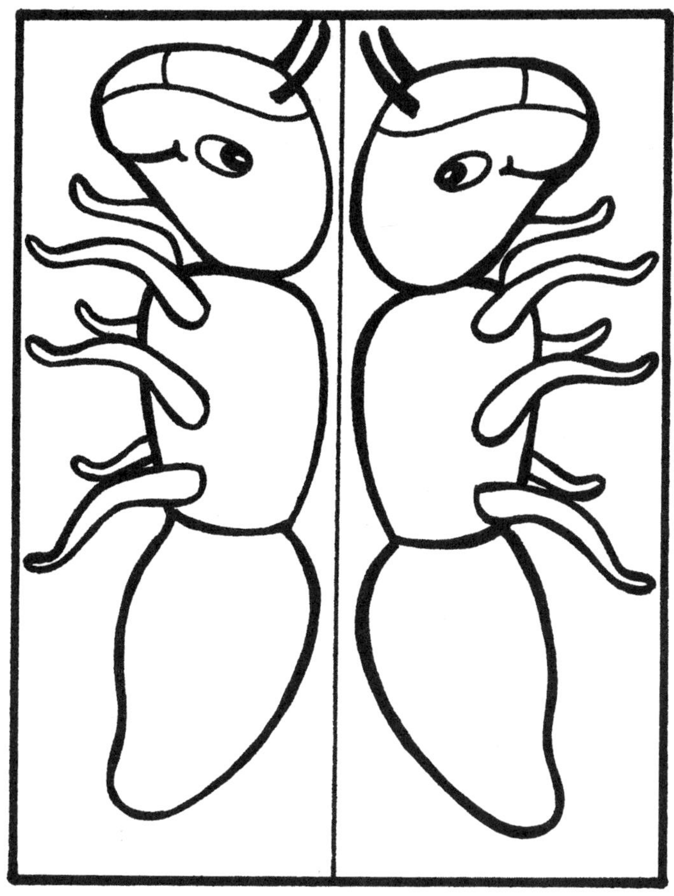

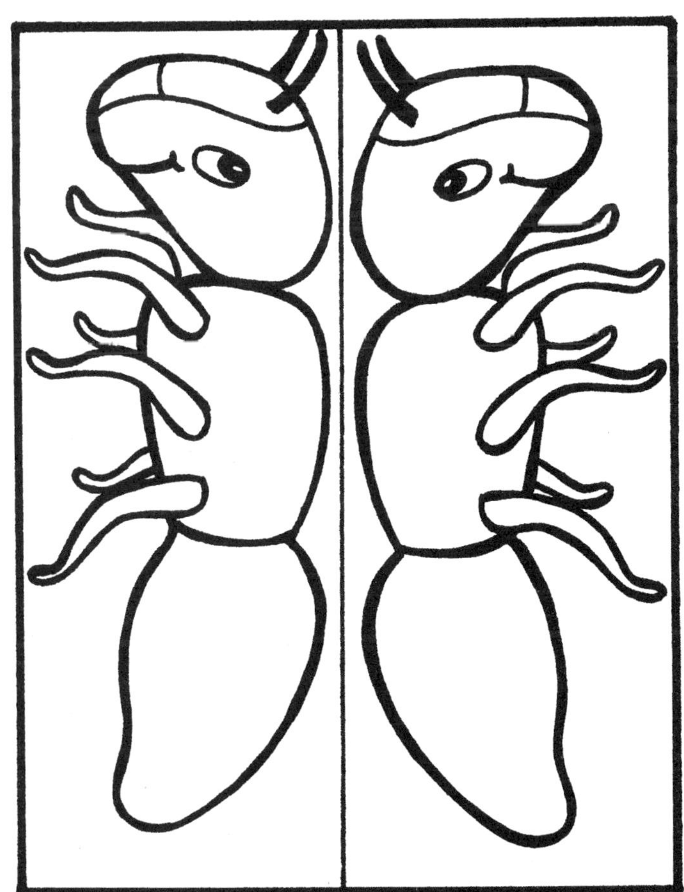

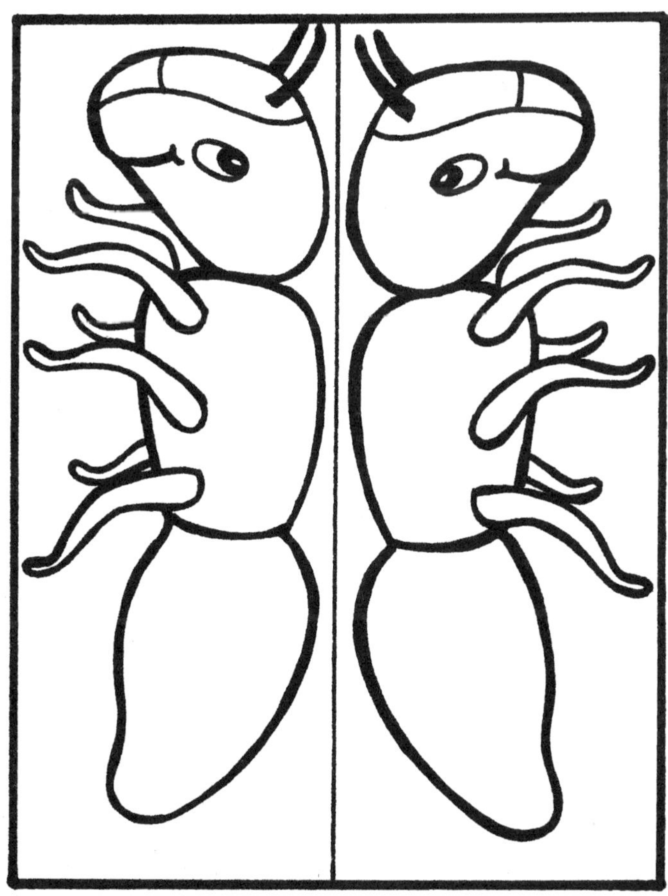

Beehive and Honeybee Patterns

bees

fold

1

2

3

4

5

Hen Pattern

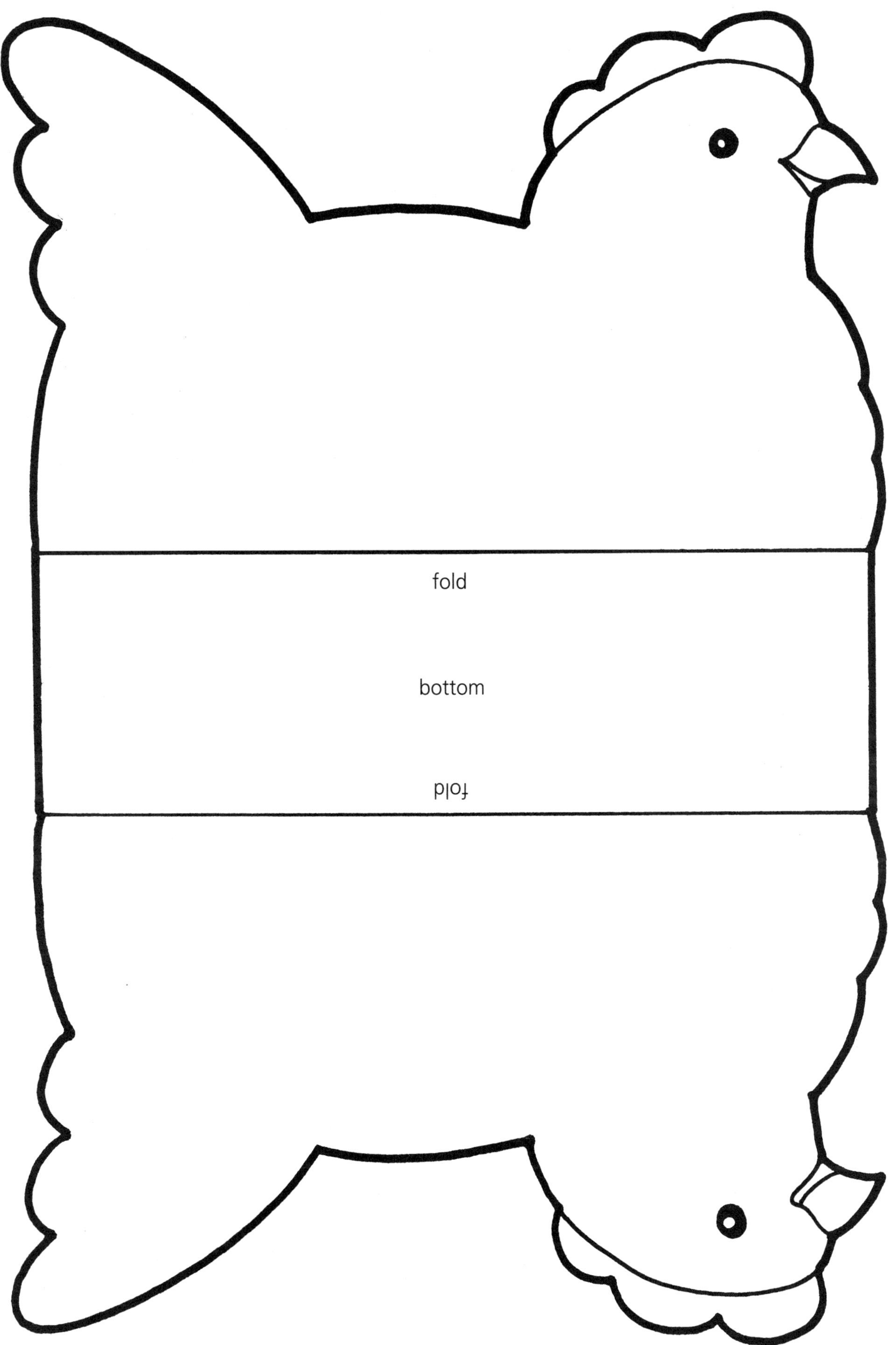

Rooster Patterns

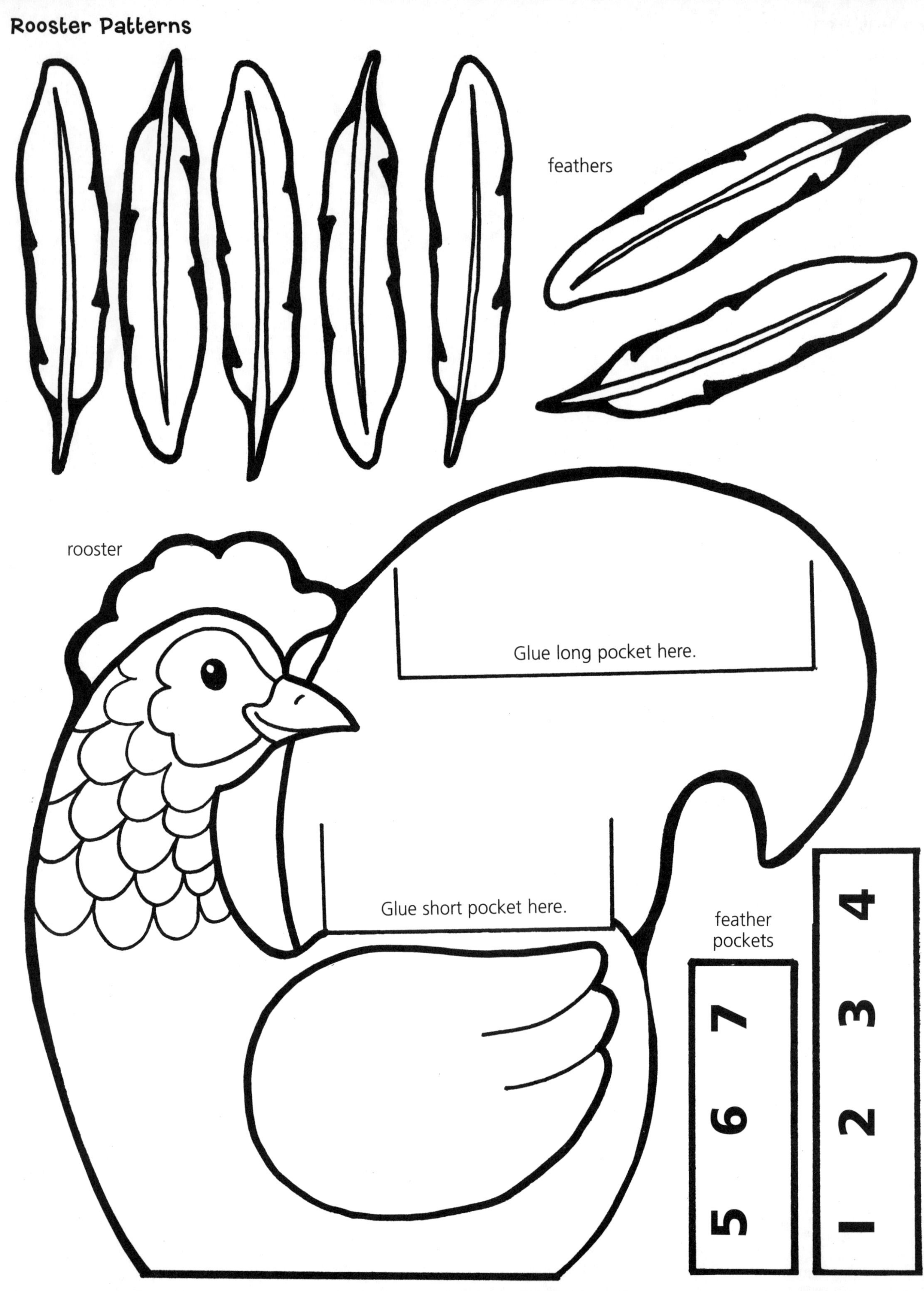

Octopus Tentacle Patterns

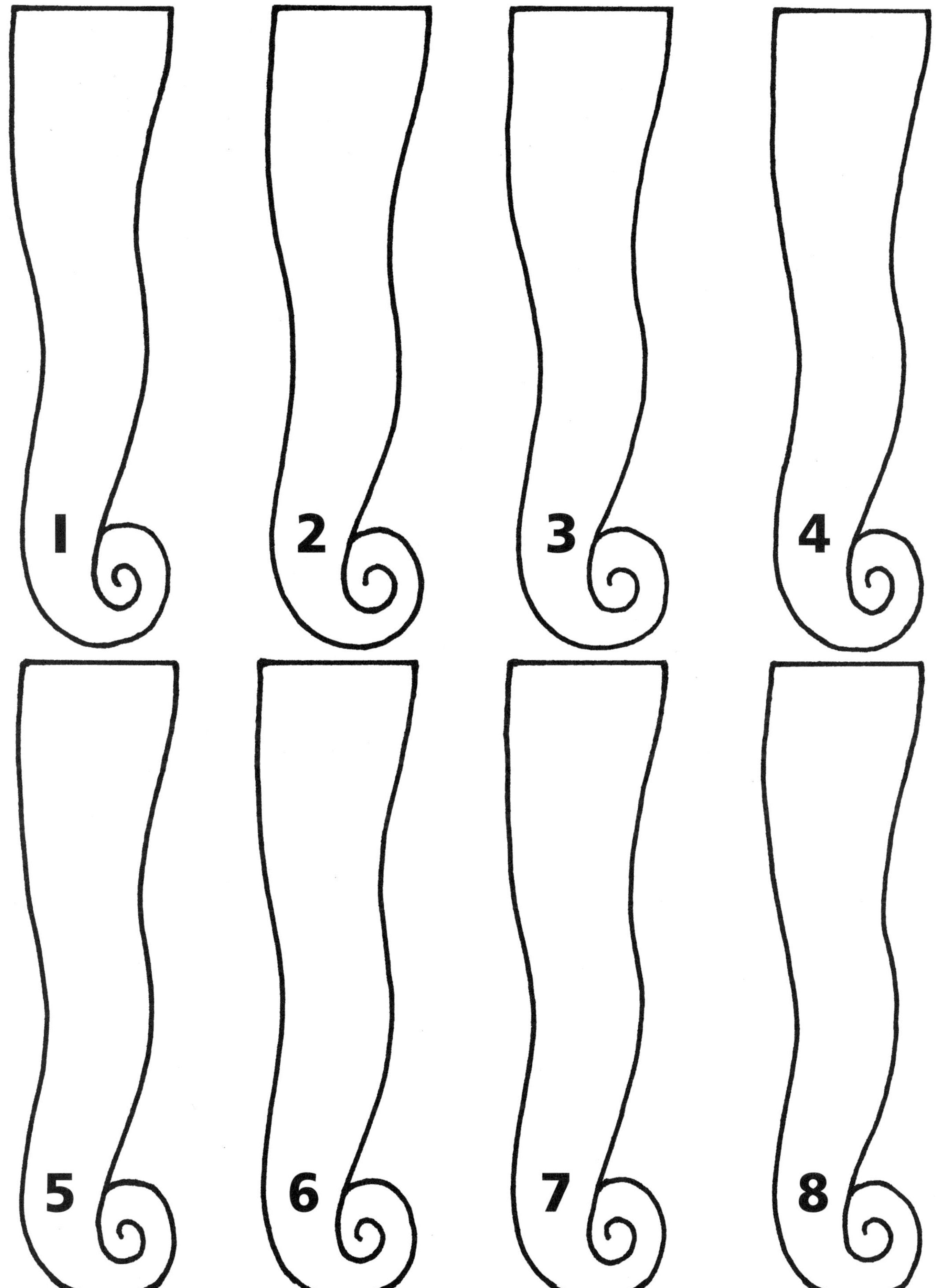

Gator and Fish Patterns

head

legs

Fold and glue.

Fold and glue.

Fold and glue.

Fold and glue.

tail

fish strip

fold

1

2

3

4

5

6

7

8

9

Tree and Birds on a Fence Patterns

Clothesline and Sock Patterns

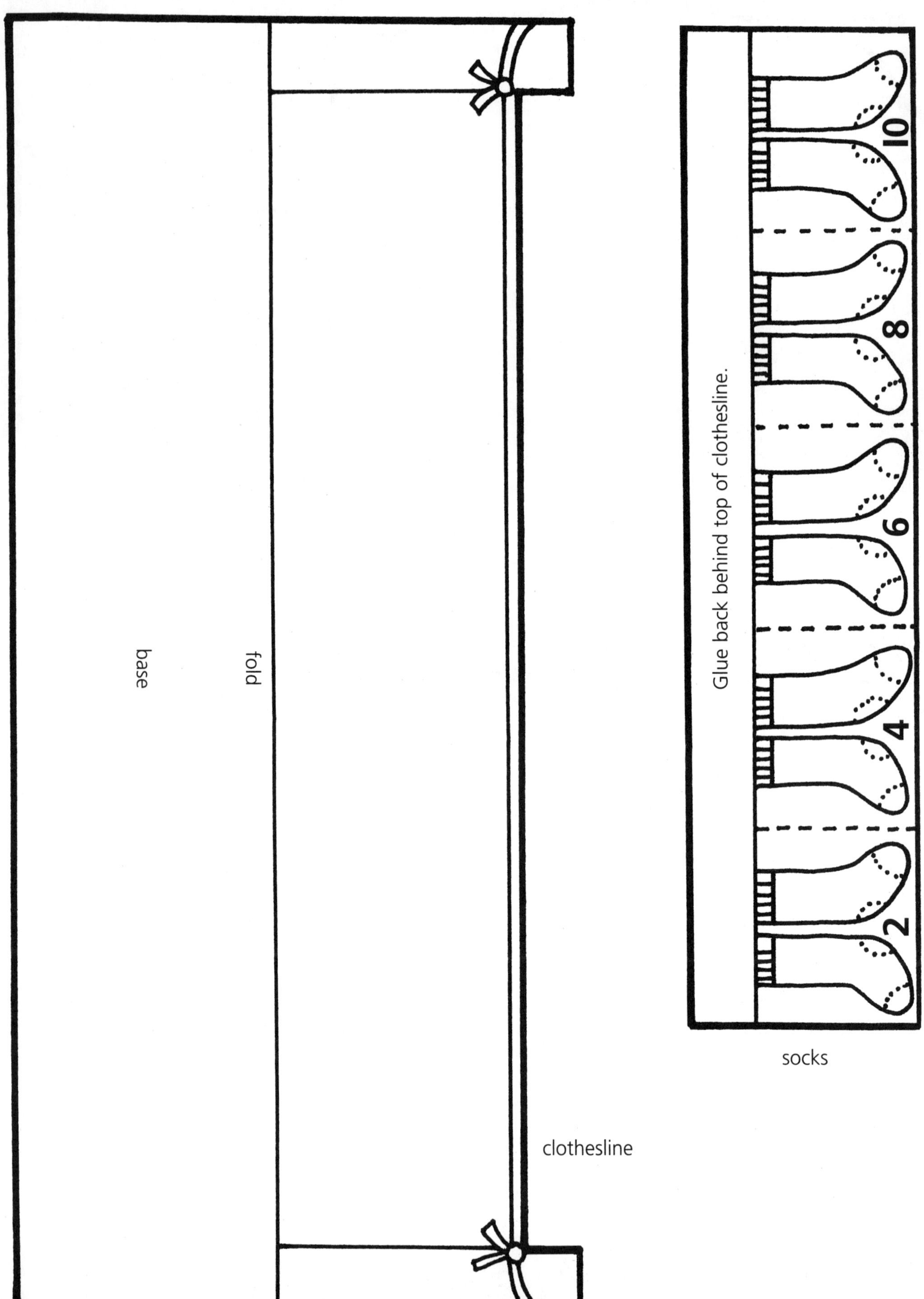

Wallet Patterns and Nickel Cards

wallet front

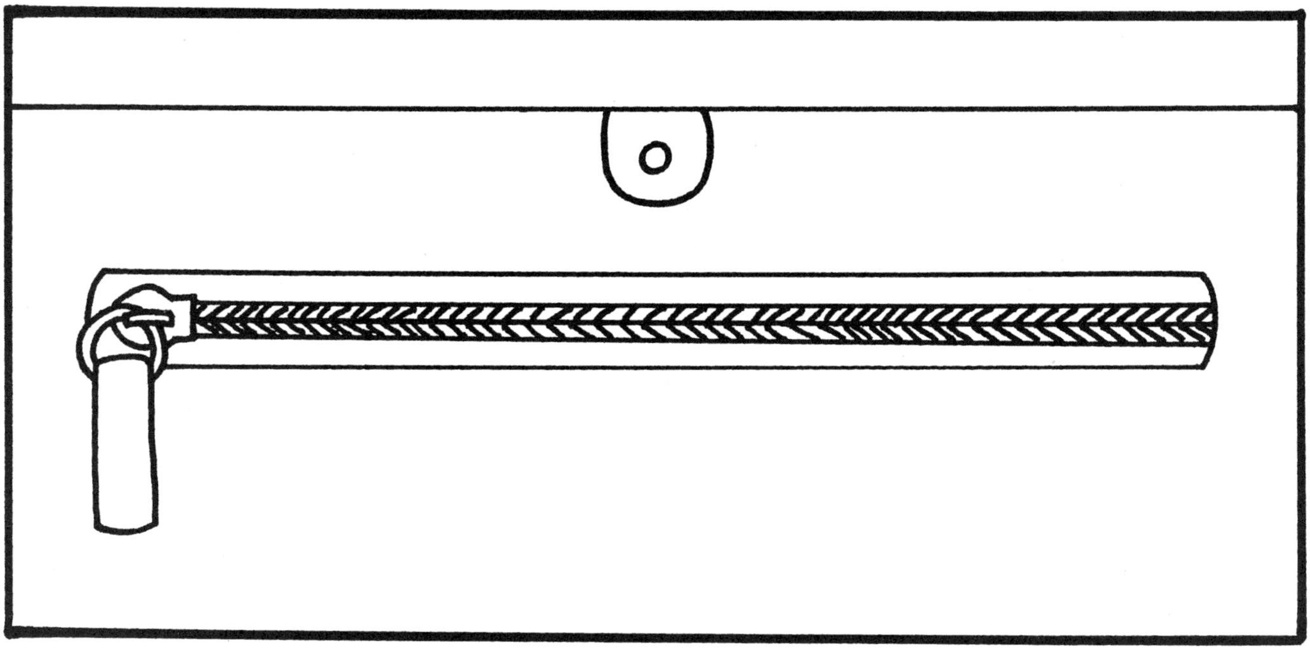

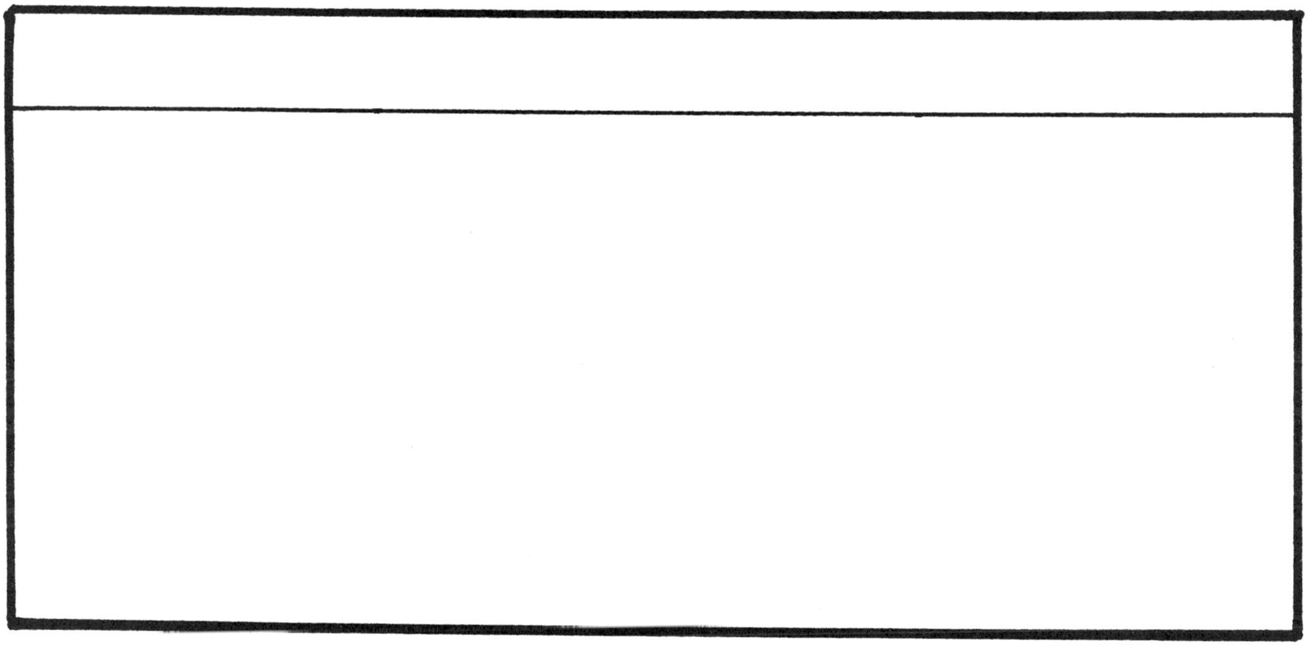

wallet back

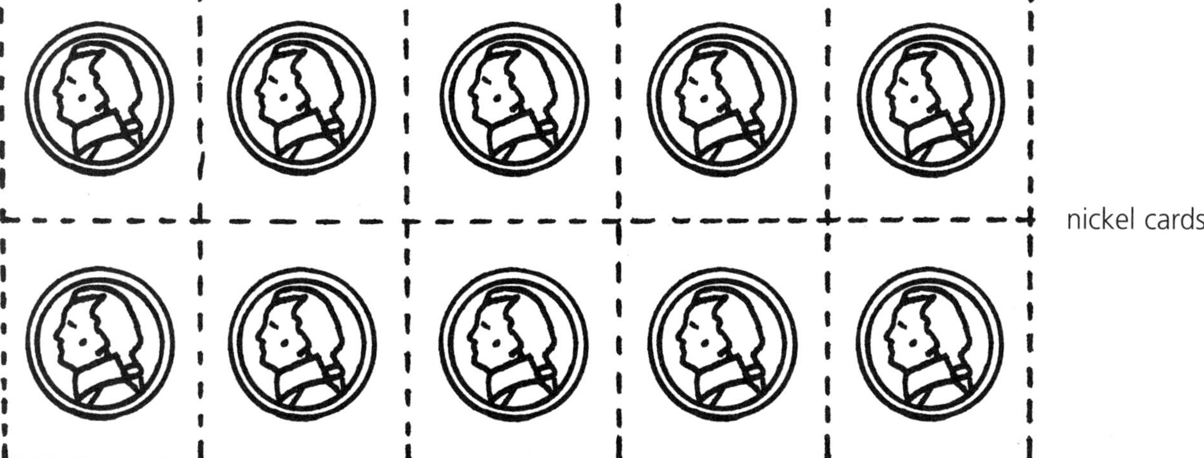

nickel cards

Cookie Jar and Cookie Patterns

COOKIES

Race Car Patterns

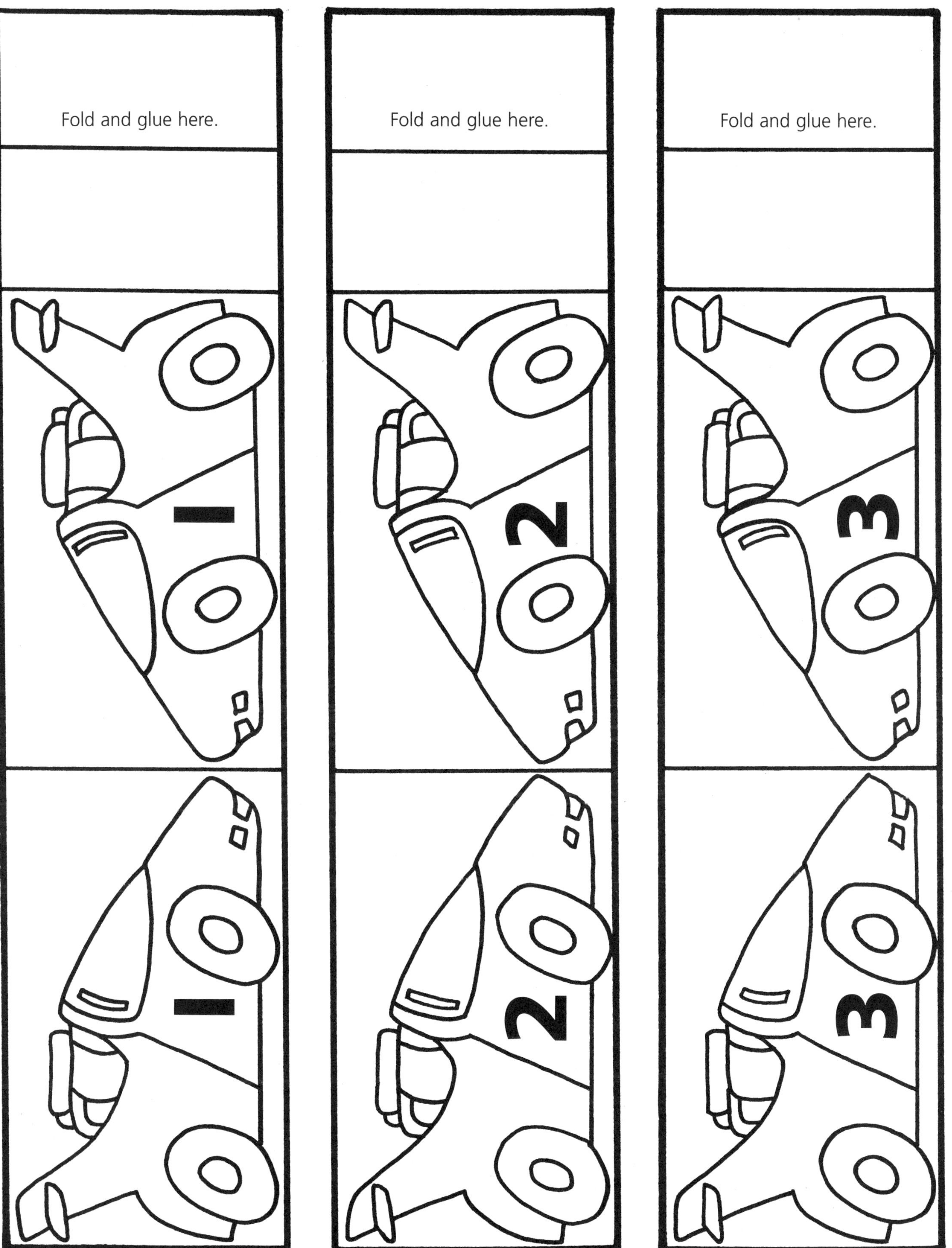

Merry-Go-Round Horses and Robot Patterns

Rectangle Pictures

Ship Captain, Hat, and Diamond Patterns

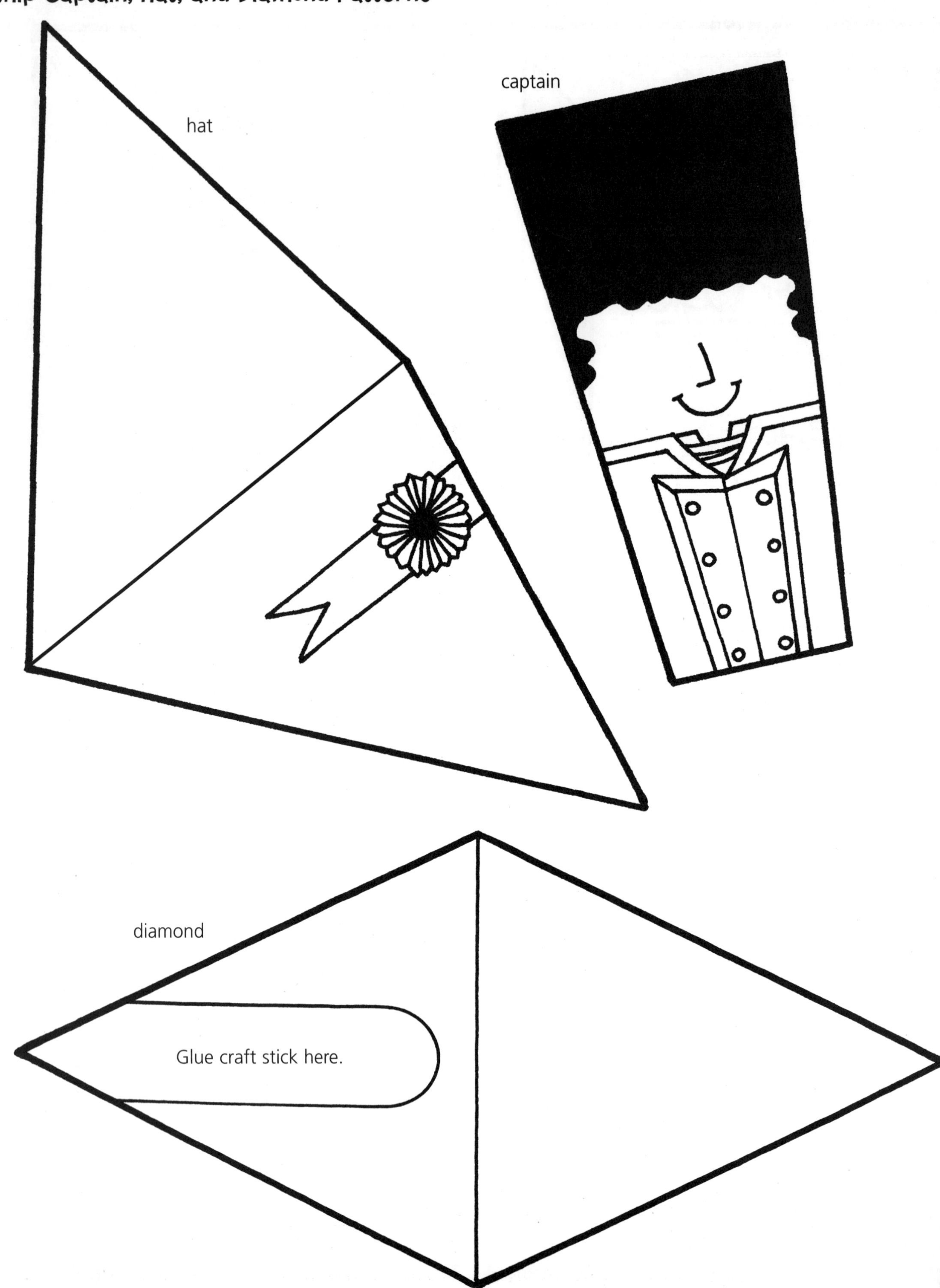

Three Bear Patterns and Letter Cards

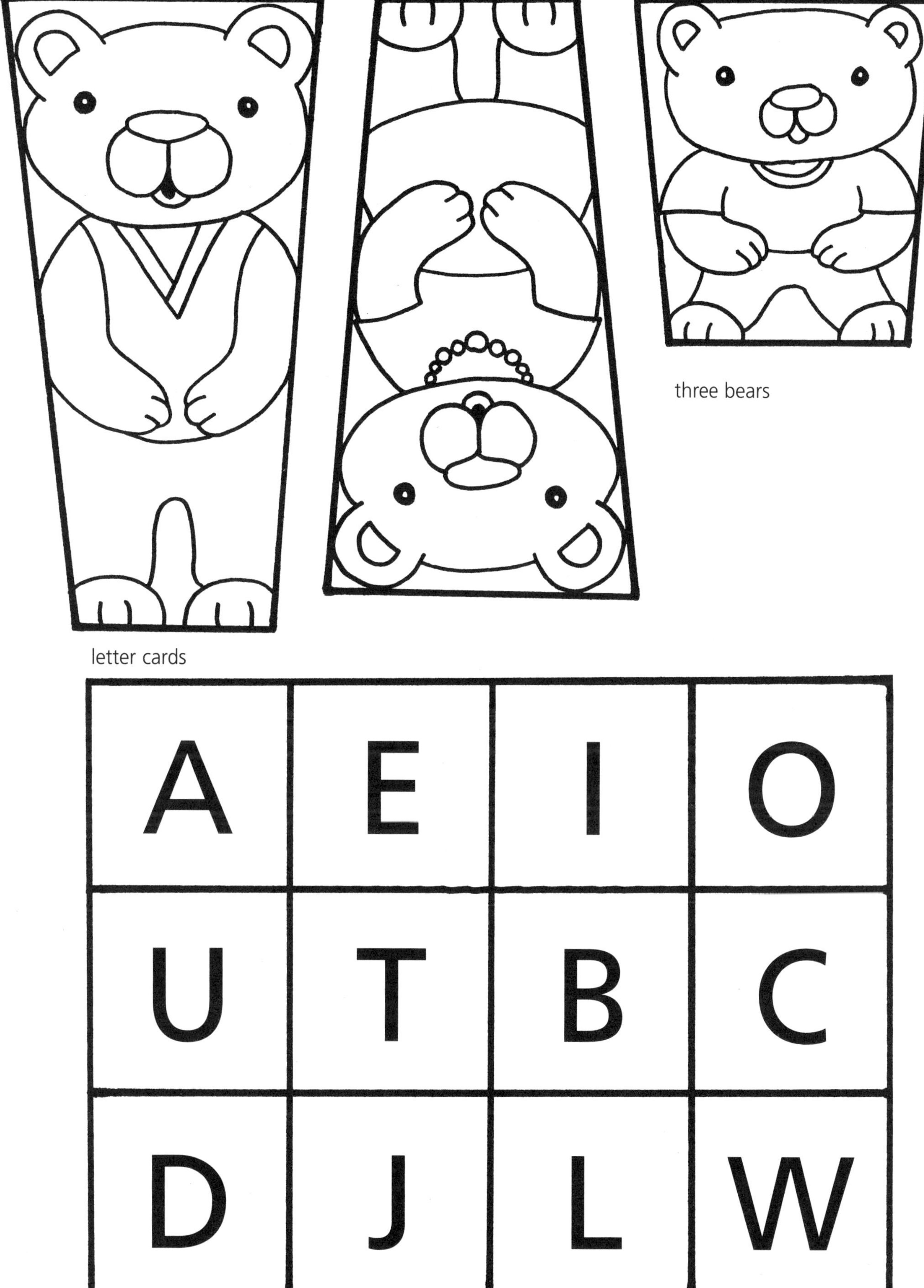

Moving Truck and Box Patterns

U-Move

truck

boxes

Letter Box Patterns

Glue D here.	Glue T here.	Glue L here.
Glue R here.		
	D	T
L	R	

Map and Car Patterns

Glue here.

bottom

car

map

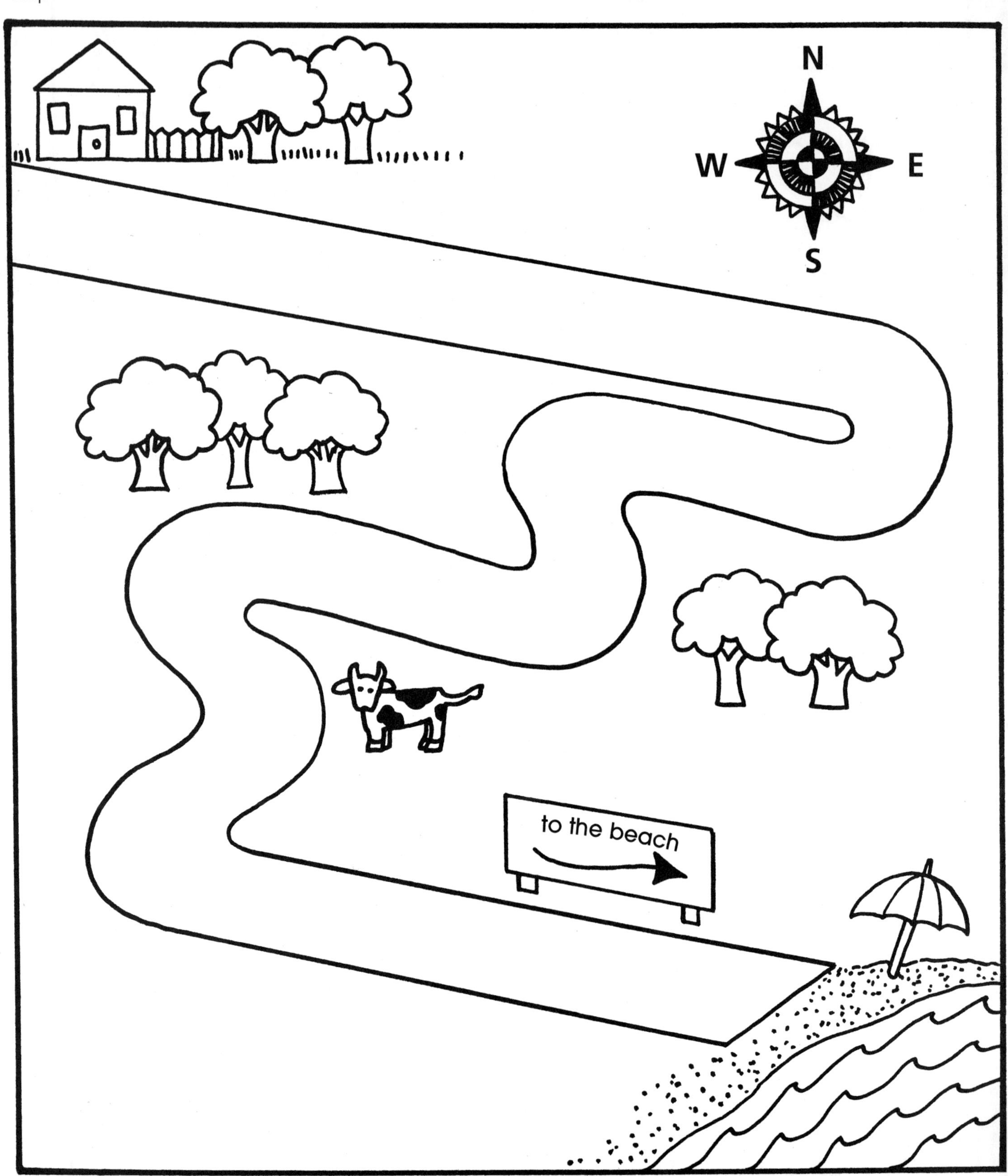

Tortoise, Hare, Racecourse, and Inchworm Patterns

racecourse

Finish

Start

inchworm

tortoise

hare

Iguana and Goat Patterns

iguana

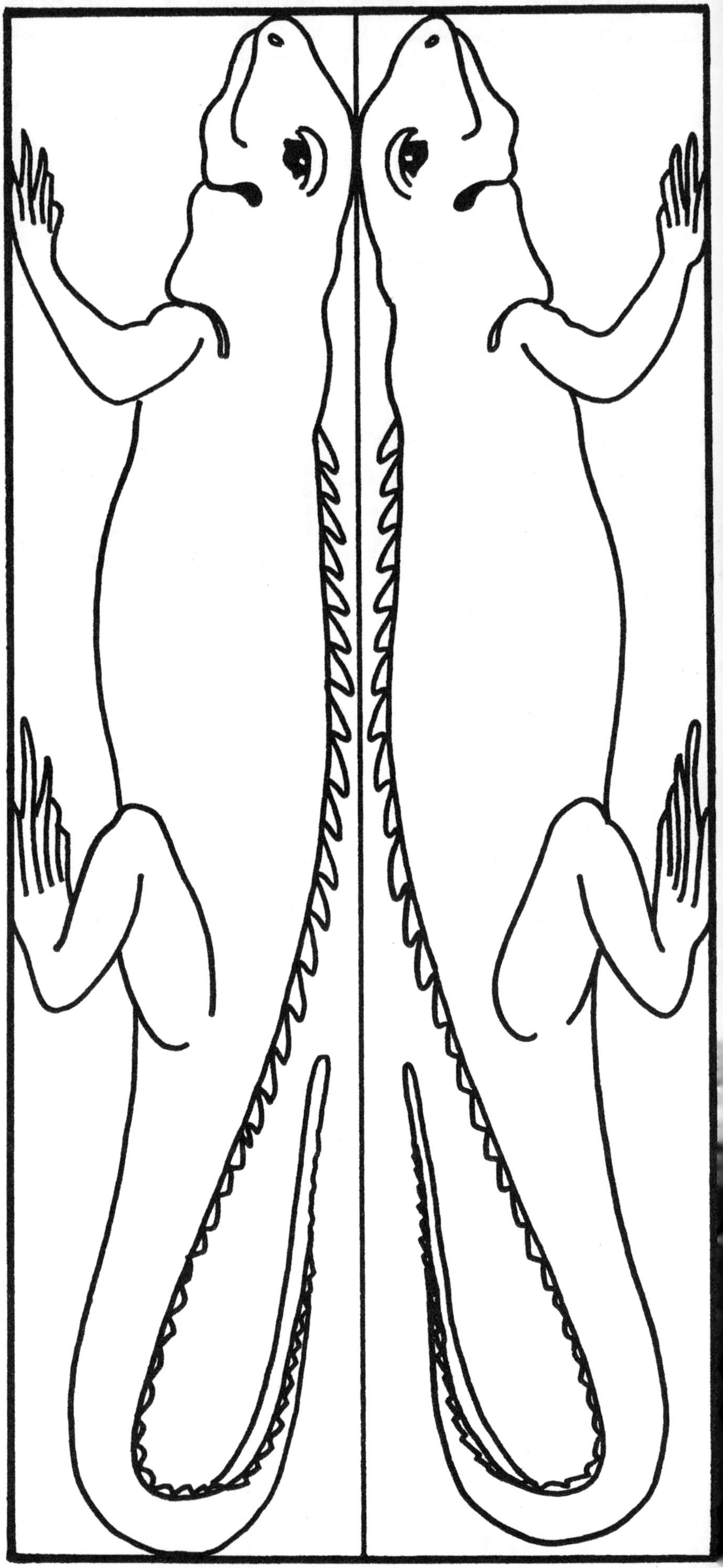

goat

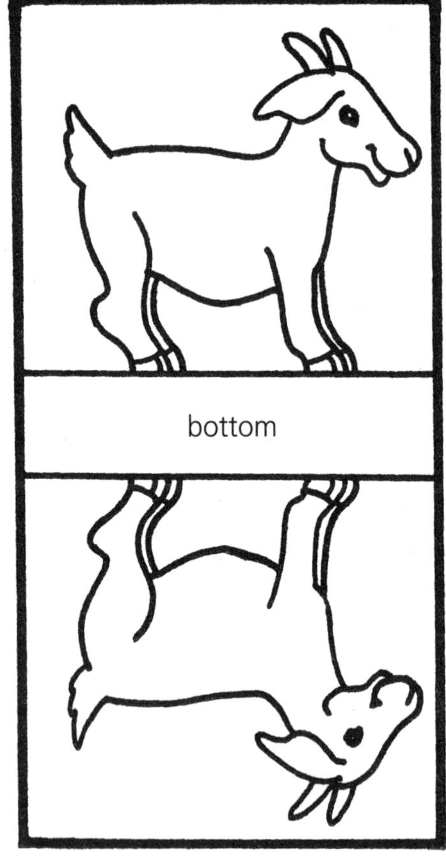

Bridge Pattern

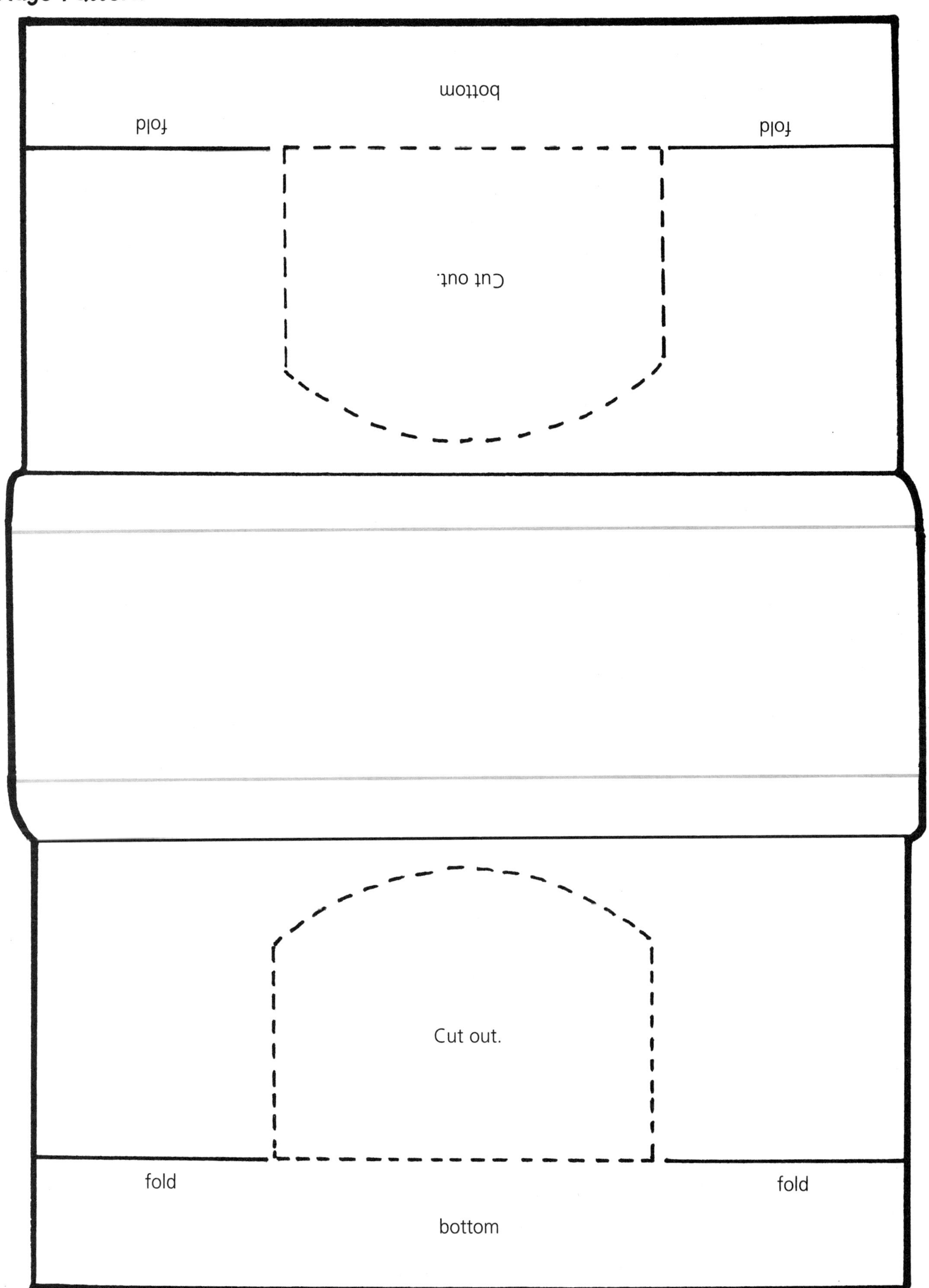

Kangaroo Patterns

Dolphin Patterns

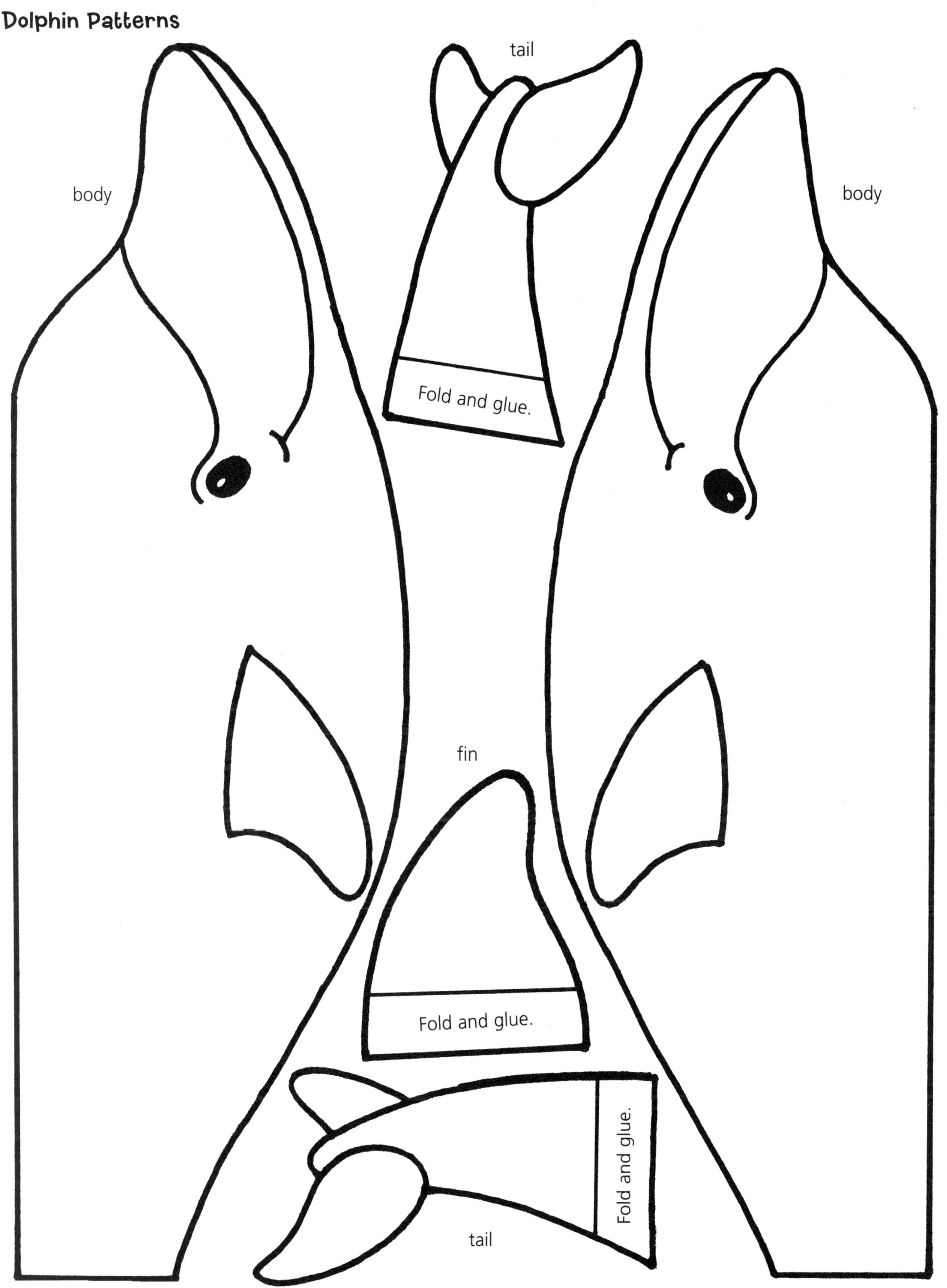

Ladder, Firefighter, Bird, Bee, and Beetle Patterns

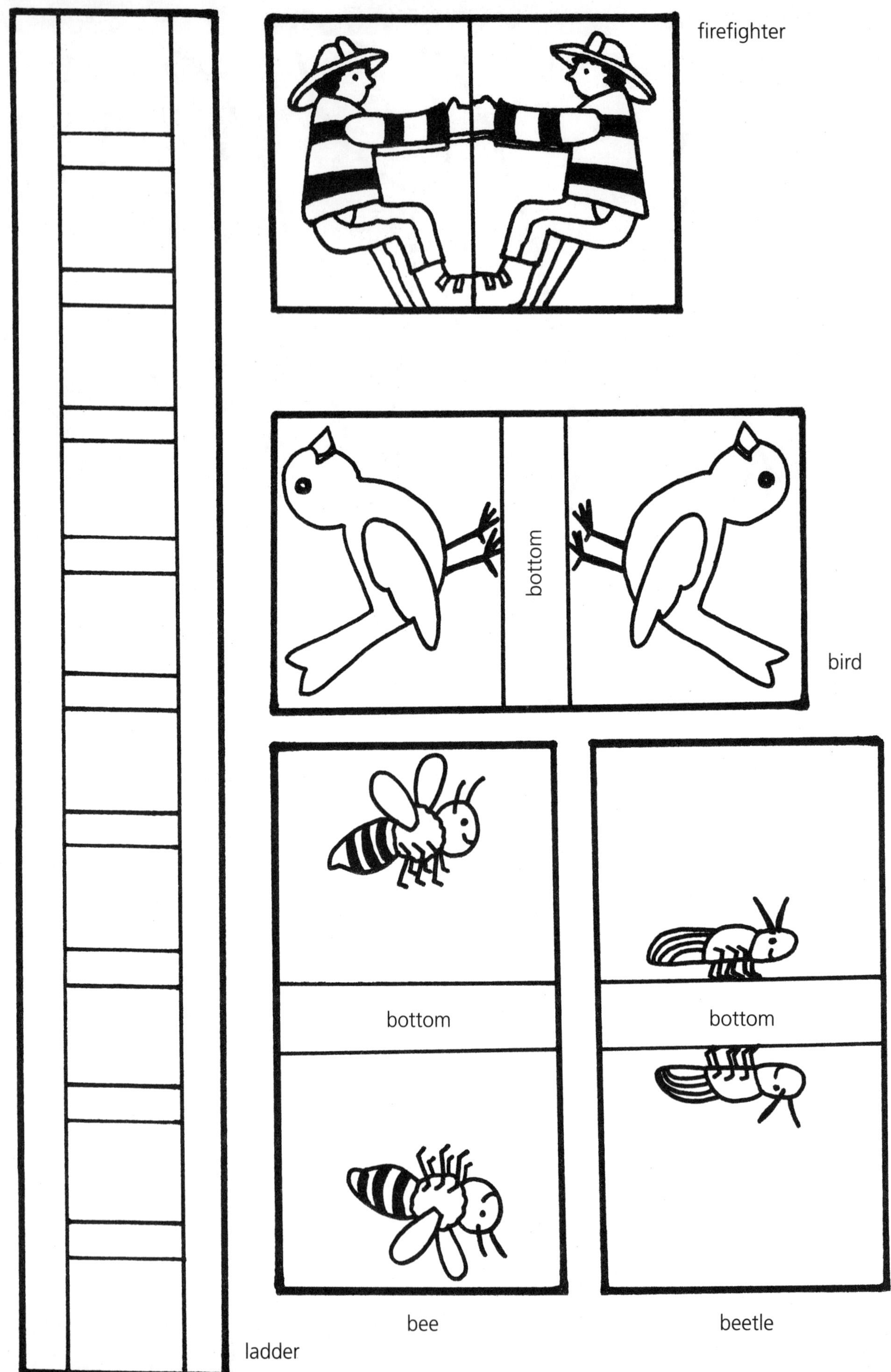

Spider, Web, and Turtle Patterns

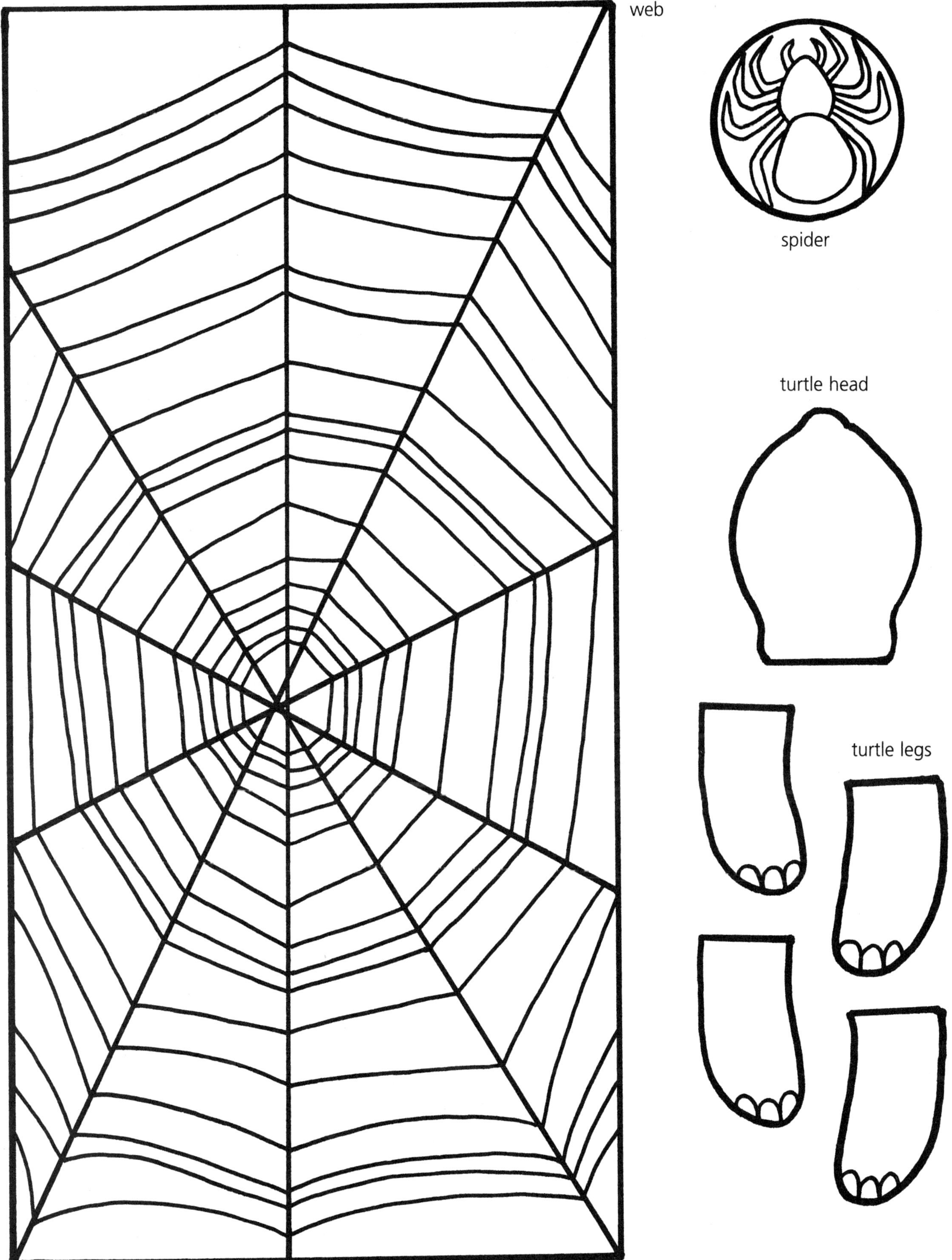

Frog Patterns

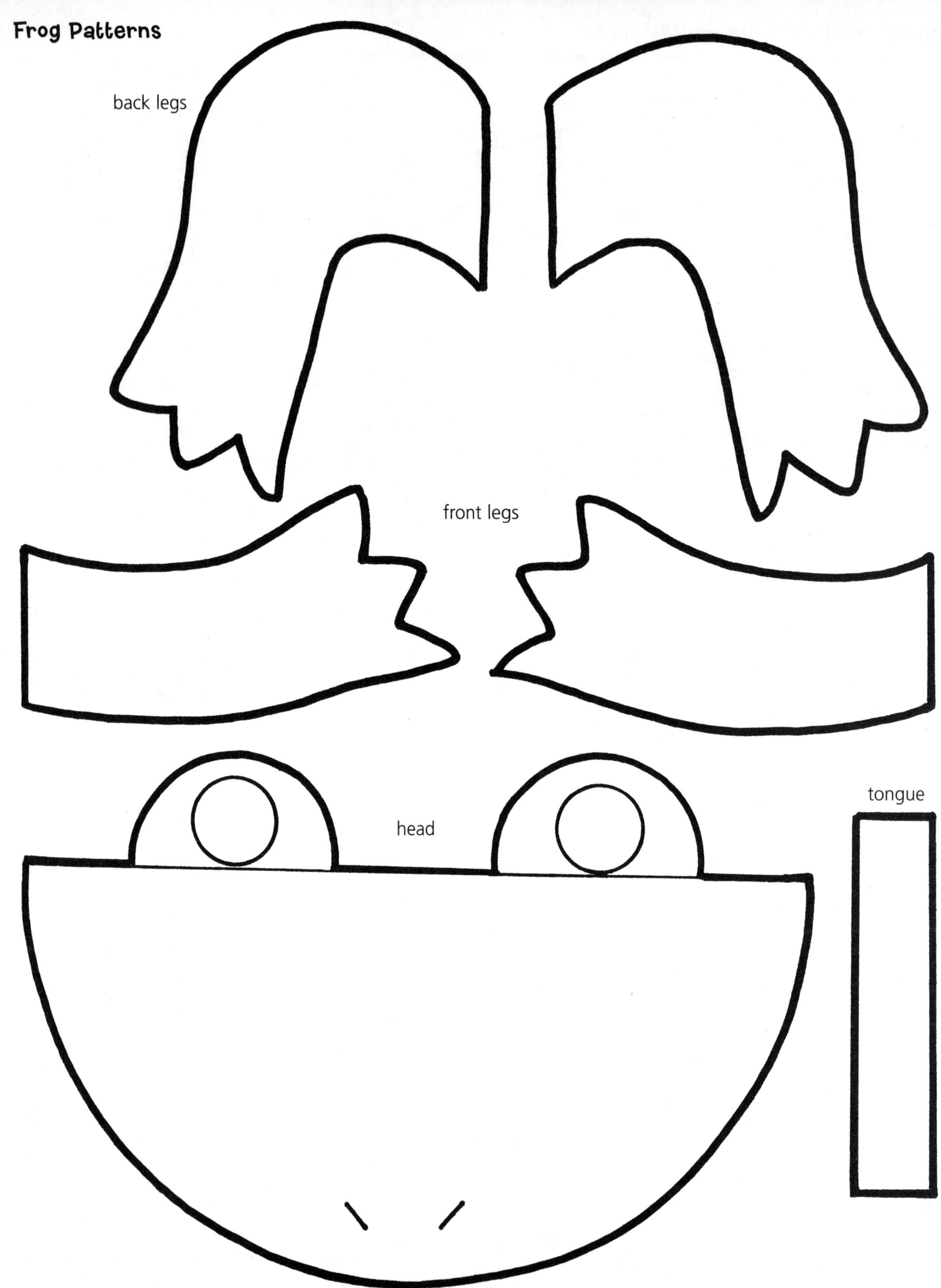

Mouth and Firefighter Patterns

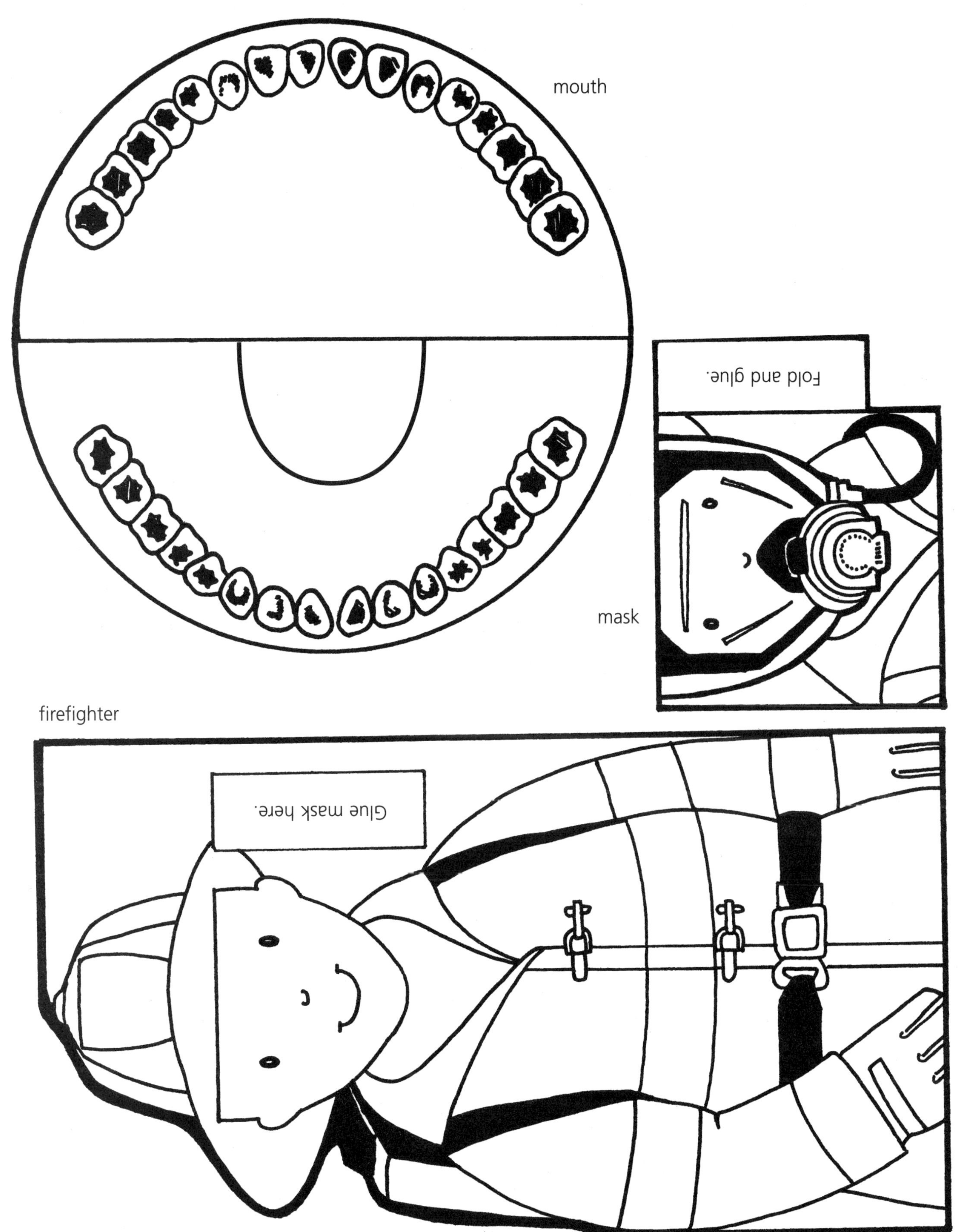

Barn Pattern

Animal Wheel Pattern

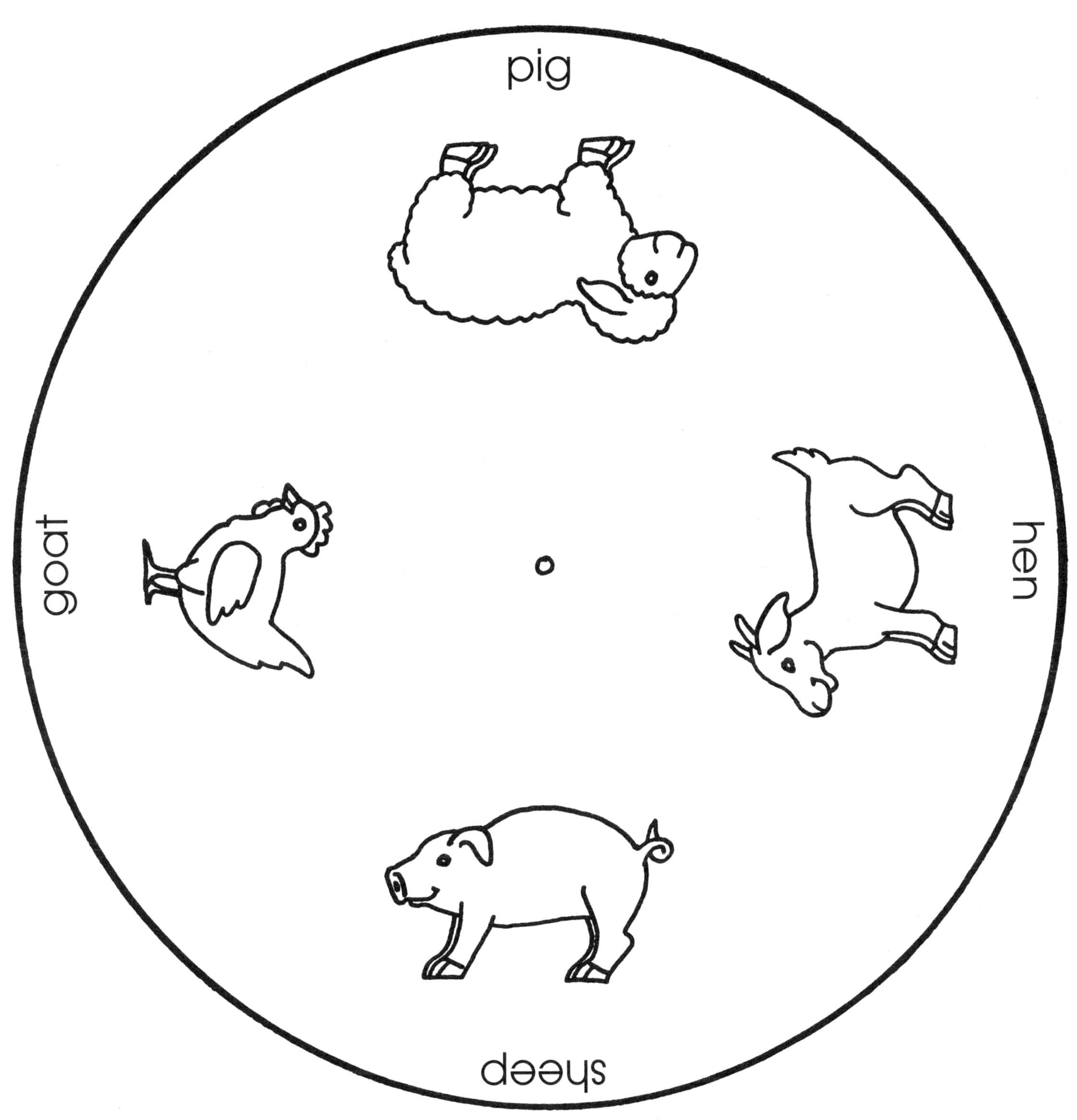

Doctor Patterns

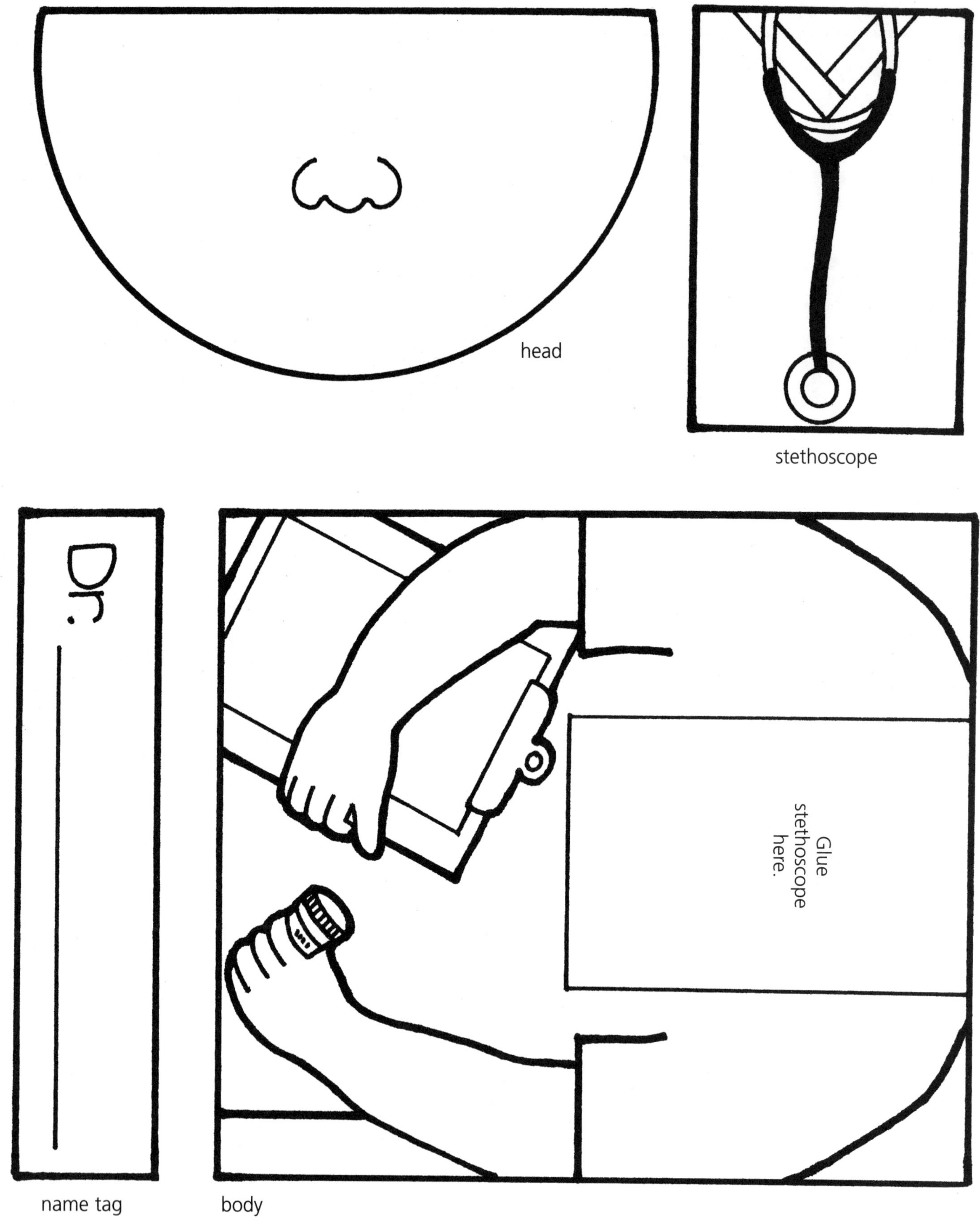

Mailbox and Mail Patterns

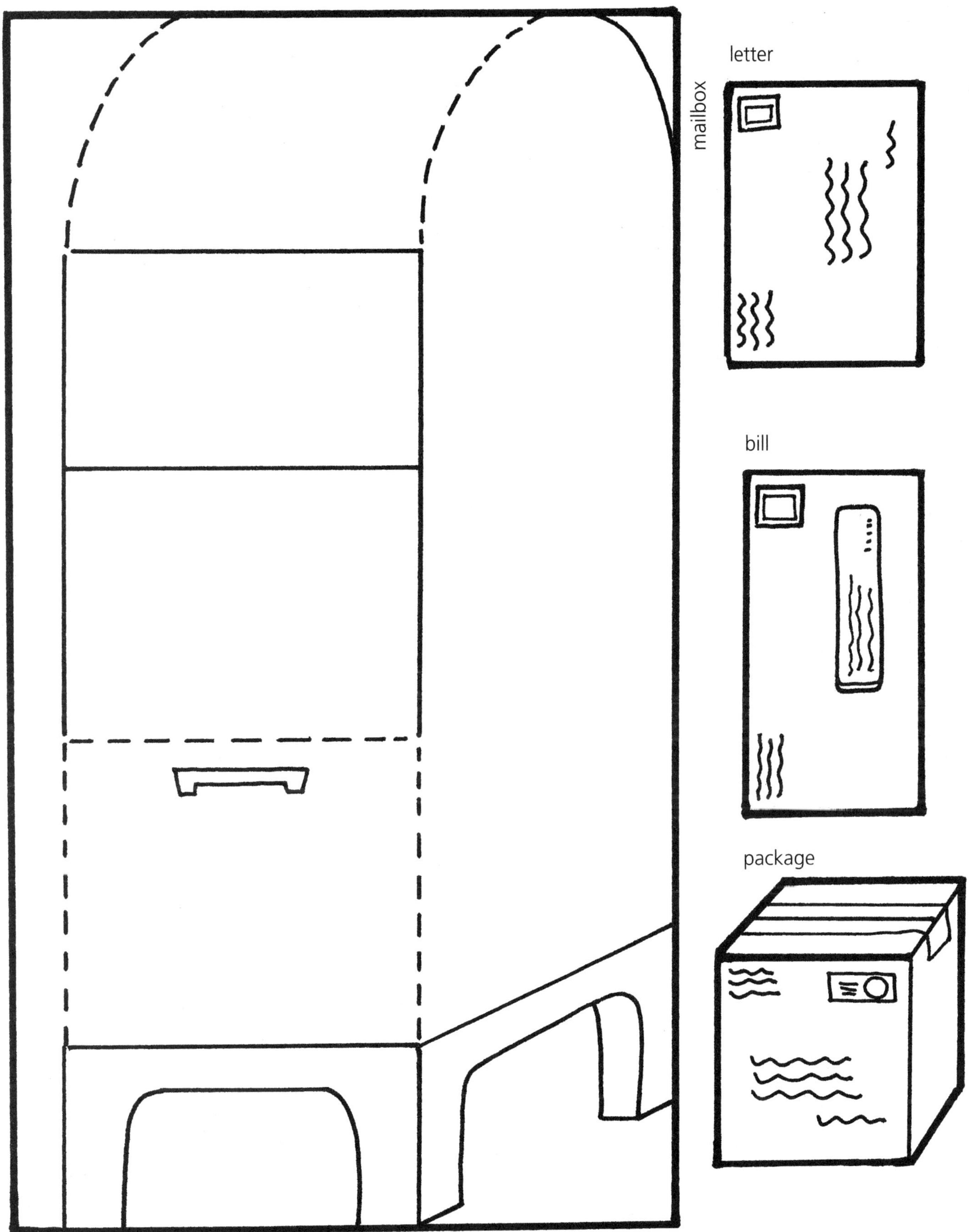

Food Cards and Grocery List Pattern

Towel, Soap, Shirt, and Four Faces Patterns

Puppet Pattern

Toothbrush and Toothpaste Patterns

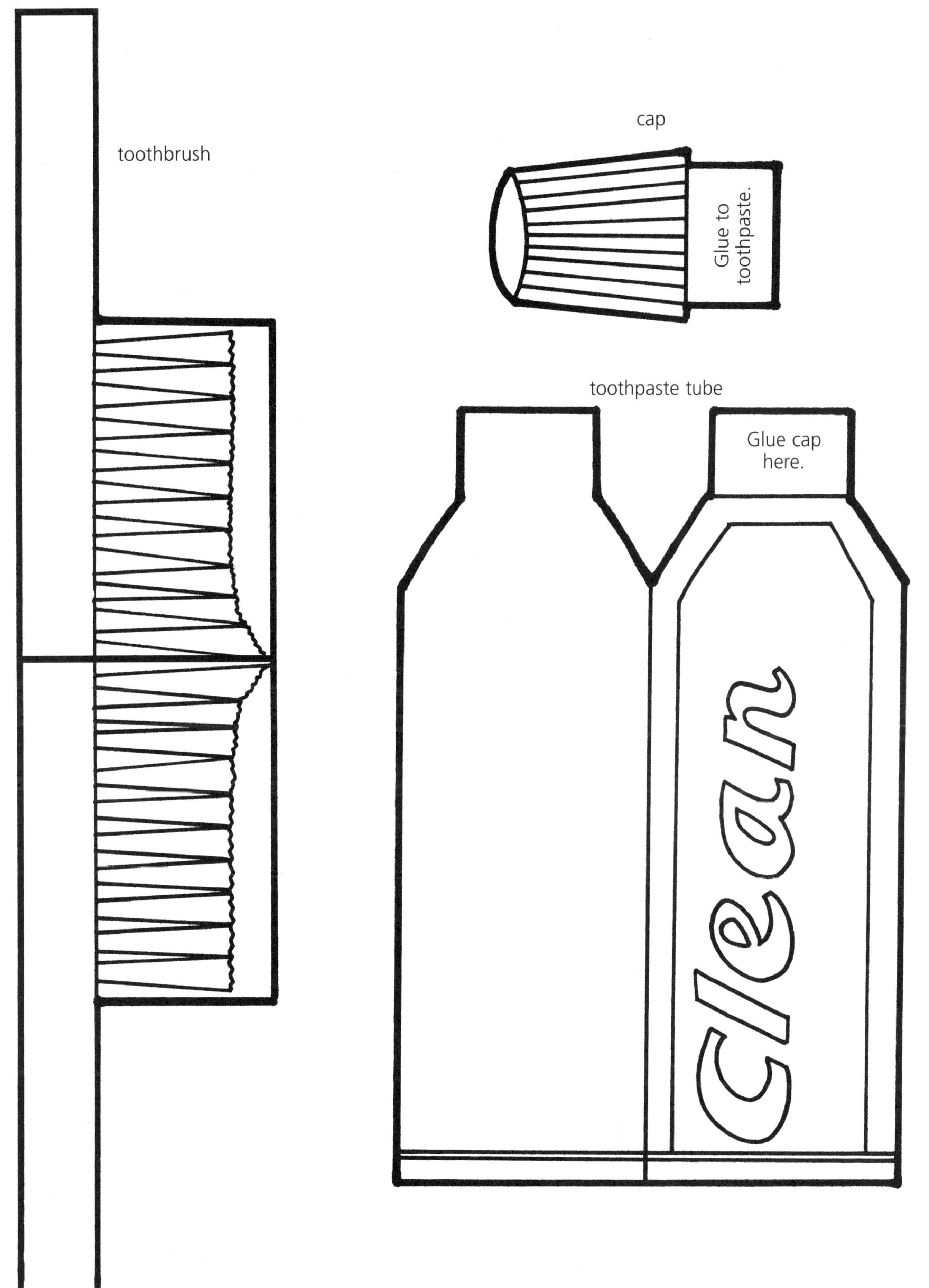

Cap and Name Tag Patterns

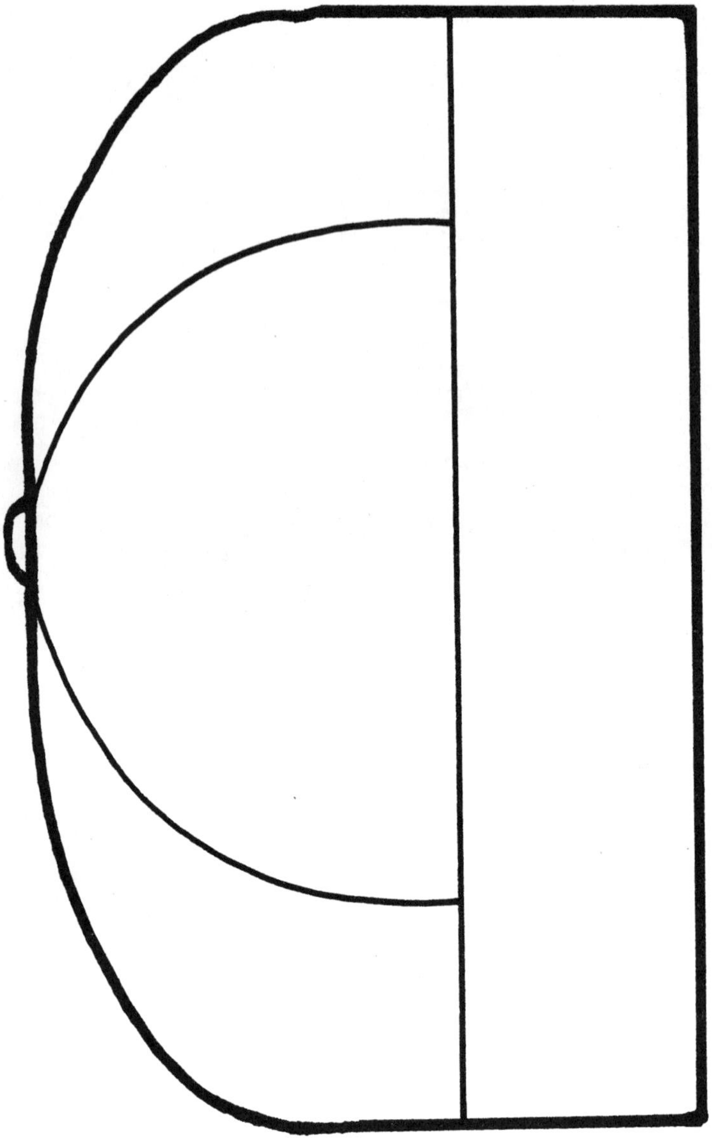

cap

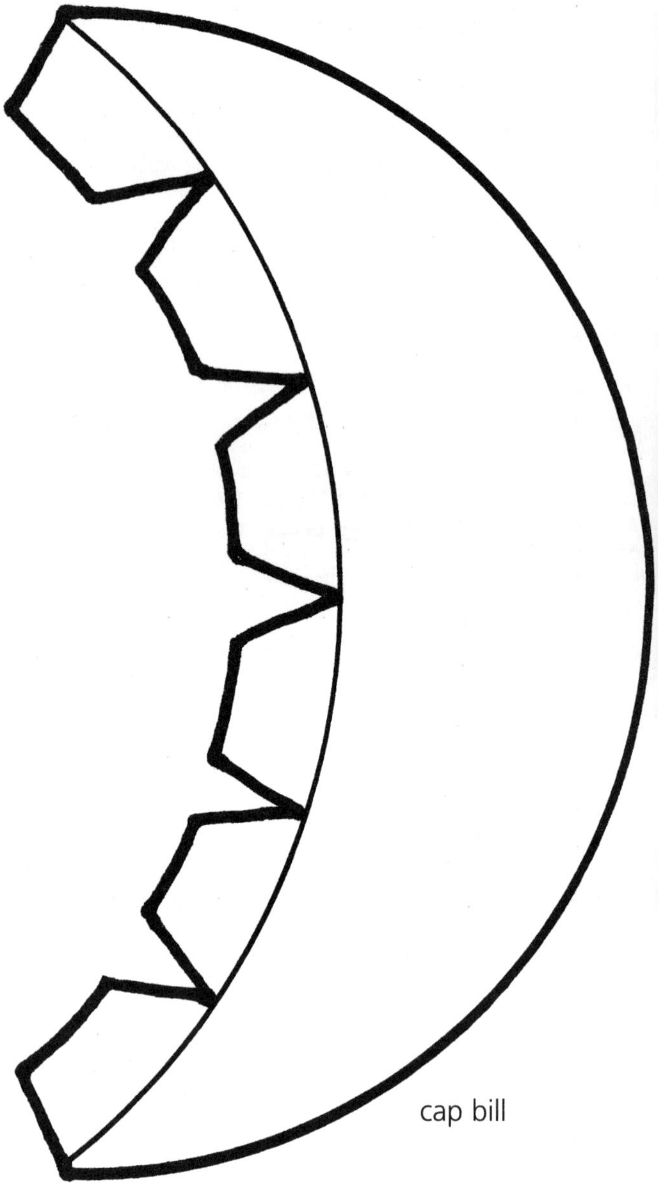

cap bill

name tag

Pedestrian Signal Patterns

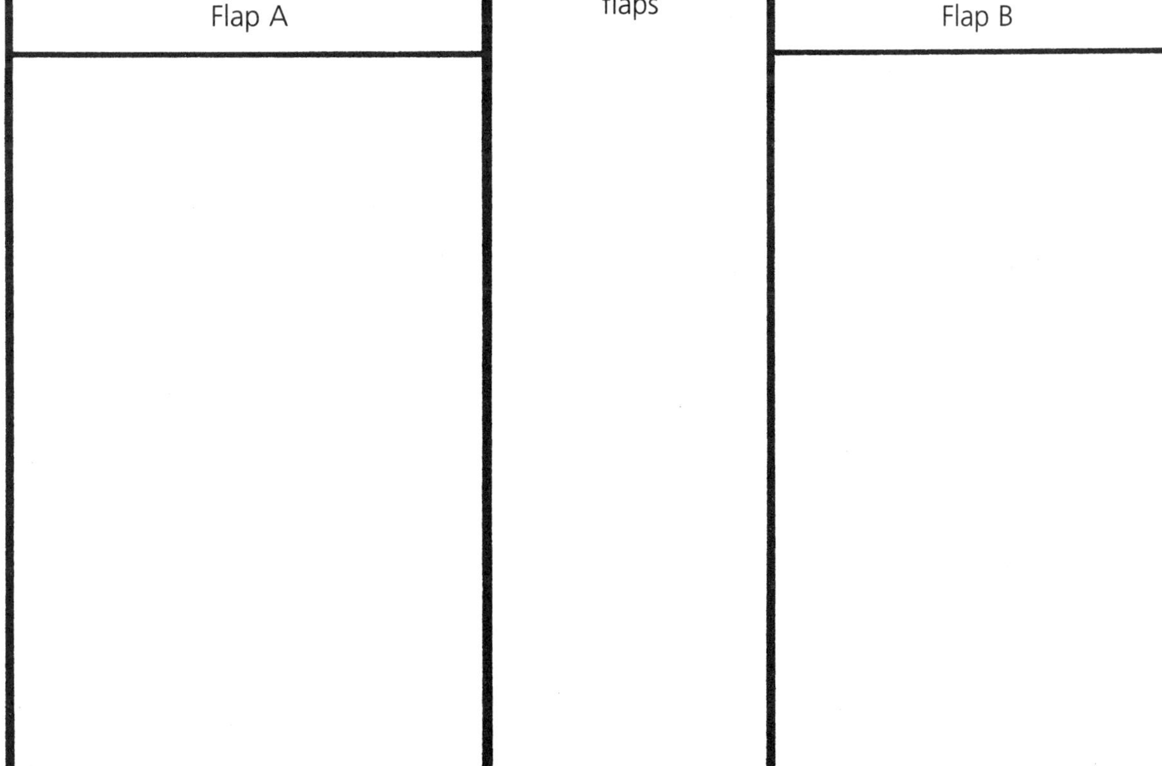

Ear and Nose Patterns and Scent Cards

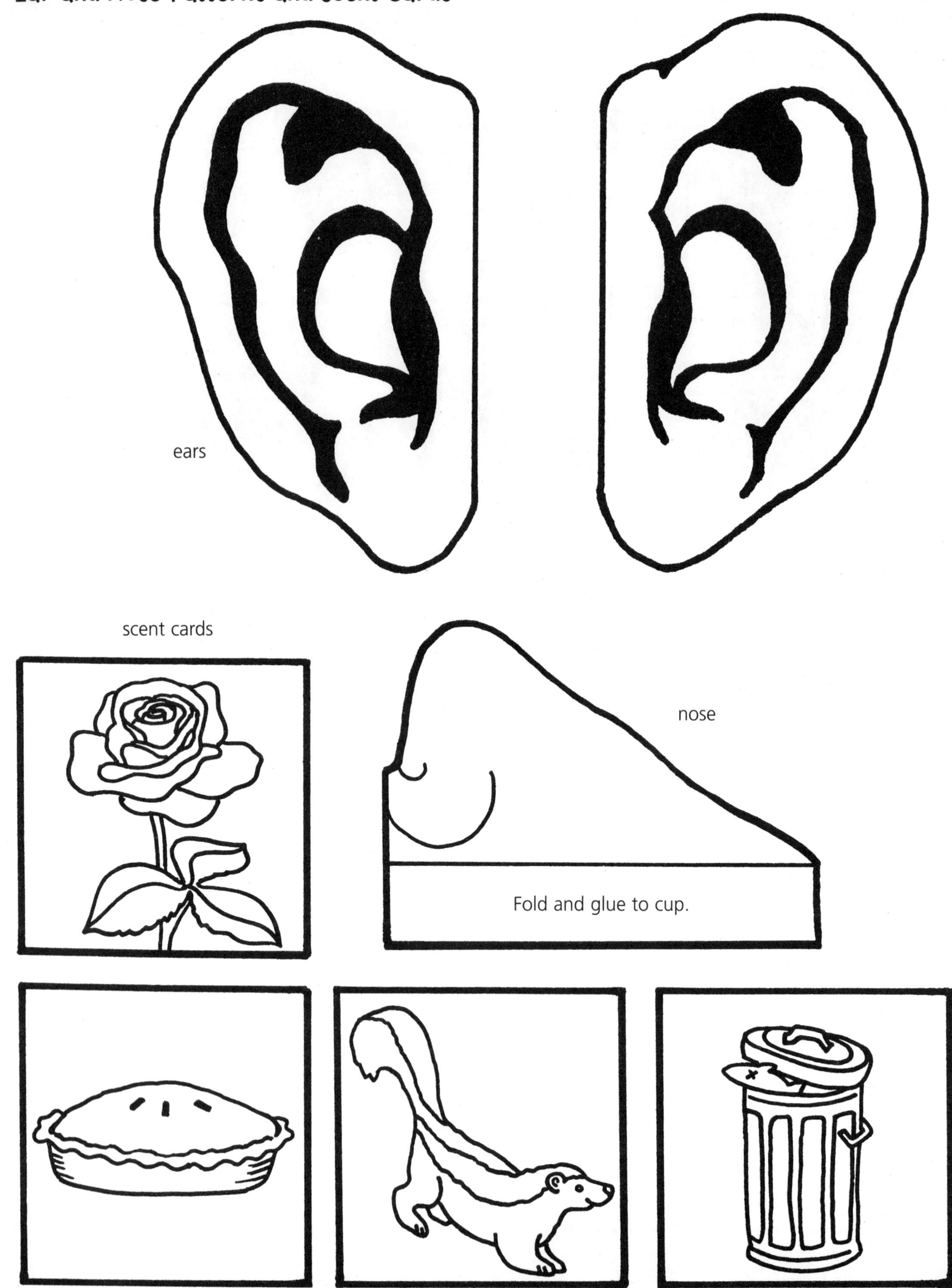

Flip Puppet, Mouth Pattern, and Food Cards

Mr. Wiggles Patterns

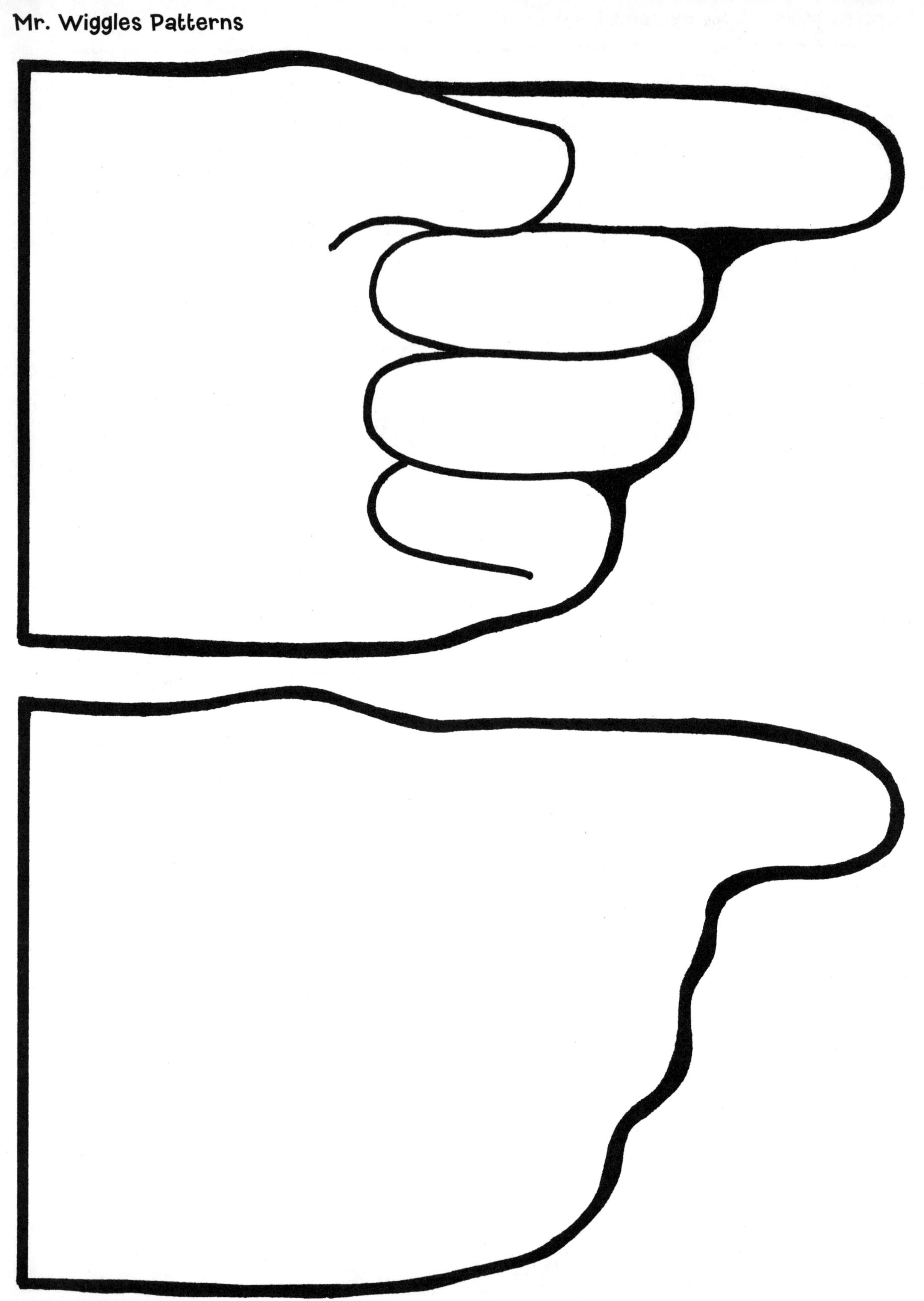

Ant, Bee, Butterfly, and Spider Patterns

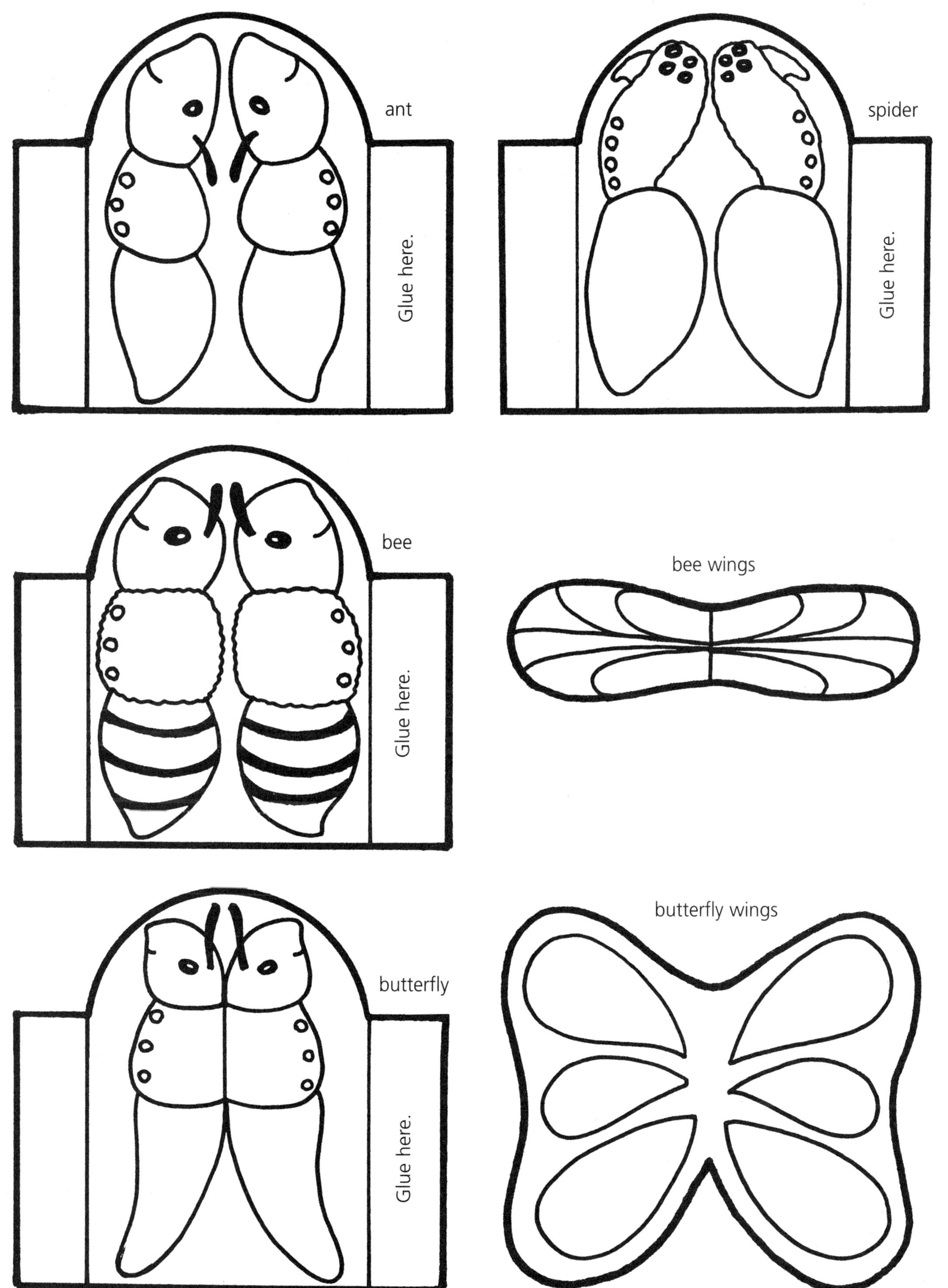

Bird and Bat Patterns

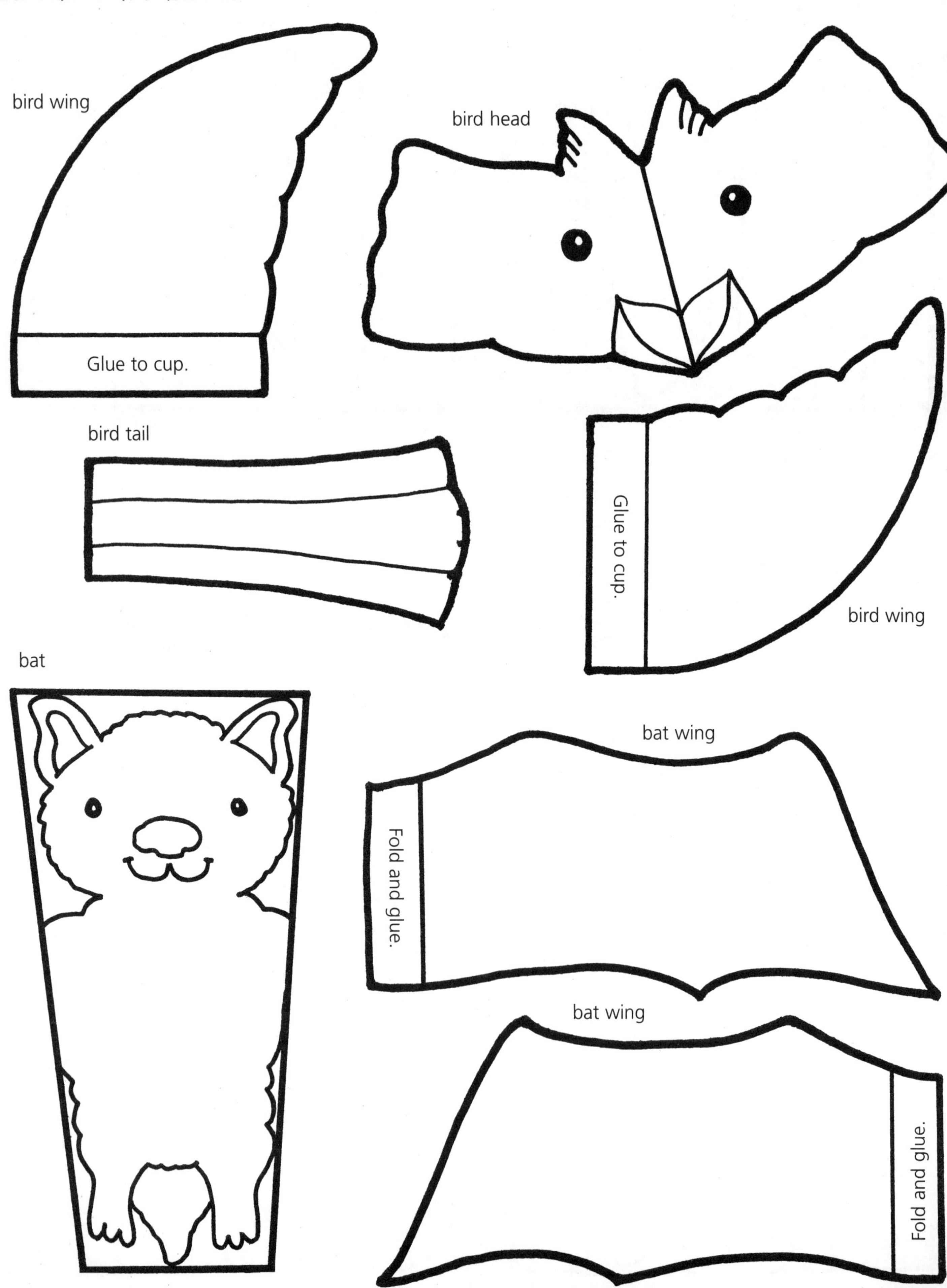

Fish Patterns

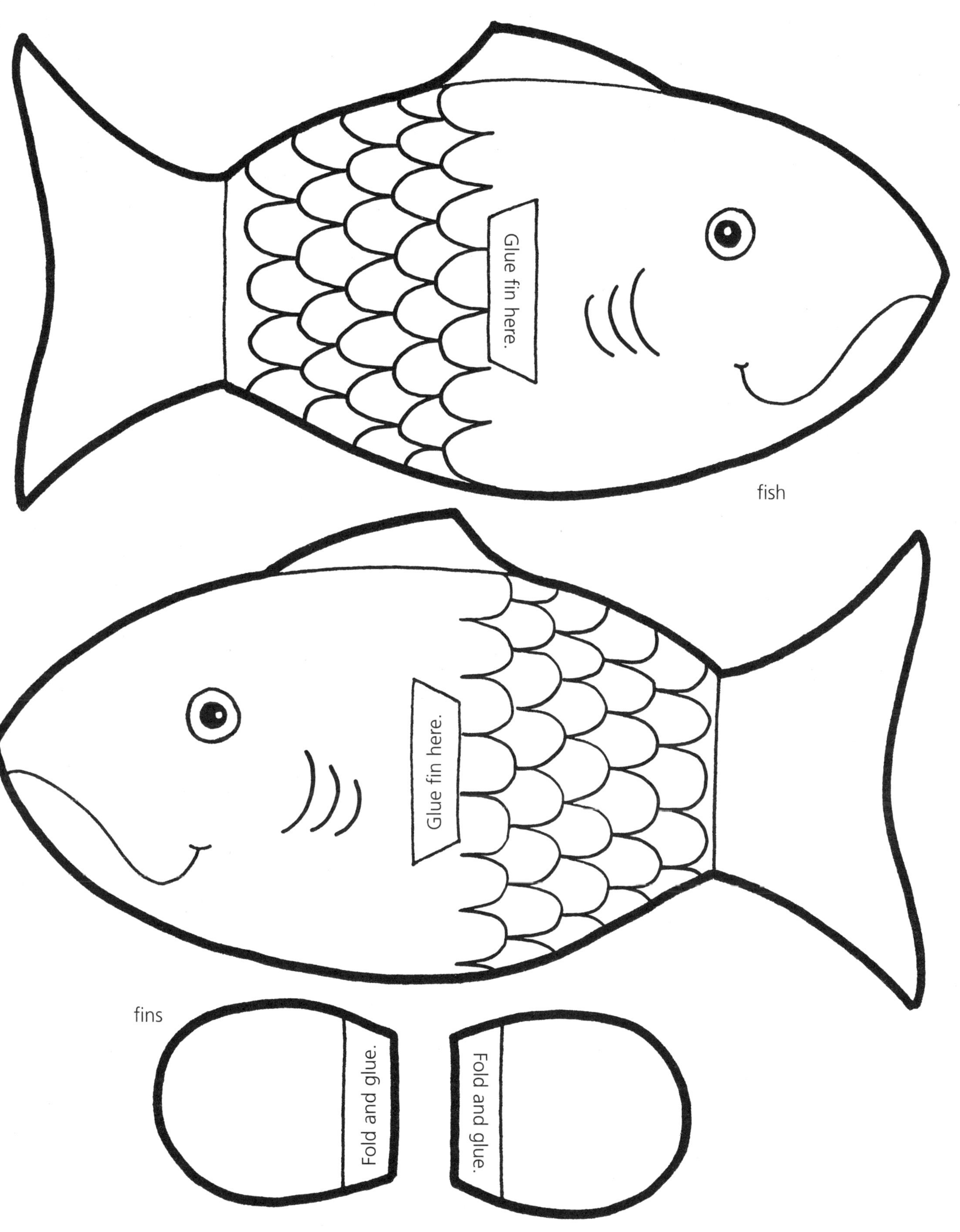

Bear, Mouse, and Whale Tail Patterns

Whale Patterns

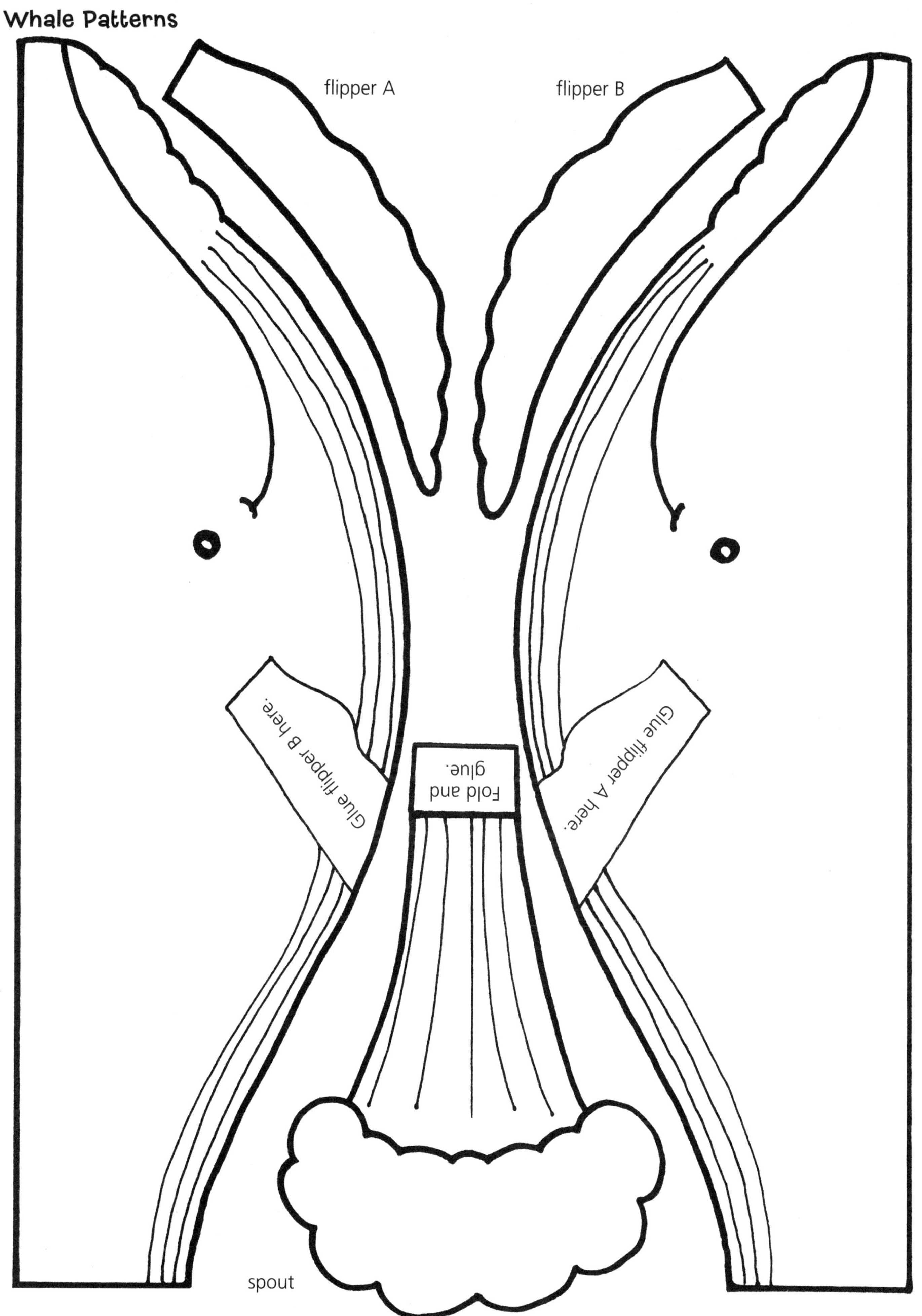

Lizard, Turtle, and Snake Patterns and Frog Life Cycle Cards

frog life cycle cards

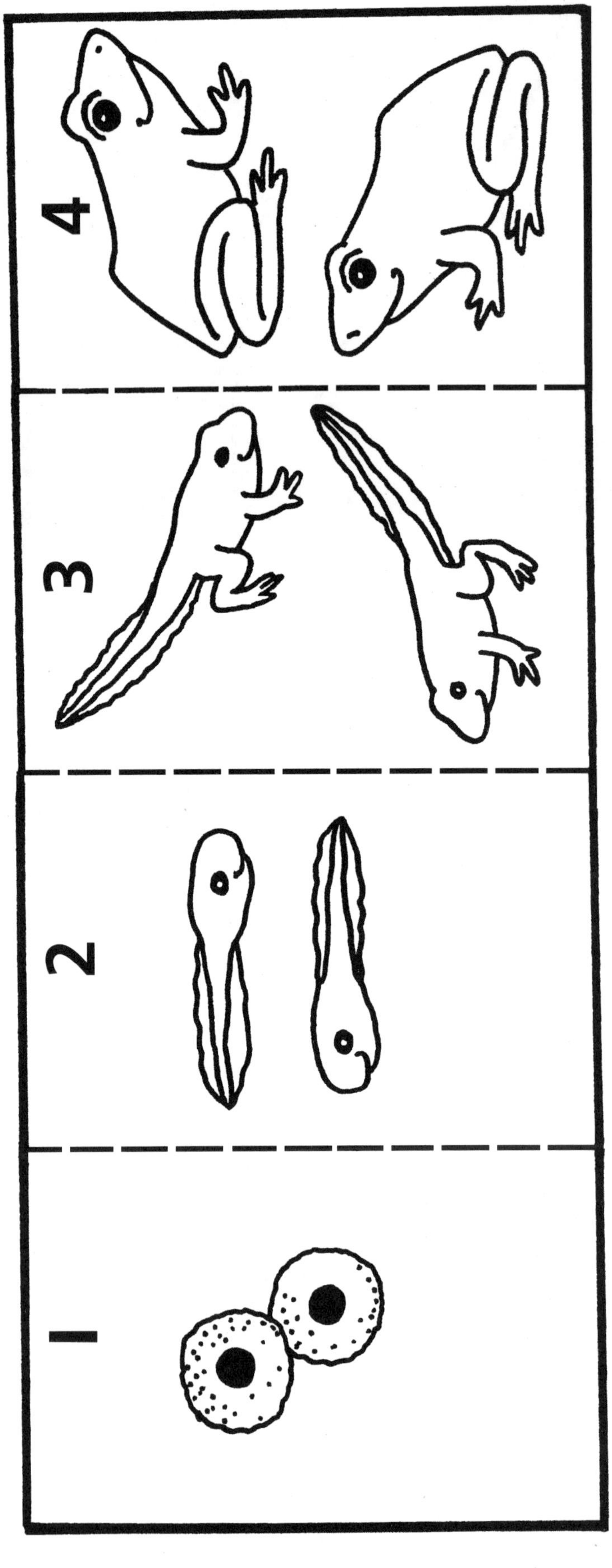

4

3

2

1

lizard

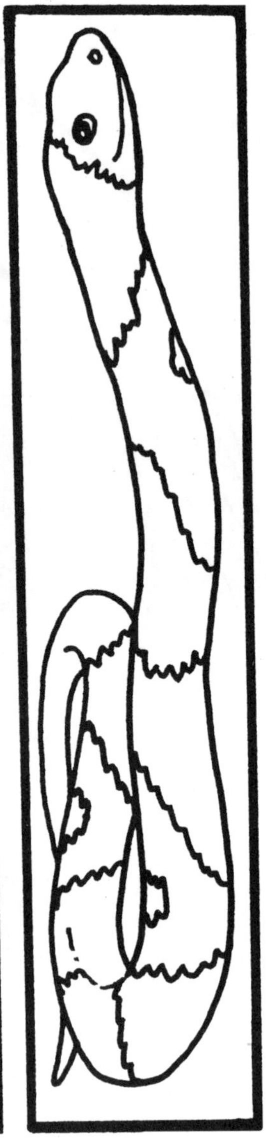

snake

turtle

A Butterfly's Life
label
life cycle cards
1
2
3
4
5
6
butterfly

Chicken Life Cycle, Stem, and Leaf Patterns

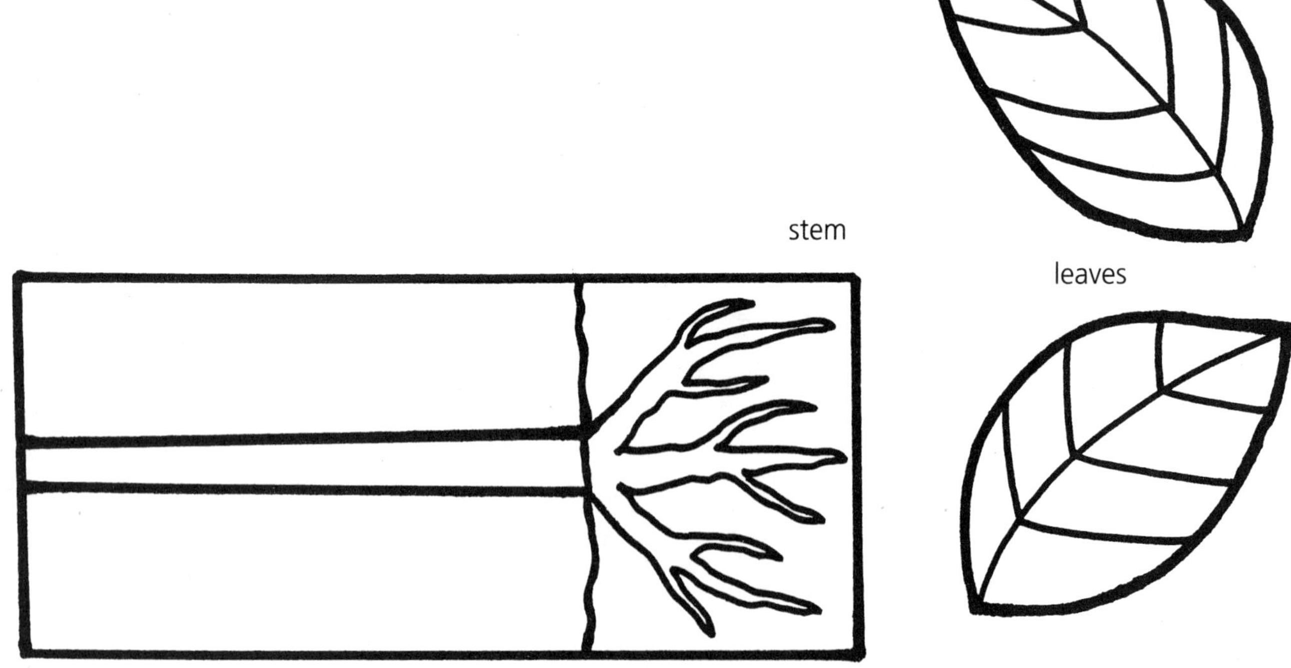

Plant Needs Cards and Flower Pattern

flower

cards

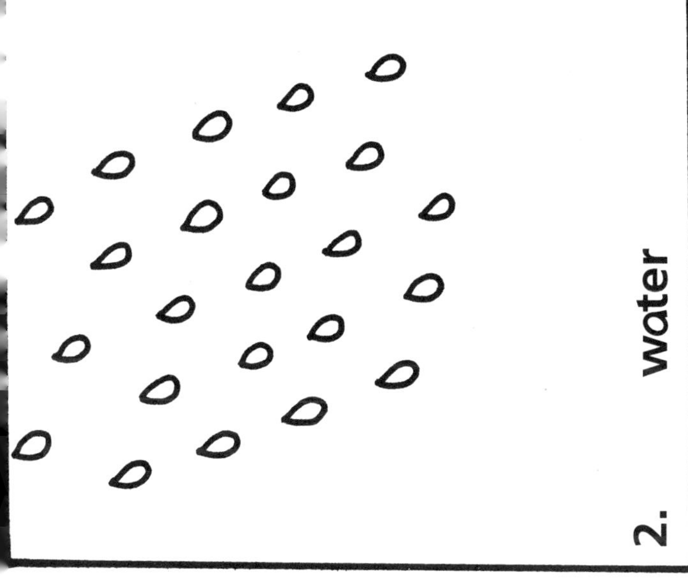

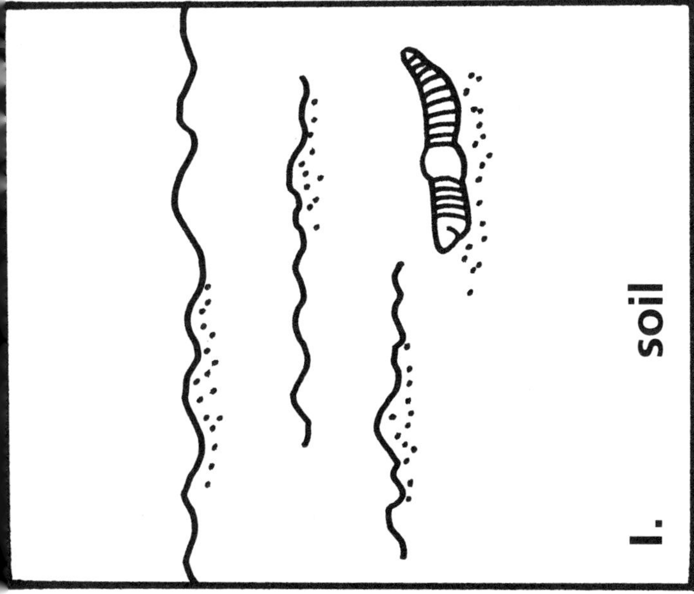

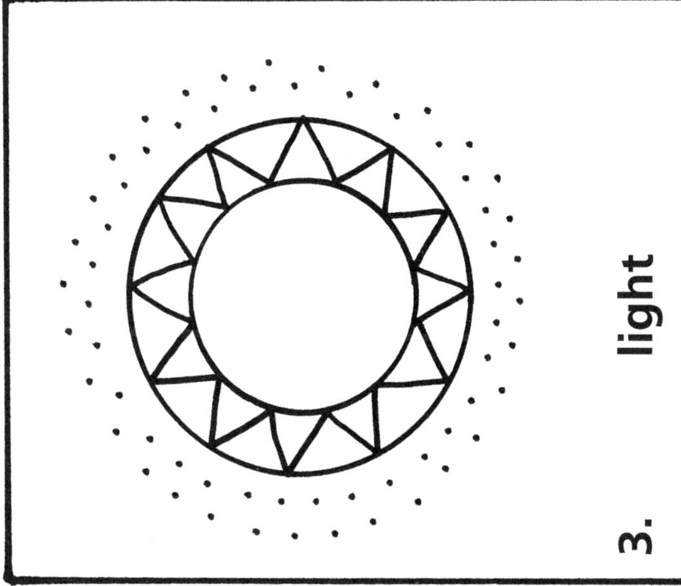

Water Cycle Patterns

The Water Cycle

The Water Cycle

bottom

Glue here.

sign

cards

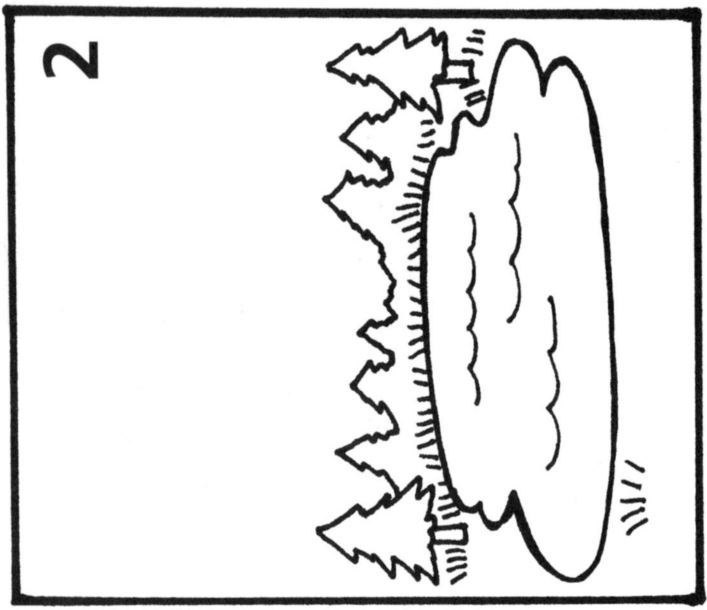

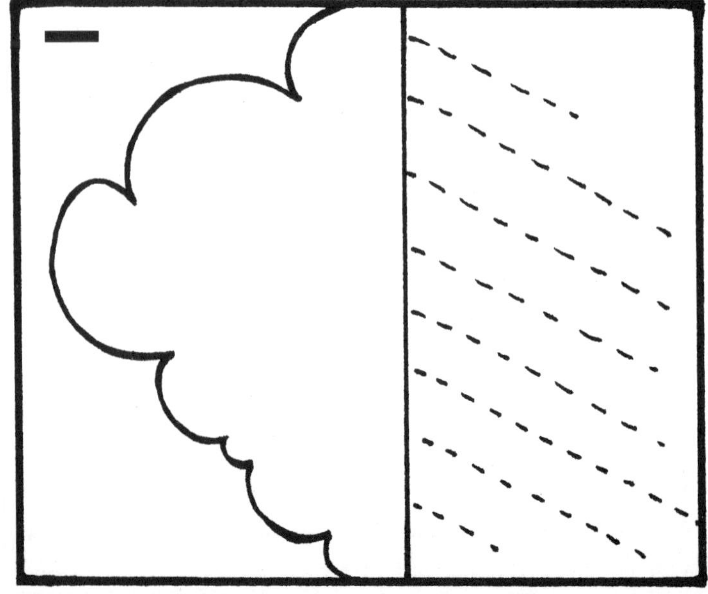

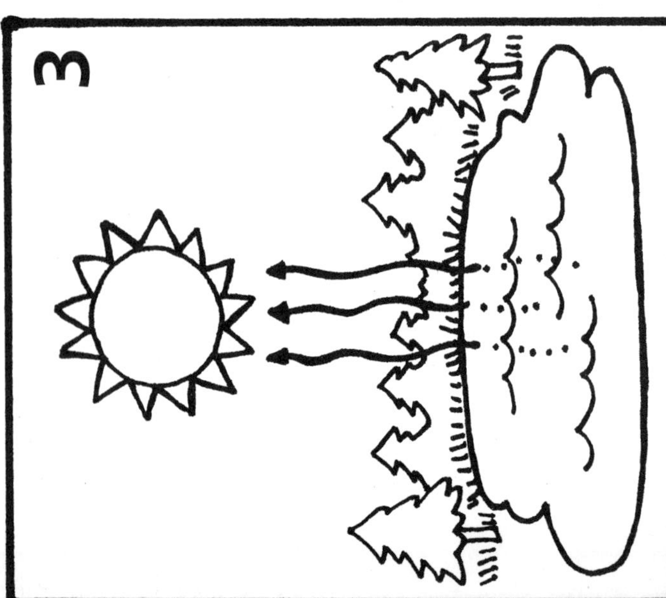